Welcome to Elm Street

ALSO BY WAYNE BYRNE

Burt Reynolds on Screen (McFarland, 2020)

BY WAYNE BYRNE AND NICK MCLEAN

Nick McLean Behind the Camera: The Life and Works of a Hollywood Cinematographer (McFarland, 2020)

Welcome to Elm Street

Inside the Film and Television Nightmares

WAYNE BYRNE

Foreword by Mick Strawn

McFarland & Company, Inc., Publishers
Jefferson, North Carolina

ISBN (print) 978-1-4766-8452-9
ISBN (ebook) 978-1-4766-4479-0

LIBRARY OF CONGRESS AND BRITISH LIBRARY
CATALOGUING DATA ARE AVAILABLE

Library of Congress Control Number 2022010048

© 2022 Wayne Byrne. All rights reserved

No part of this book may be reproduced or transmitted in any form or by any means, electronic or mechanical, including photocopying or recording, or by any information storage and retrieval system, without permission in writing from the publisher.

Front cover: Robert Englund as Freddy Krueger, the title character from the 1991 film *Freddy's Dead: The Final Nightmare* (New Line Cinema/Photofest)

Printed in the United States of America

*McFarland & Company, Inc., Publishers
Box 611, Jefferson, North Carolina 28640
www.mcfarlandpub.com*

For Ang, Pat, Jen, and Freddy

Acknowledgments

I would like to thank the following for the generous sharing of your memories and archives:

Nick Benson, Andre Ellingson, Robert Englund, Steven Fierberg, Bill Froehlich, Mick Garris, Lisa Gottlieb, Jacques Haitkin, Tuesday Knight, Bobby Lesser, Tom McLoughlin, Dennis Maguire, William Malone, Bradford May, Nicholas Pike, Declan Quinn, Chuck Russell, Craig Safan, Jack Sholder, Mick Strawn, Tony Timpone, Roy H. Wagner. This book wouldn't be what it is without any of you.

Thanks also to Annie Bardach, Nancy Englund, Paul Farren, Lucinda Lewis, David McGiffert, Nick McLean, Adam Rifkin for all the help.

Huge love to my dearest friend, Amanda Kramer. Your support has been boundless throughout this project and beyond. Thank you.

Table of Contents

Acknowledgments — vi
Foreword by Mick Strawn — 1
Introduction — 3

1. Wes Craven and the Nightmare of America — 7
2. The Monster Goes Mainstream — 44
3. Welcome to Primetime, Freddy! — 115
4. The Birth, the Death, and the Resurrection — 152
5. The Main Event and the Remake — 183
6. The Legacy of *A Nightmare on Elm Street* — 194

Chapter Notes — 209
Bibliography — 215
Index — 217

Foreword
by Mick Strawn

I had finally caught up on some sleep and was in the process of finding a parking spot for the cast and crew screening of *A Nightmare on Elm Street 3: Dream Warriors* when Chuck Russell, nemesis for the last five months of my life and the film's director, was just stepping off the curb on Beverly. I was feeling pretty forgiving, so I graciously allowed him to live as he crossed the street in front of my car. Later that evening, halfway across the theater lobby and halfway through the film, I happened to cross the path of a certain *LA Times* reviewer. I'm withholding his name for purposes of chivalry, but his initials were K and T. Chivalry is indeed dead. We did literally run into one another. I, desperate to pee, and he, desperate to flee, were both a bit stunned and wound up facing each other spluttering. To break up the awkward moment I introduced myself. He reciprocated and we chatted for a moment in which I asked him why he was leaving so soon, as the film was only barely through the second act. He then told me, in the most patronizing voice he could come up with on such short notice, that he had seen enough of the film to be able to trash it and that I had done my part and so he was on his way to go do his, as if another bad review of another independent horror film was his duty. The funny twist to that was his final review wasn't that bad and he said nice things about the work of my sister C.J. and me.

But it raised a good point. This is the way it was in the '80s: as Rodney Dangerfield put it, we couldn't get any respect. In retrospect, most of us weren't housebroken and we were too busy creating the Second Golden Age of Horror to give a shit anyway. I used to claim that producers would underpay me because they could look in my eyes and know instantly that I would have done it for free, but I was hardly alone in that. We were an army of misfits, we built crazy sets, amazing creatures and created the most twisted stories for people like ourselves who weren't just an audience but die-hard fans, who went back and saw our creations again and again. But we were also the gutter of Hollywood. We played among ourselves and occupied a social status sandwiched in between porn stars and late-night TV lawyers, and most of us made considerably less money than both.

Cut to: genre conventions, horror film festivals, millions and millions of dollars in merchandise, thousands upon thousands of horror films made every year; I can't even begin to list the number of ways this genre has exploded. We are now respectable and the sought-after survivors of horror's Second Golden Age. I cannot tell you how bizarre it feels to be a part of this world. I am constantly awed, often humbled, and occasionally scared of this fandom. And the undisputed King of this world is Freddy Krueger, the bastard son of a hundred maniacs. This is not up for dispute, just a fact. I don't have to count the ways that he is King, after all, as Wayne Byrne is here to do it for me. In this book, Wayne reassembles the heart of these incredibly complicated films by using the filmmakers' own words to paint a picture. Okay, in the case of *A Nightmare on Elm Street 3* the picture is burning and on *A Nightmare on Elm Street 2* maybe it should be. But Wayne remains true to Elm Street history, walking the tightrope between crew, cast and production, and often on fire himself.

So, put the kids to sleep, let the cat out, pour yourself a beer and, using your replica Krueger claw to turn the pages, dig in and enjoy…

Mick Strawn (courtesy Mick Strawn Collection).

Mick Strawn is a production designer and special effects artist whose credits include A Nightmare on Elm Street 3: Dream Warriors, A Nightmare on Elm Street 4: The Dream Master, Freddy's Nightmares, Critters 2, Leatherface: Texas Chainsaw Massacre III, Candyman, Boogie Nights, *and many more.*

Introduction

"The first one was scary, but the rest sucked!"
—Drew Barrymore, *Scream*

Not true, Drew! But we will allow horror maestro and *Scream* director Wes Craven this ironic exaggeration of a general consensus, as the originator of *A Nightmare on Elm Street* no one has more authority to poke a little fun at the expense of the films that followed his own than he. However, one is always ready to argue against ignorance of the qualities of the remainder of what is arguably the richest, most thematically significant and aesthetically brilliant horror series of the post–New Hollywood horror franchise boom; in fact, you are about to read nearly 100,000 words in defense of such. Wes Craven was without doubt the most intelligent and socially conscious horror filmmaker of his generation, but this is not a book about Wes, it is about the industrial context, cultural relevance, and legacy of his creation. But the specter of his genius, intellect, and influence looms large over the proceedings and that is because the themes within his uniquely drawn commentary on American society, represented here by the fictional idyllic Midwestern town of Springwood, are the very ideas that have informed the entire franchise, and which have inspired me to write this book. I take this approach in respect to Craven's interest in the myriad social and psychological themes that have informed much of his oeuvre, from *The Last House on the Left* and *The Hills Have Eyes* to *Shocker* and *The People Under the Stairs* right up to the *Scream* quartet. Craven's critical and sometimes satirical commentaries upon the American milieu provides what may otherwise seem like merely effectively made slasher films with a greater level of depth and intelligence. Of course, when it gets to certain entries in the *Nightmare on Elm Street* franchise, the special effects, the wicked humor, and the elaborate set pieces were indeed the priorities of the filmmakers rather than cerebral or intellectual notions.

While charting the production of the films and analyzing the themes inherent, this book also considers the larger importance of a franchise that has continually fascinated me since childhood. The indelible image of Freddy Krueger grabbed the attention of my six-year-old self as I was perusing the shelves of the Screen Test video store in my hometown of Naas, circa 1989, and I was duly beguiled by what I saw as a most entertaining bogeyman. These days it would probably be unthinkable that someone of such a tender age could engage with the dastardly adventures of a hideously disfigured child killer, but while my schoolhouse contemporaries were kicking a round object about a field, or perhaps at home learning calculus, I was busy obsessing over videotapes of the horror icons of the 1980s: Freddy Krueger, Jason Voorhees (of *Friday the 13th*), Michael Myers (of *Halloween*), The Tall Man (of *Phantasm*), the Crites (of *Critters*), and the Ghoulies (of, well, *Ghoulies*). In the Ireland of 1989, Freddy could be found everywhere. His memorable image adorned the shelves of video stores while a surfeit of branded *Elm Street* ephemera flooded our budget markets: water pistols, plastic gloves, rubber dolls, lunchboxes, and t-shirts. It really was a great time to be a young Freddy fan, as *A Nightmare on Elm Street 3: Dream Warriors* was released on home video just before *A Nightmare on Elm Street 4: The Dream Master* rolled out into theaters and as *Freddy's Nightmares* was making its debut on our TV screens, appearing every Friday night at 11 p.m. on the new Sky One satellite channel. The latter has a particularly special place in my heart and the scope of its chapter here is testament to such, having discovered its illicit delights while my parents were busy being entertained by the Irish chat show and cultural institution *The Late Late Show*. After enjoying episodes of *Hunter*, *Unsolved Mysteries* and *WWF Wrestling Challenge*, and before being marched to bed, I was able to catch a tantalizing, almost forbidden, glimpse of *Freddy's Nightmares*. It was thrilling, and it inspired my awe of Freddy Krueger and the world of Springwood; here was a villain who was funny and endearing enough that you could embrace the darker elements of his monstrous personality without being truly scared or traumatized by the material presented. Unfortunately, the show has been largely forgotten, to the point of its DVD release being unceremoniously canceled by Warner Bros. due to lack of sales and interest, but as you will see in the ensuing pages, it hasn't been forgotten by me or many of those who made it. While there are those who celebrate it, there are those who are somewhat embarrassed in discussing it, resigned to its largely negative place in the *Elm Street* canon. But as *Freddy's Nightmares* introduced me to the whole world of *Elm Street* and instigated a love of the genre, I have endeavored to pay it some due respect for instilling in me the belief that horror fiction is best experienced when we are young, before we become cynical and terrified of real-world problems like political unrest, poverty, illness, and life's other assorted maladies.

One of the unique functions of this book is that it presents an alternate look at the history of the *Nightmare on Elm Street* franchise, featuring tales never told before. If you care enough to be reading this, you may already be privy to the vast discourse available on *Elm Street*, it having been covered in detail in many previous documentaries and books, those which so often feature the same stories, maybe tweaked a little, perhaps exaggerated, or toned down, depending on the mood of the piece. Of course, some of those stories are re-told here, though in a different context and to highlight themes and ideas that I have felt were underexplored in previous considerations of the franchise. I am proud to include brand new perspectives and stories from those who have never or rarely appear on record discussing their involvement. In the ensuing pages, you will hear from directors, cinematographers, production designers, actors, and other professionals who worked on the sets of these films, either in front of or behind the camera. These insights take the *Elm Street* fan on a journey into the creation of this art that we adore, whether it's the themes and subtexts of the respective narratives, the style and aesthetics of the various filmmakers, or the immense effort that went into the production and special effects which make these films such a visually rich extravaganza. This book is a rare glimpse into the dynamic of personalities, the unique artistry, the sheer intelligence, and the intense labor that goes into the making of a major horror franchise.

1

Wes Craven and the Nightmare of America

"He's dead because Mommy killed him."
—Marge Thompson

The town of Springwood, Ohio, is idyllic Midwestern America. Perfect suburban streets are lined with fine middle-class housing which are adorned with white picket fences, carefully manicured lawns and rose trellises creeping up their two-story façades. This is safe, wholesome, clean-living America. But looks can be deceiving, for Springwood harbors a dark past, one which threatens to undermine the cozy image it has struggled to maintain for the last two decades. In the mid–1960s, Springwood was plagued by the menace of Freddy Krueger, a local man who kidnapped and killed twenty children from the area. Krueger was arrested at the scene of his crimes, the boiler room of a decrepit factory, though he didn't remain in custody for long as despite the damning evidence presented at his trial he was let go on a legal technicality. A drunken judge and a misplaced signature on an arrest warrant led to a miscarriage of justice and to Krueger's premature release. Devastated, grieving, and angry, a group of Springwood parents reacted with swift, brutal, and justified vengeance. Forming a mob, they traced Krueger back to his boiler room hideout, confronted him and doused him in gasoline before setting him aflame. The vigilante murder of Freddy Krueger soon becomes a malignant town secret which infects the collective conscience of the parents for years to come, rotting their morale and inducing an anxiety which is self-medicated with drugs and booze as a dissociation from the reality of their actions. The complacent bourgeois milieu of these citizens had begun to unravel ever since Krueger annihilated their lives and the innocence of Springwood, but their violent reaction results in things getting a whole lot worse for them and the generation of children who did survive.

Now in the early 1980s, the remaining children of Elm Street are teenagers, and they are experiencing some sort of unexplained collective psychosis. A group of friends including Nancy Thompson (Heather Langenkamp), her boyfriend Glen Lantz (Johnny Depp), Tina Gray (Amanda Wyss), and her bad-boy lover Rod Lane (Nick Corri) have all begun dreaming of a hideously burned man in a striped sweater and fedora hat. In their slumber, the teens find themselves wandering in a hissing, steaming industrial boiler room where the sinister figure terrorizes and taunts them to the point that these nightmares become so bad that they endeavor to stay awake and combat their fatigue with coffee and pills. But the razor-fingered specter plays upon their youthful weaknesses for decadence and debauchery, and one particularly fateful night proves the beginning of the fierce battle between the teens of Elm Street and the legacy of their parents' immorality. "Morality sucks!" says a chaste Glen as he overhears Rod and Tina have sex, during which she is brought to howl in orgasm and leading her to coo, "Jungle man fix Jane." After drifting off in post-coital bliss following their illicit teenage tryst, Tina is slashed and killed in her sleep by an unseen force. All the evidence points to Rod, whose criminal record, violent tendencies and reputation for delinquency are enough to make him a prime suspect; that he was seen brandishing a small gardening fork earlier in the evening doesn't help his case.

Wes Craven directs Amanda Wyss in *A Nightmare on Elm Street* (Photofest NYC).

1. Wes Craven and the Nightmare of America

One of the investigating officers is Lieutenant Donald Thompson (John Saxon), Nancy's father. Donald uses his daughter as bait in capturing Rod, who is duly arrested for the murder of Tina, but the teen is later found hung in his jail cell, apparently the victim of suicide, though actually another victim of the vengeful spirit. In the aftermath of the two deaths, Nancy details the man of her dreams to Donald and her mother, Marge (Ronee Blakely). Spooked by Nancy's description of a man who closely resembles the town's old nemesis, Freddy Krueger, Marge admits to her daughter that years ago she, Donald, and several of the town's parents were the ones who tracked down and killed the maniac in a moment of revenge. Marge informs Nancy that Freddy killed twenty neighborhood kids and that "the lawyers got fat and the judge got famous," even showing her daughter Krueger's offending glove, evidence of their vigilante action which has been hidden in the Thompsons' furnace all these years since. Nancy now realizes she is caught in a vicious cycle, that Freddy is wreaking vengeance upon the children of those who murdered him in retaliation for his own misdeeds. It is not long before she witnesses Glen succumb to Freddy in his sleep, after which she becomes determined to fight the fiend in a battle where the lines between dreams and reality are blurred. If Nancy can bring Freddy into the real world, she is no longer vulnerable to the elastic rules of his realm; if he is to be flesh, he is to be mortal.

The man cast in the most crucial role of Freddy Krueger is Robert Englund, a classically trained actor who tread the boards performing Shakespeare and Shaw before moving into film work in the mid-seventies with small roles in major studio pictures such as *Buster and Billie* (Daniel Petrie, 1974), *Hustle* (Robert Aldrich, 1975) and *St. Ives* (J. Lee Thompson, 1976). Further work in the independent and B-movie horror realm ensued, making memorable appearances in Tobe Hooper's *Eaten Alive* (1976), Gary Sherman's *Dead and Buried* (1981) and the Roger Corman–produced *Galaxy of Terror* (1981). *A Nightmare on Elm Street* director Wes Craven recalls his

Nancy (Heather Langenkamp) becomes vulnerable to Freddy Krueger.

initial meeting with Englund, whose slight physical demeanor wasn't what the director initially envisioned for the character of Freddy Krueger:

"When I was casting Freddy, Robert Englund came in and he was this little guy who didn't look at all what I thought Freddy would look like and he was able to approach the role with complete lack of worry that anybody would look at him and say, 'ooh, there's horrible stuff inside of you!' He just didn't give a damn about anything like that. He just reveled in the role and that really is what made Freddy work."[1]

In the pantheon of great horror villains throughout cinema history, there is a particular actor inextricably linked to each of those classic movie monsters thanks to their unique ability to bring their own distinct personality and style of performance to the respective role which has made them become part of the fabric of Film. Think Bela Lugosi as Dracula, Boris Karloff as Frankenstein's Monster, Lon Chaney, Jr., as The Wolf Man. And while there have been plenty of iconic bogeymen born of the horror genre during the past fifty years, including Jason Voorhees (of *Friday the 13th*), Michael Myers (of *Halloween*), Leatherface (of *The Texas Chainsaw Massacre*), no single actor has embodied the soul of contemporary horror cinema, or brought such distinctive characteristics and unique qualities to the performance of a single movie monster as Robert Englund has done with his rendering of Freddy Krueger.

"All of us horror movie monsters—Bela Lugosi, Boris Karloff, Vincent Price, Christopher Lee, and so on—we all have this great gift," Englund says, "and that is we became a logo for a story or a franchise that people love. So I'm the logo for the *Nightmare on Elm Street* franchise, and even if I sucked in one of them, I'm still the logo for the whole *Nightmare on Elm Street* experience. Every week there's a new action figure and a new illustration, a new painting and a new graphic novel or a new cartoon depiction of Freddy; he lives on in that merchandising and in the imagination of these artists and I get the benefit of that because it has been good for my career and it has helped make me international. And even though I'm the logo, I think it's the more surrealistic elements of Freddy that are the real hook; the idea that our most private and intimate thoughts and our imagination can become infected by this evil as a result of something our parents did is an idea that resonates with many people."[2]

A Nightmare on Elm Street was Wes Craven's seventh feature film. His name was both revered and notorious after having already amassed a body of work which was respectively lauded and reviled, the latter due to some infamous legal run-ins of several of his early works. *The Last House on the Left* (1972) and *The Hills Have Eyes* (1977) caused a significant stir with the British Board of Film Classification in Great Britain after having become embroiled in the widely reported Video Nasty panic of the early 1980s due to their depictions of extreme violence; this resulted in the films being legally unavailable in the UK and Ireland for decades. However, such furor and moral outrage would undermine the genuine directorial skill and keen intellect at work in the films. Craven's previous career in academia, having taught English and humanities, served him well when it came to conceiving thematically significant works, including those previous films but particularly so with *A Nightmare on Elm Street*, in which he would parlay his interests in sociology and psychology along with the vivid memories of the fears and anxieties of his youth. Another most chilling influence behind the surreal 1984 picture was a very real incident related in a series of *Los Angeles Times* articles published throughout one particular year in the 1970s. Craven details the chilling true story that grabbed his attention:

"Essentially they go like: some young man, usually of Southeast Asian origin, had been reported to have died in the middle of a nightmare. The first two I clipped without thinking too much about it, and the third one had really the nub of a story in it. Basically this kid, he and his family had come out of the relocation camps in Southeast Asia, I think Cambodia or something like that, and they were now in the United States living somewhere in California and he had been troubled by severe nightmares and they had increased in intensity to the point where he had told his family that these don't feel ordinary. His family tried to counsel him and tell him that we came out of this terrible background and nightmares are part of your psyche trying to deal with that. But he increased in a sense of trying to say, 'this doesn't feel normal, it feels too real.' At a certain point they had a doctor prescribe sleeping medicine and his father insisted he take it. It turns out he had taken them under their supervision and as soon as they were away he'd spit them out, and they also discovered later that he had a coffee pot in his closet where he kept black coffee to stay awake at night. So this had gone on and at a certain point he decided to stay awake and not sleep, and obviously the family thought he was having something like a nervous breakdown. After about three days he would be downstairs watching television all through the night, but then they went down and found him asleep on the couch and the father brought him back to his bed and the family thought, 'thank god, he seems to be sleeping peacefully,' and they all went to bed. Later that night they heard screaming and thrashing about and they went into his room and before they could get to him he fell down dead. Stone dead. The family had to have an autopsy done and there was no sign of heart failure, no sign of why he had died."[3]

With an eerie premise rooted in such mysterious real-life trauma and tragedy, it is no wonder that *A Nightmare on Elm Street* struck a chord with audiences and has become part of American film history and culture, as well as a massively successful commercial enterprise. Beneath the immediate fantastical horror film context, Craven's themes are universal and speak to both everyday fears of familial failure and of greater societal breakdown. Robert Englund notes the allegorical nature of the film to be evident in the film's title, and considers the weight of the words "Elm Street" to mean so much more than meets the eye:

"When you think of 'Elm Street' there are many connotations to those words. In elementary school, in grades One through Six, you begin to learn to read in these reading groups at a certain period of the day, and the primer, the book that you are taught from very early on, is about a family in which the two kids are called Dick and Jane, and they have a dog named Spot and a cat named Puff, and their parents are simply referred to as Father and Mother, and they all live on Elm Street. The books are filled with very simple words with lots of repetitions and illustrations depicting a wholesome milieu, the ideal family existence, much like what the people of Springwood aspire to. So that's a subconscious reference in the 'Nightmare on Elm Street' title. But then there is also Elm Street in Dallas, Texas, and that is the street on which our beloved president John F. Kennedy was assassinated. We don't know for sure who was involved and what really went down, but something very ugly happened on that day in November 1963. At that moment of time we were going through the beginning of our Civil Rights era, but then our president was killed and that changed everything; then they killed Martin Luther King and then we had Vietnam. So that is the last moment of American optimism, it was the loss of American innocence, it was our loss of trust, and the beginning of our incredible cynicism; it was the rise of conspiracy theories and of arch conservative lines and even a resurgence of the Ku Klux Klan. It saw a little bit of Jim Crow coming back and saw ugliness creeping into the American soul. And so the Nightmare on Elm Street is really the Nightmare of America."[4]

Indeed, the American Dream of a safe, comfortable middle-class existence being turned upside down is part of Craven's vision of an American Nightmare here and in other films, wherein he ruminates on the destruction of civilized society and how erstwhile civilized people can be encouraged to violent behavior by external influences. The director has been continually fascinated with looking behind the seemingly innocuous elements of such a life, peering behind the doors of polite society and suburbia, as if entering into the pre-conscious or sub-conscious of the people who reside there to uncover the darkness behind the façade of civility. The traumatized middle-class families of *The Last House on the Left* and *The Hills Have Eyes* are driven from being rational, progressive, idealistic people to those who resort to acts of extreme violence in reaction to their traditionally safe and exclusive world being invaded by the feral, anarchic underclass as depicted by Krug and company in the former and the Jupiter clan in the latter. In the petit bourgeois world of Springwood, Freddy's filthy, unruly presence within the ornate homes of the upwardly mobile similarly creates utmost fear and anxiety. The very opening shots of the film are set in a grimy industrial space, far removed from the sterile streets of Springwood that we will be privy to; this is Freddy's lair, the boiler room in which he enacted his depravity. Here we see him welding deadly blades to the molded fingers which he has attached to the tatty and torn glove, a deadly makeshift weapon which becomes a stark symbol for the corruption of innocence. From there we are elliptically taken into Tina's nightmare wherein the pretty teen struggles to navigate this hissing hellscape in which the sounds of children and animals wailing abound, before Freddy appears and frightens her awake. Tina's disturbed sleep alerts her mother, whose concerns are cut short by her impatient, lusting suitor summoning her back to bed. "You got to cut your fingernails or stop that kind of dreaming," is the apathetic response of Mrs. Gray. Tina is later killed while her mother enjoys a weekend away in Las Vegas with said boyfriend.

While his films are presented in the form of horror, Craven uses adroit satire to make his most damning critiques of the society presented. The culture clash between seemingly civilized and uncivilized elements of our communities is one which Craven considers in several films throughout his career, though these ideas are presented with more subtlety in *A Nightmare on Elm Street* than they are in the aforementioned two earlier films and in later works such as *The Serpent and the Rainbow* (1988) and *The People Under the Stairs* (1991). Craven often metaphorically presents the uncivilized as the working-class while the middle-classes are represented in a heightened, absurdly idealized form of civility. Just look at the social implications in depicting

Tina's boyfriend Rod as a rough Latino rogue who carries himself with bad-boy bluster, "a musician type" who we learn has previously been arrested for drugs and brawling. All of this is in contrast to the well-mannered all–American middle-class kids he is friends with and who represent the average profile of those who populate Springwood throughout the series, with it being a town of limited ethnic, economic, and social diversity. It becomes typical of Freddy to manipulate and toy with his victims according to their own sense of identity and place in the world, and in setting Rod up as the killer of Tina he knows it will be easy for people to believe Rod would transgress, given his rebel attitude and propensity for violence. Even Tina's aforementioned referral to him as "jungle man" could be taken as a sly class dig at his proletariat status. Rod's home is the only one we are not privy to and given how Craven rendered the character we can infer that he is from another, perhaps less-affluent side of Springwood. In essence, Rod is the perfect scapegoat for Freddy, and for the town of Springwood.

"Wes deals with Class," Englund says, "especially in the first film. Our first victim, Tina, the person you don't expect to die, is supposed to be the girl with a bad reputation; she is supposed to be slightly lower class so that she can be contrasted with Nancy, our strong survivor girl and heroine who is comfortably middle-class by comparison, even though the Thompson parents are divorced. Both Tina and her boyfriend Rod are supposed to be from the wrong side of the tracks, and Rod was especially depicted as such; his character is in contrast to Glen, played by Johnny Depp, although interestingly enough, Johnny originally went in for the part of the bad boy, but he ended up playing the safe suburban kid, Glen. The story I heard was that Wes's daughter, who was working on the set as an intern, got one look at Johnny and said, 'Daddy, if you don't cast him I'm leaving home!'"

Englund continues, "Freddy also didn't fit into Springwood, he didn't fit into the idealized American society, because he represents everything that polite society abhors. The symbolism of Freddy is that of 'Child Killer.' Those words, 'Child Killer,' they are almost poetic, I mean you could imagine a hardcore punk band being named 'Child Killer,' you know: 'Tonight, at Madame Wong's West: The Clash supported by The Child Killers!' And when you apply those words to Freddy, what is he doing? He is killing children. And what are children? They are the future. Freddy is killing the future. He is that unexplained and undiscussed evil. Some people really want to get specific into his backstory and label him as a pedophile, but he is just a child killer, he is killing innocence, he is killing the future."[5]

Freddy's Nightmares director Tom McLoughlin considers the villain's heinous abuse of innocence to be a key element of the film's effectiveness. "Where Freddy came from is an awful and creepy thing: he abused our most vulnerable of society. And so by grounding the film in something so awful and truly terrifying makes it much more frightening because the terror comes from a very real, very dark and horrible place. And it is set in everyday life, in places that are recognizable to us, whether it's our bedroom or a suburban street, these places that traditionally make us feel secure but which are invaded and no longer feel safe. Nobody is free from Freddy and the evil he represents; even after the vigilante group track him down and get their retribution, punishing him in this horrific way, the memory of his evil and the fear that it creates is so great that he can return to haunt the dreams of their kids and get them at their most vulnerable. There is much more of a psychological core to the Elm Street franchise than the other horror franchises of that era."[6]

A Nightmare on Elm Street cinematographer Jacques Haitkin concurs: "I think what's at the core of the piece is that which is at the heart of cinema: it is an investigation of moral ambiguity. Right there in Wes Craven's original film is a story about evil hitting supposedly good people and those people become vigilantes in the name of their children, so there's a blurring of morality. What has made it universally resonant at its core, if it comes down to one thing, it's that very theme of moral ambiguity."[7]

Craven's commentary on the parents' actions, the resultant moral implications of such, and how that affects the children of Elm Street would indeed become the central theme for the rest of the series, though how obvious or how subtle that theme is depicted depends very much on the respective director and their approach to these elements that Craven had implanted in the first film. Familial breakdown and the attendant anxieties of the children is a crucial narrative thread of the entire Elm Street franchise. Having been the child of divorced parents, Craven parlayed his adolescent vulnerabilities and need for his parents to stay together into a discourse on the failed family unit, and noted as much when he said, "Family is the best microcosm to work with, if you go much beyond that you're getting away from a lot of the roots of our own primeval feelings."[8] In the film, we learn that Tina's father left his wife and daughter ten years prior, in the aftermath of the vigilante action that killed Krueger, and as the film unfolds Craven introduces us to the multiple neuroses of the various elders of Springwood, revealing the psychological and marital breakdowns of those who were involved in the act of illegal retribution. The Thompsons are one of the couples who have suffered estrangement since their involvement in the Krueger killing. Like other parents of Elm Street, Marge is depicted as emotionally distant and chemically dependent; she is an alcoholic. Ronee Blakely informs her role as Marge with a tremendous sense of melodrama which may seem overegged in comparison to the straight performances of the other actors, though her histrionic rendering of the troubled matriarch actually plays exquisitely into the film's subtext of social hysteria.

All of the characters that Nancy relies on for support are stymied by some physical or emotional crippling which hinders them from helping her. In her mother's case it is alcohol mixed with denial, and while her father is more practical and attuned to his daughter's emotions than his ex-wife, he is still bound by established rules of law and he logically refuses to believe that Freddy could return from the dead to attack his daughter and her friends. Ultimately, the parents' ignorance is the cause of their children's' malaise. In their suspicion and incomprehension of Nancy's warnings, Glen's parents allow their son to become even more vulnerable to Freddy, as seen with the ignorant assertion by Glen's father that "you just gotta be tough with these kids" and his subsequent refusal to listen to Nancy's desperate pleas to wake Glen and save his life. This oblivious and somewhat old-fashioned parental response foreshadows the trauma of another teen in *A Nightmare on Elm Street 2: Freddy's Revenge,* when a father orders the same kind of patriarchal punishment when he says, "what that kid needs is a good goddamned kick in the butt," just before Freddy administers an ultimate butt kicking upon the unfortunate teen. The boozy dissociation of the parents of Elm Street is a self-destructive act to shield them from the feelings of guilt and from acknowledging the troubling effects that their dark secret history is having upon their children in the present. Each film in the *Nightmare on Elm Street* franchise offers up myriad failed marriages and disastrous examples of ill parenting, that which is emphasized by divorce and misuse of alcohol and pharmaceuticals, all of which is seen to contribute to the emotional demise of the children, that which precedes their physical demise at the hands of Freddy.

"Yes, the adults are all depicted as flawed," Englund agrees, "divorce, single moms, pregnancy out of wedlock, drug abuse, alcoholism, that's all in there and it was a time in the 1980s when we were beginning to see the effects of divorce, which had really boomed in the 1970s. Now, the libertines and modern French people would say that you should have a mistress, that no one shouldn't be pre-occupied and that it shouldn't matter, and they're probably right, and I understand that it is probably worse to be stuck in a sham marriage and have that effect the children, especially if there is fighting and domestic abuse occurring, but we do know that children of divorce do not take it well. There is a staggering statistic of damage being done psychologically to young men who grow up without fathers in all communities. If there is shared custody then that damage can be diminished, but that culture of divorce was really starting to affect American society by the 1970s; people thought it was a good thing that if the marriage isn't working then we can just go get a divorce. In the 1950s if you got a divorce there was a certain stigma attached to it, people were a little more hesitant because society would take this stiff upper lip approach to marriage and see it through. But then divorce became much more prolific in the 1960s when it became an automatic thing to do if you thought you weren't happy for ten minutes, and that's the way it was through the '70s and '80s and that is reflected by Wes here. He had seen and experienced that as his own parents divorced and then he too became divorced. As a society we started seeing the result of a lot of divorces and that's part of the subtext and so prevalent a theme in the *Nightmare on Elm Street* films. You see a lot of single parents in the *Nightmare* films and you will notice that their children are not happy."

Englund continues, "Freddy is a symbol of everything that can rot the family unit, he is a threat to the love, health, sanity, senses, and stability that holds a family together. Now I don't think that the twelve- or fifteen-year-old boy watching these films and enjoying the great death scenes or the special effects is really thinking about these themes on that kind of intellectual level, but I do believe they are experiencing them, just like the kids in the movie are surrendering to their subconscious which is infected by the evil of Freddy Krueger. And I'm not sure if everyone picks up on some of the symbols that are in there, especially European audiences because, as I mentioned, 'Nightmare on Elm Street' means the Nightmare of America. The way that theme is embodied in the films is by the depiction of the decline of the American Family, and we see many broken and fractured homes in the Elm Street series. There is also a loss of innocence, and particularly the loss of innocence of young women, and I'm not talking about rape, but in seeing the world for what it really is. I have always said that there should be a class in school called 'Life's Not Fair' because we know now that you can work hard and be honest but somebody can cheat, or somebody stupid and lazy can still get ahead of you; life isn't fair."[9]

Craven further explored ideas of class, social anxieties, and gentrification in his work beyond *A Nightmare on Elm Street*, most obviously in his 1991 satirical horror *The People Under the Stairs*, which is perhaps his most scathing takedown of bourgeois adherence to the accumulation of wealth and haughty suspicions of those of other, lesser, social status. The white middle-class landlords, the Robesons, are portrayed as a deranged and incestuous couple who call themselves "Mommy" and "Daddy" while looking like something that crawled off the *Leave It to Beaver* set; the heroes are the poor, disenfranchised black community who have disrupted the prosperity of the kinky capitalist cannibal couple that is forcing poor minority families out of their homes.

Further bourgeois dreams are shattered in *Scream* (1996) as the disruption of the family unit is the catalyst for a killing spree when the home of young rebel Billy Loomis is broken by the extra-marital affair of his mother, thus inspiring the traumatized son to embark on a murderous rampage targeting the comfortable middle-class lives of his schoolmates. In *Deadly Friend* (1986) teenage boy Paul Conway and his mother arrive to their new house in the absence of a husband-father figure, thus setting the community's curtains twitching. Paul introduces his closest friend, a science experiment robot named BB, to his beautiful new neighbor, Samantha "Sam" Pringle, but his wise metallic companion senses a malevolent force in the presence of her brooding father, Harry. The alcoholic patriarch scowls in Sam's direction upon her introduction to the new neighbors. We soon learn that Harry is possessive and jealous, given to domestic violence and, as suggested via a dream sequence, prone to sexually abuse his daughter. Harry cuts a slovenly figure, lying on the couch watching television and drinking beer until he decides to expose his daughter to further assault

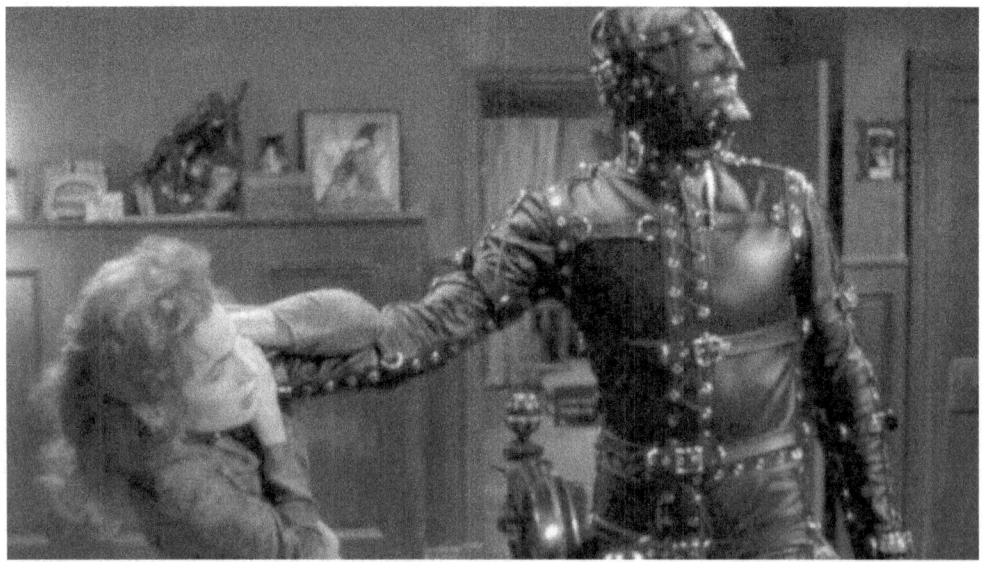

Kinky capitalists, the Robesons (Wendy Robie, left, and Everett McGill) in *The People Under the Stairs*.

and humiliation. Even in suburban paradise, Craven doesn't allow for anything as cohesive as a complete family unit. Once again, his milieu of middle-class Americana sees young characters flounder in broken homes poisoned by chemical dependency, domestic abuse and emotional indifference. *Deadly Friend* was Craven's first major studio picture, and a difficult production for the director who was used to more creative autonomy on his independent productions, enduring a battle with Warner Bros. over the tone of the film as the studio demanded a higher concentration of horror. Interestingly, it is the studio-mandated additional footage that gives the production more of a Craven distinction and which ties the film in thematically with other works in his oeuvre.

"Wes Craven was the Professor of Horror," says Tony Timpone, former editor of the legendary horror magazine *Fangoria*. "He came from an educational background as an academic and school teacher. He didn't grow up on horror films, he came to them later in life due to his religious upbringing in which he wasn't allowed watch movies as a kid. So Wes brought an outsider's perspective and an intellectual's perspective to horror movies and he really elevated the genre because of that. He was a very smart, educated man and in these films he is talking about important issues: family, society, and everything else. So what you have are films which are very capable of giving us a good scare but also capable of giving us something to think about. There was always some deep psychological underpinnings to Wes' films because he also wrote most of them, so they are coming directly from him."[10]

The year 1989's *Shocker* saw Craven further exploring the idea of dreams and the relationship between our subconscious world and our real waking lives. The introduction of a medium such as television is here seen as an extension of the dream world, a nebulous surreal realm in which anything can occur. This was another film

Sam Pringle (Kirsty Swanson) and her abusive father, Harry Pringle (Richard Marcus) in *Deadly Friend*.

which considered the chasm between one generation and the next within a family, a division of ideals between a father and son, or rather a son and two fathers—the adopted father and the real father. Craven wanted to examine the conflict between those two generations, and he saw those as representing the generations on either side of the Vietnam War.[11] It was a discord between those who could accept and condone the violence, and those who wouldn't; the old-fashioned morals of the elders clashing with the more liberal and conscientious ethics of the post-counter-cultural youth. Craven also wanted to explore these familial themes in *Shocker* because of his experiences with his own father, who died when the filmmaker was young but whose legacy of rage lingered long in the memory of his son. Notably, many father figures in the Elm Street franchise have short fuses and Craven rendered the villain of *Shocker*, Horace Pinker, as someone who tries to manipulate his son's fear and to guilt him into believing he is cut from the same corrupted cloth as he, thus inheriting the same amorality to carry on his legacy of evil—the sins of the father assumed by the next generation. Like *A Nightmare on Elm Street*, the parents of *Shocker* have broken the commandment of "Thou shalt not kill" and have left their children with the emotional and physical fallout of their actions.

The man responsible for crafting the distinct visual aesthetics of *Shocker* and the first two *Nightmare on Elm Street* films is Jacques Haitkin. An alumnus of NYU and subsequently a fellow of the American Film Institute, Haitkin cut his teeth on the early films of Martin Brest (*Hot Dogs for Gaugin*, 1972; *Hot Tomorrows*, 1977) as well as various B-movies, and brought with him a keen intellectual approach to his cinematography that married well with his director's sociological horror and his desire to craft a unique visual world that the film required. He affirms that there is far more going in these films than the mere surface horror on which they are sold:

"These are existential films, Wayne. It is there in *A Nightmare on Elm Street* and it is there in Wes's other films; he was always touching upon a deeper, existential theme, it's not just superficial horror. The photography of the film is in service to the narrative and the narrative is the higher purpose. We are trying to touch an audience's hearts and minds, so my approach is to look deeply into the script, to look deeply into the characters and situations, the conflict and themes, and I then base my cinematography on those guiding lights; it is those elements of a film which are the higher purpose of cinema. I've been a screenwriter and story consultant, which many people mightn't know about, and so the story is key to me. I've always been a story guy as much as I have been a photography guy, so Wes and I talked about the themes of the film a fair amount. Although, once we rolled up our sleeves and got into the work of figuring out the sets, the lighting, the look of the film, and that kind of stuff, you kind of bury those intellectual ideas; you don't forget them but you hold them internally and allow it to spread out as you make choices, they are always resonating within you as the production comes together. It's not talked about that much once we get into the operational parts of making the film, you certainly don't have those kinds of esoteric discussions on the set during production because once you're there it's all about execution.

Wes had a much more morbid take on things; he had a disabling condition when he was in high school, it was like a viral meningitis where he experienced a temporary paralysis and he was bed-ridden during some of his high school years. He shared this with me, not in deep detail, but his point was that the high school years are an imprinting time and this disease had a big effect on his perspective. He went through some difficult times growing up. In contrast, I had a very easy life: happy parents, middle-class, no adversity, so I'm not a dark, brooding person. If I were to direct a film it would definitely be a comedy, not horror, but the reason I love horror is because it's deep and there were substantial themes here which required so much custom design work to be done to make the illustration. It was very challenging, I learned a lot on the Elm Street pictures, not only about the craft but about my artistic intent and how to interpret it. So why I love horror films is not because of my sensibilities, it's because those films are intelligent, they are very labor intensive from a mechanical and design perspective, there is a lot of original stuff that you have to figure out how to do. How I ended up part of all this is because I was on the list of names. Wes and the guys at New Line interviewed all of those people but I just hit it off with him. I had a 35mm reel, edited very carefully, and it was not easy to get the footage back then, and you had to rent a screening room to show your reel, and that's exactly what I had to do to get *A Nightmare on Elm Street*. I rented a room and screened my demo reel for Wes, and then a few days went by before he visited me and we had a couple of meetings before I got the job. Hiring a cinematographer is like hiring an actor, you are going to be spending a lot of time together and that collaboration is going to have a major impact on the outcome of the final film."[12]

The introductory shot of Nancy and her friends arriving for school is definitive of Haitkin's distinctive style, creating a lucid atmosphere where the audience is never quite sure if they are experiencing a dream or reality, an aesthetic approach which would become essential for the film series and television show to come. Here, Haitkin introduces us to the angelic little girls singing the haunting lullaby, "One Two, Freddy's Coming for You…" in a soft, heavily diffused image that suggests a dream state, only to pan right to herald the arrival of the teenagers as the frame focuses sharply to denote the shift to reality. It's a masterful move, setting the visual tone of the film and the entire franchise in a single shot. Haitkin agrees and explains:

"I designed that shot! That was a very, very special shot that required five people simultaneously operating the camera. How we did it is there was a speed change done in the camera, there's no post-production on it; everything you see, from the diffusion to the diffusion being taken away, the slow-motion going to regular motion, the tracking and zooming, it is all done in one single camera move without a cut, from beginning to end. The conception of it is great. Wes conveyed to me what the scene was to be and I went to that location, figured out where I'd have to put the kids, how we'd have them drive up, what lenses I would use, and I pitched my idea for the shot to Wes and we worked on it together from there. He totally got it and he was very patient, because it was a complicated shot, especially for 1984; to be doing speed changes in the camera was not achieved by pushing a button, we had alligator clips and wires connecting to the camera and there was this prototype device made for us by Claremont Camera to change the speed while adjusting the iris to compensate perfectly. When you do a speed change in a motion picture camera the exposure changes automatically, and because you're spinning slower you have to compensate with an iris change, but because the change is so gradual you can't do it manually, you have to have a machine telling the iris how much speed change there is. So we had what was called the Speed Aperture Computer and it was a separate device hooked up to the camera that had pretty much never been used before and we were testing a prototype to execute that shot. I also had custom-made filters that were fifteen inches by five inches—five inches wide to fit inside the matte box—and I personally painted those filters in a graduated fog from clear to very dense. I had a camera assistant take this filter which was fifteen inches long and he'd start at the heavily diffused end and then slowly, physically, pull the filter through the box, slowly lightening up the fog based on how I graduated it by eye. I bought these pieces of glass custom-made, then I got into a shop and started fussing around with sprays and cleaning and testing until I had two or three filters that were the ones I wanted to use. So altogether I had someone pull the filter, someone change the aperture, someone working the zoom, somebody pulling focus, somebody dollying the camera. That shot was a big deal!"[13]

Another striking example of Haitkin's use of elliptical leaps into the dream world is the scene in which Nancy is drifting off in class during a particularly somnambulant reading of Act 1 Scene 1 of Shakespeare's *Hamlet*, during which she experiences a haunting vision of her slain friend Tina in a body bag. Tina is beckoning to Nancy to follow her to the hissing boiler room below. To a certain point we are not quite sure if we have crossed over into a dream or not because the filmmakers haven't signaled the audience through any aesthetic heralding of such, as there are no old-fashioned waves or dissolves to suggest a transition into a surreal realm, but when Nancy exits the classroom the school hall resounds with the subtle howl of wind as well as the rustle and crunch of falling leaves, and we are certain that we are now in Freddy's playground of the subconscious.

The ghostly apparition of Tina (Amanda Wyss) leading Nancy to the boiler room.

"That's a perfect example of what Wes once said to me," Haitkin states, "which was 'I don't want to be able to tell the difference between the dream world and the real world.' That school scene is one of the really good uses of that subtle shift, because we see her in the classroom where she slips into the dream but we don't realize it, and we didn't change the lighting, or maybe we just tweaked it and made very subtle changes, and then she sees Tina and you know then that Nancy is in the dream world. And then she follows Tina out and we see the leaves falling even though we're in the interior of the school, so we know for sure that Nancy is in peril. In pre-production one of the things I pitched to Wes was a look for the dreams so that the audience would know they've entered a dream. And that's typical of a cinematographer, trying to make a distinction with these obvious nightmare sequences. But Wes said, 'no, I'm going to slip into dreams and people won't know that they're in a dream, so I don't want to have any effect popping up to let people know they are leaving reality and entering the dream world.' And he was so right. That's why he's the author of the piece! And he didn't have to argue with me, once I listened to Wes's idea I knew immediately that was the right way to do it, and it even took me down a rabbit hole which allowed me to go even further with my own ideas, because now I realized what the journey is. Once I had my cues from Wes about how the dreams were not going to be delineated other than with a subtle surrealistic shift I knew we found our voice. Wes's voice is the voice of the film, and he and I were singing a duet."[14]

Haitkin's visual rendering of Springwood sets up the neat visual dichotomy that dominates the aesthetic of the franchise: the hazy, sun-drenched, idyllic Midwestern exterior world in contrast with the dark, industrialized interiors of the nightmare realm and the shadowy basements of the subconscious. Together, Craven and Haitkin draw attention to the ugliness behind the shiny veneer, using light and shadow to underscore the secrets kept, the social ills ignored, and the dark side of life behind the picket fence.

"It was a conscious thing," Haitkin affirms, "the idea is to put expression in the lighting and the framing to evoke the emotion, and so each shot has its own values. Sometimes the overriding value of a shot is the surprise part of it, perhaps a scare, or it may be an expositional story component. Every beat and every micro beat of a story is informational and the question is its emotion and meaning: is it a scare, or is it a beat that's leading up to a moment of suspense? You look very deeply at the values of a shot because you're making an illustration with all of these flourishes and out of all these building blocks, and every block counts. At the professional level, there's a lot of deep thinking about the storytelling. It's like words, you form a sentence by choosing the right words in order to communicate, and how we speak them conveys a certain communicative signal; it's the same here: you look deeply for the meaning in every single beat and every single shot and then when you have a series of shots combined it takes on a further meaning, like phrasing in music or in writing."[15]

Freddy's Nightmares director Mick Garris, too, notes the juxtaposition of the bright suburban world of prettified living rooms and trellised façades in contrast with Freddy's nightmare netherworld: "It is 'Norman Rockwell Goes to Hell.' Wes's theme of juxtaposing the two sides of Springwood is something that David Lynch used so well in *Blue Velvet* and it's one of my favorite themes. It shows up in a lot of my work as well. You have this idealized vision of what America is, small-town Americana, and then you turn it on its ear; literally in the case of David Lynch finding the detached ear in the lawn under the wistful image of the sprinkler. Wes is doing that here too, he is going beneath the surface of this idealized image of America and he is finding the truth that it is an ugly fucking place."[16]

Robert Englund concurs: "In Springwood you have these pristine suburban ranch houses with the beautiful manicured lawns and the sprinklers and white picket fences, but Freddy exists in these homes, in the bedrooms of the teenagers as he lingers in the imagination and the subconscious of the offspring and the relatives of the vigilantes that burned him alive. Because two wrongs don't make a right, he hasn't gone all the way to Hell, he is somehow having his revenge from some kind of strange purgatory where if you think of him and think of the truth, of the terrible crimes of this man who is whispered about, who perpetrated it, he can get to you and you can become infected by the 'Nightmare on Elm Street,' by the Nightmare of America and the loss of innocence."[17]

Craven would also indulge his themes outside of the cinematic canvas, bringing his ideas to the place which is not only of sight and sound but of mind, that is to say he took his vision to television, particularly to *The Twilight Zone*. In 1985, two decades after Rod Serling's television masterpiece ceased after five seasons, CBS revived the show for a new generation of cult aficionados, sci-fi buffs, and horror hounds alike. The network was tentative in bringing the show back for the 1980s; the original had not been a runaway commercial success and the very title itself came with unfortunate connotations after the 1983 film version became mired in controversy because of the accidental on-set deaths of actors Vic Morrow, Myca Dinh Le, and Renee Shin-Ye Chen and the resulting legal fallout. Morrow and the two child extras were shooting a dangerous scene for director John Landis' segment of the film, during which a helicopter lost control and devastatingly collided with the actors. A criminal trial ensued, but the film was a financial success regardless, and so CBS were keenly aware of the long-term marketability of the property, something that Serling wasn't, having sold his rights to the network and from which they profited large with its success in syndication. The series would attract some of the biggest names in fantasy, sci-fi, and horror literature, including George R.R. Martin (*Game of Thrones*), Rockne S. O'Bannon (*Alien Nation*), J. Michael Straczynski (*Babylon 5*), Harlan Ellison (*Star Trek*) and Alan Brennert (*The Outer Limits*) and also brought in some heavyweight auteur filmmakers of the New Hollywood era whose cultural cachet wasn't what it was ten years prior, but whose presence on the show lent it some serious filmmaking credibility: William Friedkin (*The Exorcist*), John Milius (*Big Wednesday*), Peter Medak (*The Changeling*), Jim McBride (*David Holzman's Diary*), Claudia Weill (*It's My Turn*). The show would also prove a showcase for the hottest emerging talents in town, such as Joe Dante (*Gremlins*), Martha Coolidge (*Valley Girl*), Atom Egoyan (*Next of Kin*), and one Wes Craven.

Twilight Zone cinematographer and director Bradford May recalls the series being a boundless playground of the imagination for some of the most creative people in the industry, one in which filmmakers could flex their artistic muscle without corporate restraint. "CBS didn't regulate the show, it was like Camelot," May says.

"We had all these great writers and we brought in these amazing directors and actors, and what we were doing is essentially making a new movie every day, or sometimes twice a day, as some of them could be as short as ten minutes while others could be thirty-minute episodes. There was no pre-determined style on how to shoot the whole series; it wasn't like a regular show that retains the same style and has recurring sets, because every story of ours was different, every director had his own vision, and we shot every one of them like they were a different film. And Wes was our very first director. Our producer, Phil DeGuere, was instrumental in bringing in all of those great filmmakers and I remember being at his house going through all these names when Wes Craven's name came up. He wasn't yet the pop-culture horror icon director that he would become; at this point *A Nightmare on Elm Street* wasn't long out, and it certainly wasn't yet a franchise, nor had Freddy Krueger become this huge name in horror. Wes had just made a number of good, small independent horror films and we thought he would be a good director for this show, and he proved to be excellent. A remarkable man and filmmaker. The first thing he did was the episode 'A Little Peace and Quiet.' Then we filmed 'Shatterday,' which starred Bruce Willis. At this point Bruce was just starting *Moonlighting* and we all just knew he was going to go on to be a huge star. Wes was used to small non-union crews so this was a different kind of situation for him. But Wes and I had a good creative relationship. I read the scripts, so I knew what was required of the story and I was well-prepared for anything Wes might have needed and he trusted that if he wanted some unusual kind of shot that I would get it for him. We both approached things from an intellectual level but once I'm on the set I'm more guttural, I'll just get in there and get the work done."[18]

While Craven addressed the familial malaise often and usually in the context of the horror genre, perhaps his most sincere address of such is his *Twilight Zone* episode, 'Her Pilgrim Soul.' In this story written by Alan Brennert, Kevin Drayton is a computer scientist who finds himself in an increasingly loveless marriage to wife Carol. She pines for a child, but he is disinterested; she uses emotional blackmail, invoking his previous enthusiasm for the idea of having a child, perhaps uttered in the throes of courtship, and blames his preoccupation with work for his dereliction of domestic duty. One of Kevin's projects is a computer hologram which can virtualize inanimate objects he programs into the system, so he and his colleague Dan are therefore shocked to discover the emergence of a human fetus floating within the holographic column. Being that neither of the men programmed the fetus, both leave for the night baffled, only to return the next morning and discover that it has matured into a baby. Growing at the alarming rate of ten years per day, the child grows up through various stages of life within a few days, during which Kevin becomes infatuated with the woman it becomes, Nola. As she approaches death, Nola reveals to Kevin that he is the reincarnated soul of her partner who died in his grief after she perished after the miscarriage of their child. This revelation leads to Kevin's sudden awareness of his ignorance to his wife's needs and to his marriage. The episode displays an astounding tenderness in Craven's handling of such sensitive material, but his empathy for the yearning of family stability and unity would be no surprise to keen followers of his career.

Anne Twomey as Nola Granville in Wes Craven's 1985 episode of *The Twilight Zone*, "Her Pilgrim Soul."

"Working on *The Twilight Zone* didn't exactly help Wes's career," says May, "but it did show he could do dramatic and poignant things like *Her Pilgrim Soul* and do it well. He was all about the inner feelings and the subtext of his stories, which are deep and very emotional, and this episode really allowed him to explore that more openly. Wes wasn't a surface level kind of guy, he was very much an intellectual, and he even spoke like a professor. He was a gentle guy and he was very soft-spoken. As a director, he was not pushy in any way, nor did he rule with a big stick. He approached directing just as he approached storytelling, with high intelligence. That is evident in the themes of his work and you could see it in the deep approach to working with actors; he had a unique sensibility in getting really rich performances from them. Wes went on to great success, and he actually asked me to shoot some of his later feature films but I was usually always tied up on another show, but what the *Twilight Zone* did for him was allow him to hone the skills that bit more; he went on from there to really define his brand and to become this pop-culture icon."[19]

And a pop-culture icon he would become indeed, though Wes Craven's status as a revered symbol of contemporary horror wouldn't truly be cemented until the release of *Scream* in 1996, the second horror franchise that he would steer to triumphant box office success. Following *A Nightmare on Elm Street*, Craven embarked on a series of interesting films, such as the mid-career quartet of *Deadly Friend*,

The Serpent and the Rainbow, *Shocker* and *The People Under the Stairs*, but none of those generated the kind of fan fervor or box office receipts of the Elm Street franchise, even though they are respectively entertaining, singularly crafted works which continued to ruminate upon Craven's favorite themes. The 1994 Freddy revival *Wes Craven's New Nightmare* is an ingenious work, but it was lost on audiences who were perhaps jaded of being visited by Freddy, having been supposedly killed off three years earlier in *Freddy's Dead: The Final Nightmare*, or perhaps they were just not yet ready for its unique kind of intellectual intertextual treatise on horror storytelling. The film's financial performance wasn't good, yielding only moderate results which made it the poorest box office performer in *A Nightmare on Elm Street* history. A similar fate awaited his next film, the Eddie Murphy horror comedy, *Vampire in Brooklyn*, another commercial misfire, despite the presence of the bankable star. It would take the sleeper phenomenon of *Scream* to bring Craven to true mainstream relevance, introducing him to a whole new demographic of teen audiences while appealing to film-savvy Gen Xers who were wise enough to recognize the in-jokes and self-reflexivity of the ironic murder mystery. The film's success revived Craven's career and led to three sequels, all directed by him, and a television series for MTV.

Wes Craven died on August 30, 2015, of brain cancer. He leaves an immeasurable legacy, one so profoundly admired, studied and celebrated it is hard to deftly summarize in a paragraph, but then again, to discuss the entire *Nightmare on Elm Street* franchise in this book is one's resolve to celebrate and acknowledge the mammoth mark that the filmmaker left upon the horror genre and within the history of American Cinema. Craven himself once considered the impact that his most memorable and adored creation would leave upon his legacy: "When I die the obituary will be, 'best known for inventing Freddy Krueger.' It'll be something like that, they'll summarize my entire career with it and I think for Robert it will be, 'The man who played Freddy Krueger.' No matter what else you do in life, it's one of those things, the film has its way with you." [20]

Wes Craven (Photofest NYC).

> *"Something is trying to get inside my body!"*
> —Jesse Walsh

Springwood is the new home of the Walsh family, which includes 17-year-old Jesse (Mark Patton), his sister Angela (Christie Clark) and his parents, played by Clu Gulager and Hope Lange. They have just moved into 1428 Elm Street, the former Thompson household and it is here that Jesse begins experiencing his own teenage traumas of sexual anxiety and insecurity when he starts having nightmares that feature the taunting specter of Freddy Krueger. The house begins to undergo unexplained supernatural phenomena, leading to Jesse and his girlfriend, Lisa (Kim Myers), to uncover the dark past of the home and the unfortunate legacy of the town of Springwood. Meanwhile, Freddy begins to play a more intimate role in Jesse's life, transcending the dream realm to enter the boy's waking psyche. By feeding off of Jesse's fears and taking possession of his physical being, Freddy can continue his reign of terror in the real world of Springwood once again.

When burgeoning film distribution and production company New Line Cinema found themselves with a sleeper hit on their hands with *A Nightmare on Elm Street*, it was only natural that they would want to milk their new cash cow. The company had previously experienced modest success in distributing cult classics such as *Reefer Madness* (1936) and assorted award-winning foreign arthouse titles before producing films such as Mark Lester's *Stunts* (1977) and John Waters' *Polyester* (1981). But with a massively lucrative property suddenly on the books, and one that had huge sequel potential, time was of the essence for New Line Cinema chairman Robert Shaye to get another Elm Street film into production. Almost a year to the day after the first film was released, *A Nightmare on Elm Street 2: Freddy's Revenge* was unleashed. Shaye recalls the impetus to roll camera on the sequel:

Freddy Krueger (Robert Englund) breaks out of the dream world and into reality in *A Nightmare on Elm Street 2: Freddy's Revenge.*

"When the film opened and it was a big success and people were actually lined up around the block, that was when we got excited, and we did at that point not only realize that this could be a franchise but kind of our bread and butter because we didn't have any product flow, we didn't have any production activities, we didn't have money. We had an office above Smith's Bar and Grill on 13th Street in University Place in Manhattan. So, frankly, we didn't have a hell of a lot. So we said, 'well at least this is something, maybe this could be viable for us,' so we hired a guy who was one of our film inspectors, a guy named David Chaskin, and an old friend of mine who had written and directed *Alone in the Dark* and who had done the very first trailer for our very first movie which was *End of August at Hotel Ozone* in 1967, we hired him to direct the movie. That was Jack Sholder."[21]

"I had a long association with New Line since the early days," Sholder affirms, "and my first feature *Alone in the Dark* was the first film that they produced; up until that point they had been a distribution company. But it got to the stage where they said distribution was getting too hard so they should go into producing and maybe start doing horror films. So I came up with the idea for *Alone in the Dark* and it actually got made. It was the first one they did completely on their own. So they knew me and I had done a lot of editing work for them and I had also directed a film called *The Garden Party*, an adaptation of a Catherine Mansfield short story that went on public television and won a bunch of awards. I knew how to put a film together, especially as an editor. At the time you had all sorts of people working on low budget horror films and a lot them didn't know what they were doing and they'd shoot these movies in such a way that you couldn't really put them together; they would be missing pieces. Bob Shaye used to say to me, 'well at least we know you'll get all of the pieces.' Whether the pieces would be any good, that's another thing, but I'd give them all the pieces and they'd have a movie. And that was all that they wanted, their expectations were low; their head of distribution was this old-time cigar chomping guy who knew every drive-in along the Mississippi and he said he hoped *A Nightmare on Elm Street 2* would do 70% of what the first movie did, so that's the kind of expectation people had for a horror sequel."[22]

Sholder, however, wasn't New Line's first choice of director, as it made sense for them to approach the originator of the saga, Wes Craven. The director became briefly attached to the project but bowed out after several weeks of pre-production, as he recalls: "The first film was not conceived as the beginning of a sequel, by myself, it was an idea that had a beginning, middle, and end. So when New Line set off to make a sequel to it, *Nightmare 2*, they sent it to me and asked me to be part of it because the relationship was cordial, and I couldn't see it in that script, I mean I just felt like things happened in that script that were just being done for some silly special effect and I felt that there were some basic mistakes, such as bringing Freddy out into daylight and into the room with … let's say the pool scene, where you had him running around with teenagers that were taller than he was. I just felt like that was not what the essence of the character was or the smart way to do it, so I passed on that. Jack Sholder, who I know, did a very good job on it."[23]

"Wes was supposed to direct it," Sholder confirms, "that was the plan, but regardless of who ended up directing it, New Line just wanted to get another film out with the words 'A Nightmare on Elm Street' in the title, so it was a case of 'go make a movie and put '2' on the end of it!' They just wanted to cash in on the original title. At that time a horror sequel was considered a big step down from the original. *Halloween II* was never going to be as good as *Halloween*, as was expected. Nowadays people expect bigger and better with each passing sequel. So they hired Dave Chaskin, who worked in New Line's distribution department to write the screenplay and I guess he had a good pitch. Dave saw himself as a screenwriter even though he was working in distribution, but Wes never liked the script, he never liked the story. The original Elm Street was really an auteur movie, it wasn't a case of, 'hey I want to make a horror movie and make a lot of money,' it was something Wes was very serious about. So he had signed on to do *A Nightmare on Elm Street 2* but he wasn't terribly involved because the screenplay never appealed to him and he really didn't like the fact that Freddy was able to be present when people are awake, that violated his whole original concept. After the first film Wes was pretty hot and he didn't have to do it, and so he quit about six weeks before they were due to start shooting the movie. So the train had left the station."[24]

Even Sholder had reservations about directing the sequel, as when New Line Cinema offered the film to him his first reaction was to turn it down, not wanting to get pegged as a horror film director. "I certainly didn't want to do a sequel to somebody else's horror film," Sholder affirms, "I would prefer to be known as someone who, if you had a verse play by William Butler Yeats that took place in the 15th century, that I was your guy—'Call Jack!' So I spoke to a producer friend of mine who was out in LA, and I told him I had been offered *A Nightmare on Elm Street 2* and I wasn't sure about it, and he said, 'Don't be an idiot! The film will make a lot of money and you'll get a career as a film director out of it.' So I accepted the job. New Line had an office set up and they had producers out in LA, so it looked like the movie was going to happen one way or another. I had been very familiar with *A Nightmare on Elm Street* because even though I was never a permanent employee of New Line I did a lot of work with them and I hung out with them all the time. Bob and I would go out once or twice a week and we would talk about the film; I had read early drafts of the script and I would give him my thoughts and then I would see it during various phases of editing and I would offer my opinion. So I was fairly familiar with the project and I guess they figured I was someone with enough understanding of it who could jump in and get something done.

I wasn't intimidated by the idea of having to live up to what Wes had done on the first film, or the fear of killing the franchise; it wasn't a franchise at that point, it was just a sequel and there was the hope that if it did okay then they would make another one, to see how many eggs the golden goose would lay. What I was intimidated about was that I had to make this movie from a script that called for a lot of special effects, none of which I knew how to do. The special effects person was this old-time studio guy who was the head of the effects department at 20th Century–Fox for twenty years; he was an old school guy, lots of fishing wire and monofilament, all very low-tech stuff, but he knew how to do everything, so that was helpful. The idea of having six weeks to put this thing together felt like I was about to climb Mount Everest. I like to be extremely prepared because I have this fear that I'm going to walk onto the set and have absolutely no idea what I'm going to be doing. I was living in New York at the time and as soon as I said 'yes' the next thing I know I'm on a plane and I'm in LA. The whole thing was moving so fast and I had yet to cast the film and get the locations as none of that stuff had been done. Thankfully, I knew people out there in LA, I knew the Head of Production, Sara Risher, who is an old friend, and I said to her, 'so, are you bringing Robert Englund back?' and she said that his agent wants more money but we're not going to give him more money, so if we have to we'll just get somebody else. They didn't have any actors on board, which is one thing, but they had not been able to make a deal with Robert Englund yet because he wanted more money and they wouldn't give him more money because they thought he was trying to take advantage of them."[25]

"There was a problem with Robert because Robert's agent started getting wise," Shaye confirms, "They were asking for all kinds of money we didn't have and we were certainly in a dither about what to do."[26] Unfortunately, by the time New Line Cinema and Robert Englund came to agreement, the actor was not available for the first week of shooting the Freddy scenes. Because the studio dragged their feet for so long, Englund went and took another job. Sholder continues, "When we were casting for all the roles we never had a casting call for Freddy, and this is what leads me to believe that New Line were always going to cast him but were just playing hardball to see what the best deal they could extract would be. And they did cast him, but then they said, 'well, we have good news and bad news: we've hired Robert but he's not available for the first week of shooting.' We had scheduled the locker room scene for the

Actor Robert Englund (left), director Jack Sholder (center), and Freddy double (unknown, right) (courtesy Jack Sholder Collection).

first week of filming and there was only that one shot where Jesse turns into Freddy and walks out of the shower room. So people were saying, 'oh they've got a stuntman to play Freddy,' well we didn't hire a stuntman—those people are like professional actors in that they have a lot of experience being in front of the camera—this guy they hired to be Freddy was just an extra or some guy they pulled off the street who fit the wardrobe, he had a similar stature and a similar face to Robert, so he was probably picked out by the makeup people. He was basically just put straight into a Freddy mask because they didn't bother to do a molding. But when we did the shot of him walking out of the shower the guy just started walking like Frankenstein, stiff as a board, and I had to tell him to stop walking like a monster, I said 'stop it! Walk like a man!' Even though I hadn't yet worked with Robert I knew something wasn't right about the character, but I think I got it good enough. So then the following week Robert came on and from the moment he did his very first scene you could tell he had this unique power, this authority; I mean Robert Englund is not this big, powerful guy, he's a character actor and he's got this funny kind of face, an odd choice to play that character, but he has this intensity from which you can just feel the earth move under his feet. So once Robert was there, I could see what it is that he brings to the role that makes it so definitively Robert. He has a very quick mind, if you sit down and talk to him, he will cover ten topics in three minutes, his mind sort of flits all over the place. He's a hyper guy and he internalizes that energy so that it comes out in this intense portrayal of the character.

New Line knew Freddy was a really good villain, but they didn't yet know that he was what the franchise was all about. If you look at the original poster for Part 2

Robert Englund (left) and director Jack Sholder (center) converse with cinematographer Jacques Haitkin (right) (courtesy Jack Sholder Collection).

there's no Freddy on the poster and it says 'Starring Mark Patton' and I think Robert gets third billing. So New Line didn't realize that Freddy was really the star until Part 2 came out and the audience went crazy every time he would appear. You see, anybody can play Jason Voorhees or Michael Myers, they just pop up, kill somebody and disappear, and the actors who play them are buried under all the makeup and the mask—you just put those on somebody else and the audience isn't going to know. But Robert is a really good actor who understands the role and he knew exactly what to do, it was never a case of me saying, 'okay, Robert, here's how I want you to play this….' He already knew the character, so it was just a question of shading here and there and some small, minor adjustments. I would never have to tell him to be scarier or ask for a certain kind of performance. He wouldn't hold anything back and I think that's part of the enduring appeal of the character. Robert is a very smart guy and he understood what the central relationship between Freddy and Jesse was all about. But New Line was very concerned about Freddy and not very interested in a whole lot else, they never gave me any kind of guidance and never said 'you gotta do this' or 'you gotta do that,' the only thing was they said they hated the makeup and wanted a new makeup person, and so I found Kevin Yagher. Kevin did a fantastic job and ended up doing the rest of the series. The only other thing New Line said to me was that they wanted to keep Freddy dark, keep him mysterious and scary, which changed later on, but those were my only marching orders. By the time I started work on the film they had already hired Jacques Haitkin, which I was very happy about, because I was somewhere in a state between anxious and panicked for the entire pre-production period and I just worked like a dog to figure out every single shot in the movie before I got there. So it was great to have Jacques already on board."[27]

Cinematographer Jacques Haitkin returned from the original film, this time working with Sholder to create a different look than that of Craven's mise-en-scène. Here Haitkin introduces a more colorful palette, incorporating the vivid green, red and purple tones that will become a distinctive part of the visual language of the series as it progresses. And while Haitkin does retain elements of the moody and expressionistic lighting that informed the first film, his cinematography is noticeably slicker this time around, with a brighter and richer palette in place of the original film's more muted and shadowy milieu.

"When I look back at the film now I don't find it particularly good. For example, the lighting at the barbeque, that's so simplistic when you think about it, the obvious Freddy colors. It's a little embarrassing to me now and I wish I had been more subtle; but I was young and underdeveloped. Some people take that as campy now. My late wife, Anne, was my Focus Puller, and she did amazing work, her close-ups were sharp as a tack. The films got more sophisticated and I appreciate how the series developed and became this bigger thing, but Wes was an ethereal artist, his higher purpose was definitely of a more thematic, expressionistic, and surrealistic nature, and that was what the first film was all about. *A Nightmare on Elm Street 2* wasn't about that. Jack was much more of a creature effects appreciator than Wes, he was much more of an on-the-nose, 'let's create a rollercoaster and scare them!' kind of guy. He came from the editing world and knew how to construct a film, but he was less prone to share ideas on the thematic side of things; in our discussions he was more interested in telling me what was going to happen on a technical level. Take the effect where Freddy pulls back his scalp and reveals his brain, that is not something Wes would do but Jack loved that stuff, so that changed it up for me. When Jack wanted to portray that kind of horror film it meant that I too have to be a bit more on-the-nose with my photography in order to facilitate the kind of film Jack wanted. It's like a marriage where I'm the wife and I have to do what my husband tells me. You have to play nice and not get into a conflict."[28]

"Jacques could be meticulous," Sholder says, "I remember very clearly the shot where Freddy is having some fun toying with Mark Patton and Freddy has one of his greatest lines of the whole series, which is 'you've got the body and I've got the brains,' and I remember shooting that so well because Jacques spent about an hour lighting that just so the light would just hit the brain when it's revealed; he had these lights which would pinpoint particular areas with a very tiny little circle to get it just right."[29]

"Cinema is about ideas," Haitkin says, "and audiences have become quite sophisticated, so it means you have to work on an intellectual level as a cinema artist and cinema professional; if you don't then you're not in the right business. All the pros, even the hacks, know that it is important to be able to think deeply about what they are doing, because the days of doing superficial work is over. But for me, as a filmmaker, I thought like that from the beginning, so I was ahead of the curve. Being able to tell a story through your images is of absolute importance. Because you're in there as part of a team you listen to the other artists, you see where they're going with wardrobes and you look at set designs. There's so much happening in this collaborative

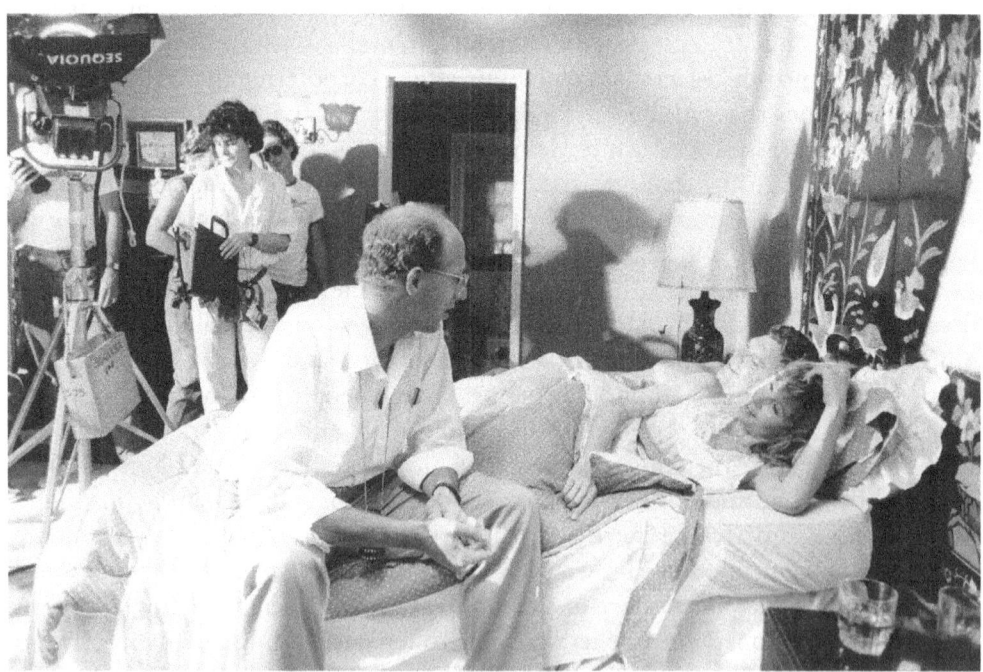

Jack Sholder directs a scene (courtesy Jack Sholder Collection).

effort and as a cinematographer I know my job is to pay attention and listen to the other artists. Jack was less-experienced than Wes, so he was a little more nervous and worried about things, but he imbued his sensibilities on the film even without verbal communication."[30]

"I was very thankful to have had Jacques shooting the film," Sholder adds, "with him there I was able to make a cinematically interesting film and he really helped get me through it all. He is a very willing collaborator and we got along very well. I had actually wanted Jacques to shoot *Alone in the Dark* but he wasn't available or was too expensive, but I really admired his work and the fact that he had already done the original gave me some confidence, knowing that I had somebody there who understood how the whole thing worked and who could make it look really good."[31]

Cinematographer Jacques Haitkin shoots a scene alongside his wife and First Assistant Camera, Anne Coffey (courtesy Jack Sholder Collection).

Haitkin continues, "That is one of the great things about the cinema, it's a collaboration, we become very powerful because of a brain trust and because of the united energy; being in this group is one of the gifts of the journey of filmmaking. It's a lot like a military operation but without all of the bad stuff. Our mission is to reach an audience and touch their hearts and minds and to entertain. And it's a very intense collaboration because the hours are long, the stakes are high, there's a lot of money involved and people are always wringing their hands because you're pushing the envelope everywhere, on labor, on time, on your budget, and then something can come along, like the weather, and completely throw you. It's very risky emotionally, it's like going out to war, and a lot of people are not suited to it. You have to be a real decision maker. I've learnt something about myself because of being in this business, and that is I'm very good at making big decisions. I can't decide on what to eat or what to wear, but big decisions? No problem! Making movies is all about big decisions. You receive hundreds of questions all day long, and every answer has the potential for disaster, so it's all important. You do need to be an expert because so many things can go wrong, especially as a cinematographer, because your expertise is out there every minute; all of those questions coming at you require a certified answer, and that certification gives everyone the confidence to move on and go ahead."[32]

Despite overcoming the mammoth task of actually getting the film in the can,

Jack Sholder and crew film the climactic scene (courtesy Jack Sholder Collection).

Sholder faced another problem in the post-production and test screening phase. Even though time has been kind to the film and it has been discovered by successive generations of fans since its release, reaction to the film wasn't always so positive. Robert Shaye found the film lacking in the essential factor of horror filmmaking: horror. But with his expertise and experience in editing, Sholder was able to rescue the film.

"At the end of our first screening Bob comes up to me and says the movie is not scary enough, so I said I would work on it and see what I could do. I was an editor for years before I became a director, so I'm very good at putting films together, I know how to do that very well, so my cuts are quite good. Most directors shoot a 120-page script and they end up with a three-and-a-half-hour movie; I shoot a 120-page script and I end up with a 110-minute first cut because I like to keep things moving along. So I went back and tried to tighten some things up and then we held a second screening and he said the movie is still not scary enough; there was no real reaction from the audience and I'm thinking part of the problem is the way the film is structured, which is basically that Freddy keeps coming out and saying 'I'm gonna do this, I'm gonna do that!' but then he doesn't do anything. And if we're talking about a three-act structure, it's not until the end of the second act when the scene in the gym happens that he does something. Bob said that we need to take that scene and move it to somewhere earlier in the film and I told him there is no way we can do that because it wouldn't make any sense to the narrative and structure of the film. If you kill off the coach earlier in the film then we can't have the other scenes with the coach and so forth, but Bob just said that we have to do something to make it scarier. So I worked on it some more."[33]

It was then that Sholder tapped an unofficial though learned source to provide feedback on whether the film finally passed muster or not: "I used to play squash a lot and there was this Hispanic high school kid who worked at the club and was a real horror film enthusiast. He saw everything that came out. So I invited him to come see the film at the next screening and at the end of it I pulled him aside and asked what he thought about it and he says, 'oh, it was pretty good' and I asked him if it was scary and he kind of shrugged and said, 'not really.' I just thought 'oh shit, this is bad!' So I got on the subway and I had about four or five stops, not even a fifteen-minute ride, and I thought how can I take the gym scene out of the end of the second act and put it in the beginning of the second act. And then I remembered there's a driving shot with Kim and Mark in the car where you can see their faces but you can't really see their lips, and I thought if I put in this new line of dialogue that would help, which it did, and so I took that scene and moved it twenty minutes earlier into the film. So now Freddy says he is going to do something and he does it; that means the next time he makes a threat you believe he's going to follow through on it, so there's more tension there. And the next screening went a lot better, so moving that scene around definitely meant the film felt scarier, and maybe that's one of the reasons the film performed as well as it did. I always find it really amusing when I do an appearance at a convention or a festival and someone tells me that the film really scared them, because for a while it was looking like we had a horror film with no horror."[34]

For the lead role of Jesse Walsh, actor Mark Patton was cast after beating off competition such as Brad Pitt and Christian Slater. Poised to be a Hollywood heartthrob,

Patton had previously starred alongside Cher, Sandy Dennis, and Karen Black in Robert Altman's *Come Back to the Five and Dime, Jimmy Dean, Jimmy Dean* in 1982, a role he had previously played in the Broadway production of Ed Gracsyk's original play. But Patton brought a unique performance and personality to *A Nightmare on Elm Street 2: Freddy's Revenge* that has drawn much attention in the ensuing decades, that which has attracted as much analysis as any of the teen leads from horror cinema of the 1980s. The reason that Patton's performance has been so scrutinized is due it being informed with the kind of feminine characteristics one would normally associate with the horror genre's obsequious tradition of the female "Scream Queen." In a subversion of the trope of having a female protagonist as victim fodder for the antagonist, Patton provides what is perhaps considered the definitive male Scream Queen performance. As such the film has developed a cult following in the ensuing years which is largely based upon the film's seeming homoerotic subtext, something which has allowed the film to be embraced by pop-cultural critics and celebrated by fans as a milestone in queer horror cinema. For years the homoeroticism of the film was kept to fans and academics to discuss and ponder, but in recent times the acknowledgment and observance of *A Nightmare on Elm Street 2* as part of the gay horror canon has in itself become part of pop-culture lore. The comprehensive 2010 documentary, *Never Sleep Again: The Elm Street Legacy*, gave screenwriter David Chaskin a platform to finally admit that the inherent homoeroticism was indeed a deliberately placed subtext in reaction to the then-pertinent AIDS crisis. Also, the 2019 documentary on Mark Patton, *Scream, Queen! My Nightmare on Elm Street*, has kept the conversation alive, and by extension, kept what was previously a more forgotten and less-beloved entry in the *Elm Street* series to be re-evaluated in such a context and to be deemed culturally relevant.

"If we re-made *A Nightmare on Elm Street 2*, that film is so right for now," Robert Englund says, "because we wouldn't have to dance around the bisexuality so much. That is something which is right there in Part 2, and obviously so, especially with the S&M bar, or the scenes with the boys in the bedroom, and there's this great moment with Mark and I where we both agreed that I was going to flirt with him and play with him and toy with his confused sexuality. Freddy gets in there like Freud and Jung, he gets into the brain and he knows everything about you. Once you have heard about Freddy, if you are a relative or a relation to the vigilante parents, whether it's whispered about in the locker room or its shared at a sleepover or a party, when you hear about Freddy he then festers in your imagination; he knows what's in your diary, he knows your secrets and your fears and he can exploit them. But there was always something creepy and darkly sexual about the series. On the earlier films, when you saw how the kids where dressed and saw how they looked, and then you saw the sets made by Mick and C.J. Strawn around them mutating. On one of the sets there was a mutated doll with blood between her legs in a baby carriage. That's the way some of those sets felt: it was violent and there was a feeling of strange, dark sexuality to them too, definitely a kind of Freudian violent surrealism that we were trying to get. Even when Freddy enters Nancy's dream and we have that simple shot of his face pushing through the wall and he is looking down upon her, he is violating her bedroom and that is a sacred, private place for an adolescent. And Freddy is in there and he's right next to the crucifix and that's a real violation, it's a very Freudian implication, and dreams and nightmares are Freudian anyway, but when you add on the extra layer of symbolism it becomes very powerful. There is always an element of sexuality with Freddy and the heroines, the survivor girls; it is some kind of Beauty and the Beast erotic chemistry occurring between Freddy and his nemeses, whether it's Nancy or Alice or any of them. Freddy represents that door into dark, dangerous sexuality, and of course Freddy plays with the sexual anxieties of Jesse in *A Nightmare on Elm Street 2*, because he's an equal opportunity bogeyman."[35]

While Robert Englund clearly recalls the theme of sexual identity and anxiety being a conscious effort of the filmmakers, some recall it differently. Depending on who one talks to from the production, the subtext is either entirely intended or the result of contemporary cultural analysis merely corresponding to the various circumstances of the production. "If you're called the 'homo-Nightmare on Elm Street' on the net by a million pre-pubescent boys, then a bunch of grown men had to know what they were doing," Mark Patton says.[36]

"None of us knew about this homosexual subtext while we were making it!" Sholder proclaims, "I was the one who cast Mark Patton and with the lead role everyone has to agree to it, so when I said I think this guy is right for the role they all agreed with me because the film really needed someone who was vulnerable, and that was the main factor in casting Mark. Him being gay, or the story having a gay undercurrent didn't even enter the consciousness. Mark was a young guy who looked like he was poised to be a star. He was a Johnny Depp kind of guy. Johnny Depp is not rugged, he's a pretty boy, there's almost something feminine about his features, and there is a feminine component to the character of Jesse. Mark had a similar kind of quality to Johnny and the girls all thought he was incredibly hot, so nobody ever thought of his casting in this homosexual context. We just needed someone with that fragility, who would be believable as someone going through an identity crisis and with the

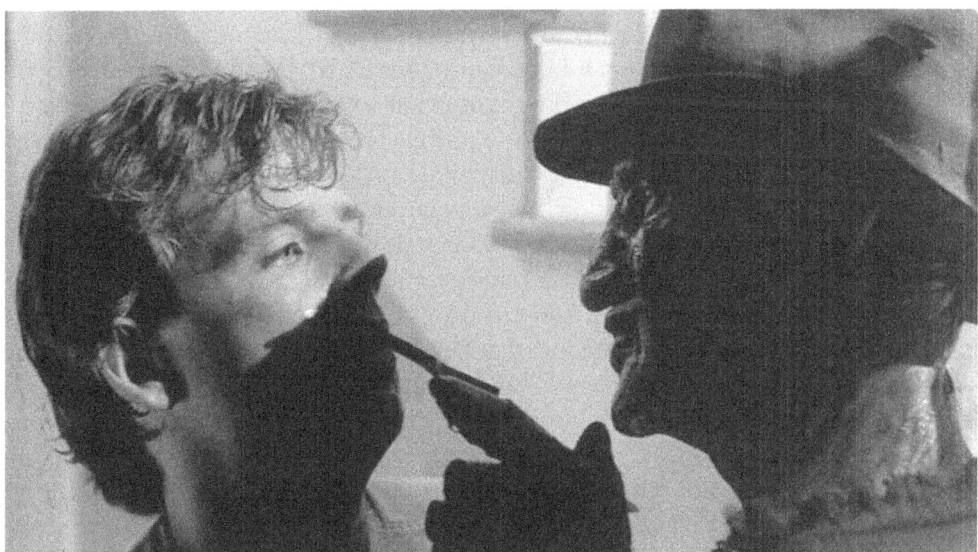

Freddy toys with Jesse (Mark Patton).

suggestion that at some point he was a victim of bullying; when you're a teenage boy your masculinity is something that people attack you with or use to bully you. That's how I saw the film: that it was about teen sexual anxiety and Robert understood that kind of tension between the characters; in fact there were some things that Robert talked to me about where he wanted to take some of the moments in the film and make them even more sexual; he wanted to do some playful stuff with Mark's mouth and other things like that but which Mark felt uncomfortable about. Robert is smart like that and is just game to go wherever he needed to go."[37]

"I remember talking about these themes on the set," Englund recalls, "but I think Jack Sholder was so pre-occupied with everything, because he had to edit the film, he had to manage the budget, and also work with the kids, that I don't he think he realized, or perhaps he has forgotten, that we discussed it a couple of times. I distinctly remember talking about it with Mark, and Kim, and Kevin Yagher my makeup man. I know for certain that I discussed it a lot with Mark because we knew exactly what we were doing."[38]

"On the Wednesday after the film opened," the director recalls, "*The Village Voice* came out with its review and I get a call from Head of Production, Sara Risher, and she says, 'Did you see the review in *The Village Voice*?' and I hadn't so she reads it to me and it says, 'A Nightmare on Elm Street 2: the greatest gay horror film of all time!' and everybody thought it was really funny and I thought it was okay if somebody wants to see it that way. I didn't really think much about the film over the years and then I was asked to participate in a thirty-year reunion that was going to happen at a convention and Mark was going to be there along with Kim Myers and Clu Gulager, so I went and that's when I really began to find out more about the homosexual interpretation, and it is where I heard Mark's story about quitting the business. Mark and I had a professional relationship but not a personal one, we just didn't really connect at all on a personal level; we got the movie done and had the cast and crew screening and we gave each other a hug and that was it. My initial reaction to the whole thing was to think it was really funny because it wasn't what we intended, but I have come to understand that the film has a lot of meaning for LGBT fans and I'm really happy about that; I do think that good art—if you want to call it art—is always open to more than one interpretation, and it is a valid interpretation. I've seen lists that people make of all the things that support their analysis of it as a gay horror film, and it's definitely in there, it's just a question of how you want to look at it."[39]

"The gay theme is not a theme that resonated with too many of us making the film at the time," recalls Haitkin, "very few people would have picked up on it. I'm certain that Jack Sholder was not conscious of it, and I wasn't that aware of it, but my late wife, Anne—who was the focus puller on that show and the first one—she was aware of it. She was the sweetest, kindest girl but she loved tracking gossip on the set. My wife and I didn't talk personally when we were working together on a film, we just talked business, but on downtime she would keep track of all the set smut and I remember her talking about Mark being a little light in the loafers, but I didn't pay attention to that kind of stuff because the crew knows better than to screw up the atmosphere on a set by getting something going that would create a problem. It was obvious that Jack wasn't aware of it and I didn't care either way, I didn't have time to pay attention to it. My wife knew I didn't like gossip or care about it, but looking back on it now I do realize that people knew. But she was respectful of the situation and I'm glad that it eventually came out. I think it's funny that Jack and I were oblivious to it, I mean we were both submerged with work and the problems of getting through the day so we didn't have time to think about it. I have heard that people comb through the film for symbolism alluding to homosexual themes, and I don't know if people are finding things that were intentionally inserted into it or if they are just attributing symbolism to things that simply isn't there. Either way it doesn't matter, because if they find something and you say you didn't deliberately put it there someone will say you did it subconsciously."[40]

Mark Patton (left), Jack Sholder (center), and Kim Myers (right) discussing a scene (courtesy Jack Sholder Collection).

Whether conscious or unconscious, it is certainly understandable as to why audiences may have picked up on some of the homosexual underscoring of the film so easily over the years, as several sequences are not subtle in their allusions to Jesse's sexual identity struggles. Aside from the entire narrative thread of Freddy coveting Jesse's body, in one scene Jesse pays a late-night visit to a gay S&M club downtown, the barman of which is played by none other than New Line Cinema chief, Robert Shaye.

"How that happened was because at one point when we were pretty far along in the casting Bob Shaye told me he wanted to be in the film. We were about two weeks away from shooting and Bob comes up to me and says, 'Jack, I'm going to play Robert Rustler's father,' and I said, 'No, you're not!' and he was like 'what?!' I told him that I need a real actor for the role because there's a lot of emotion going on in the scene where the father is on one side of the door while his son is being killed on the other side of the door and I need a real actor for this. Bob says, 'Well I'm a real actor!' and I just said, 'not really, Bob!' and he threatened to fire me, but of course I knew that he couldn't, not over that. He isn't going to fire his director two weeks before production because I refuse to hire an incompetent person to play an important role. So then I thought, well what's the most embarrassing thing I could have him do in the film? So I said to Bob, 'how about you play the bartender in the leather bar?' and he went 'okay!' and he went out looking for these S&M outfits and he was really into it. There was a place called The Pleasure Chest, which was this sex shop that sold all kinds of kinky material: chains, leather, dildos, and all the rest of that stuff. And so I told Bob about it and he went and bought all of his own gear. And with that I managed to kill two birds with one stone: I got him to drop his request about being in the film and I ended up putting him into a slightly humiliating situation. It was great and he enjoyed it. And he's good in the role too."[41] Shaye, however, maintains that "Jack could end up being a jerk from time to time and that was one of his jerkier episodes."[42]

Further such analysis of the film can point to scenes in which Jesse's track field tormentor, Coach Schneider (Marshall Bell), becomes a bound, bare-assed, towel-snapped victim of the Freddy-possessed Jesse, as well as a campy disco dance sequence in which Jesse cavorts suggestively to "Touch Me (All Night Long)" by Fonda Rae and Wish. Patton's recurring high-pitched shriek throughout the film perhaps cements him as the pre-eminent Male Scream Queen for the ages.

"I don't know whether that hurt it or not," Englund ponders, "Part 2 did great in Europe because it did stay true to and did bring up a lot of these psychosexual aspects that were hidden in Part 1. The problem with Part 2, I felt, was that they broke the sort of hard and fast bible of *A Nightmare on Elm Street*, the rules that Wes has set, which is Freddy's always in a dream; when Freddy's in reality he's really in a dream. That's the whole point, that's the joke, that's the gimmick. They tried to bring Freddy out of the dream in Part 2, which makes it a little ludicrous, I think."[43]

"I have a pretty good sense of humor," Sholder says, "if you see my other films you'll see some pretty funny stuff, in fact I should direct a comedy. The big difference between me and Wes is that Wes was a real horror film director, he didn't have a great sense of humor, whereas I have more of a sense of irony which I brought to scenes like the leather bar, which I was thought was kind of funny; the whole thing was very hard for me to take seriously, in fact most horror films are hard for me to take seriously. I mean there are things that scare me but they aren't the stuff of horror films, I'm not expecting some guy to jump out of the shadows and hit me on the head with an axe. Dying, getting cancer, and not having enough money to eat ... those things are scary! I don't really worry about some maniac appearing at my door with a chainsaw."[44]

A Nightmare on Elm Street 2: Freddy's Revenge stands out for not being a servile imitator of Wes Craven's first film, and it is a particularly unnerving entry which creates a sweltering, uncomfortable atmosphere largely due to the simmering sense of sexual anxiety that is heightened by the suggestive chemistry between Englund and Patton. Another particular reason for the taut, sinister tone of the film is thanks in no small part to its unusual score by Christopher Young, here replacing Charles Bernstein. Young's unorthodox music attracted the ear of his director, who had studied to be a classical musician. Sholder's dreams to play the trumpet professionally may have ultimately eluded him, but his ear for interesting music led to his entry in the *Elm Street* series having one of its most unsettling and distinctive scores. Sholder recalls:

"When it came time to hiring a composer I listened to a lot of different people,

Clu Gulager (left), Hope Lange (center), and Jack Sholder (right) (courtesy Jack Sholder Collection).

and I just thought this guy, Christopher Young, is really interesting and I liked that he was doing something unusual. Chris was just getting started at that point and he put a lot of money into hiring the musicians because the money he was being paid would have just been enough to pay for a synth track, which is what a lot of films were doing at that time because you can play everything on the synthesizer. But we didn't want that shitty synthesizer sound in this film and Chris felt the same way, he wanted something more orchestral, so it was a mix of both; he hired a bunch of conservatory music students who were very fine players to supplement the sound and what really made it unique was that you had this synth violin part that was mixed with a real violin section and it created this weird, unsettling string sound that gives it that unique, eerie tone."[45]

Ultimately, the film proved to be exactly the financial injection that New Line Cinema needed, grossing ten times its budget of $3 million in the U.S. alone. The evidence was in the receipts that the movie-going public were keen to embrace Freddy Krueger as the new anti-hero of American Cinema.

"The movie opened on a Friday and by Sunday it was the top-grossing film of the week," Sholder enthuses. "The reviews were all pretty positive, I mean in the context of a horror sequel. Then the phone rang and it was Dino De Laurentiis and I'm back in LA and I'm on to a career. I felt I did a good job on Part 2. If someone else had directed it, it definitely would have been a different movie, but it wasn't a personal movie for me, I didn't have a lot of input or have a whole lot of time to put into the script, my job was basically just to get it shot. The next film I did was *The Hidden* and

The cast and crew of *A Nightmare on Elm Street 2: Freddy's Revenge* (courtesy Jack Sholder Collection).

even though I didn't write the script it was something I really identified with and felt very strongly about. I just moved on. For better or worse we really made a sequel, we didn't do a slavish rethread of the first film. We didn't make a point-by-point sequel, I always looked upon *A Nightmare on Elm Street 2* as a possession movie, but we did keep the essence of what Wes was doing in the original. It's funny, people always say that *A Nightmare on Elm Street 3* went back to the formula of the original but I don't think they did, because the original wasn't that funny, Freddy was not a stand-up comedian in the first as he was in the third. For a long time people would say, 'oh, Part 2 was terrible, it broke the rules and was a big step down from the original and they re-found it in Part 3,' but people are now re-evaluating it. I've done some interviews about it over the years and I have gotten a lot of favorable comments along with some of the usual putdowns; one host of a show that I was on said, 'you have to look at this film on its own, if you look at it trying to have the same template as the original then you are going to be disappointed, but if you look at it as something different then it will make more sense,' and that is very true. It was great working on *A Nightmare on Elm Street 2*, and I still get a nice royalty check every year. We had an appealing cast, Mark and Kim were very good, Robert is really good, and it looks great; that is probably why it holds up. I'm quite pleased by the whole thing and reengaging in it has allowed me and Mark to really get to know each other and become friends. He has given me a lot of insight into looking at the film in a more serious way than I had been looking at it."[46]

2

The Monster Goes Mainstream

"It's not you. It's your parents, my parents. They burned him alive, and now we're paying for their sins." —Nancy Thompson

In *A Nightmare on Elm Street 3: Dream Warriors*, Kristen Parker (Patricia Arquette) is an anxiety-ridden teenager living on Elm Street with her pre-occupied socialite mother, Elaine Parker (Brooke Bundy). Unfortunately for Kristen, her mother also happened to be part of the mob of aggrieved parents that torched Freddy Krueger years ago, meaning she is a target for Freddy's revenge. Kristen tries in vain to stay awake at night by listening to heavy metal music and downing copious amounts of black coffee, but nothing can keep her from slipping into the dream world where she is haunted by the vengeful spirit of the man her mother helped bring down. After Freddy slashes her wrists in a dream tussle it looks as though she has attempted suicide, leading people to believe Kristen is self-harming, and so she is sent to Westin Hills Psychiatric Hospital, an asylum for children with emotional issues and sleep disorders. Once there she is put in the care of Dr. Neil Gordon (Craig Wasson), though the clinic's efforts to sedate her result in Kristen resisting fiercely until she meets Nancy Thompson (Heather Langenkamp). As Freddy Krueger's former foe, Nancy has her own tortured history in dealing with the dream demon but has since taken a professional interest in the psychology of nightmares and is interning at Westin Hills as a therapist. Nancy earns Kristen's trust after she recites the recognizable "One, Two, Freddy's coming for you" lullaby along with the troubled youngster, a moment which introduces a psychic and emotional bond between the two that will become crucial to defeating Freddy once again.

Kristen is invited to join a group therapy session run by Dr. Gordon for troubled kids who are experiencing dream psychosis and among them are the tough, aggressive Ronald Kincaid (Ken Sagoes), the sensitive, artistic Philip Anderson (Bradley Gregg), the neurotic celebrity wannabe Jennifer Caulfield (Penelope Sudrow), the fragile intellectual Will Stanton (Ira Heiden), the streetwise drug addict Taryn White (Jennifer Rubin), and the mute recluse, Joey Crusel (Rodney Eastman). During one session Kristen inadvertently uses her unique ability to pull other sleepers into her dreams, leading Dr. Gordon to suggest that they attempt group hypnotherapy to explore the possibilities of Kristen's gift and to develop their individual strengths within the dream world. We become privy to each of the teens' emotional and physical vulnerabilities, those which become weaponized by Freddy later on as he terrorizes them individually, while Nancy informs them that they are the remaining children of the Elm Street parents who killed Freddy Krueger and thus revealing the truth of the malevolent force behind their psychoses. With strength in numbers, they band together in their dreams as they attempt to fight off Freddy for once and for all, but he knows too well how to gain entry to their subconscious via their various psychological wounds, and so he plays upon their insecurities and weaknesses to remain as powerful and manipulative as ever.

After the financial success of *A Nightmare on Elm Street 2: Freddy's Revenge*, New Line Cinema were keen to cash in on their prized property. This time they would bring in some extraordinary talent to make it their slickest and most potentially commercial film to date, including first-time director, Chuck Russell, whose previous work co-writing and co-producing the psychic adventure film *Dreamscape* (1984) may have marked him out as the ideal candidate to further the adventures of Freddy Krueger. Russell recalls:

"I was a huge fan of the original *A Nightmare on Elm Street* and of Wes Craven. I've always been fascinated with dreams and using cinema to explore what happens to us when we fall into that surreal world; it has always been a passion of mine. I did a movie called *Dreamscape*, which was the first film that I co-wrote and I was also a producer on it. It starred Dennis Quaid, Max Von Sydow, and Christopher Plummer, it was an ambitious but low-budget sci-fi and is a bit of a cult film. Bob Shaye and Sara Risher, both producers from New Line, were fans of *Dreamscape*. They knew that I had worked on the script, the production and the visual effects and really liked what I had done. I was looking for my first directing gig after *Dreamscape* came out; I was still very new to Hollywood, but I acquired the rights to do a re-imagined version of *The Blob* because I wanted to create my first opportunity to direct. That is how I initially met Bob Shaye at New Line. He passed on *The Blob*, but asked me for my thoughts on potentially directing the third *A Nightmare on Elm Street*. I was thrilled

Freddy is ready for his close-up on *A Nightmare on Elm Street 3: Dream Warriors* (courtesy Roy H. Wagner Collection).

but challenged, because Wes' original was already a classic in the genre and a very original kind of horror film. But at the time, New Line was on the fence about the series after mixed results on *A Nightmare on Elm Street Part 2*.

Wes Craven and Bruce Wagner had written a script but New Line wanted a rewrite and new thoughts on the direction of the series. Actually one of the things that attracted me to the project was the opportunity to potentially work with Wes, but unfortunately, at the time Wes and New Line had parted ways. Such things happen in Hollywood, but there was a happy ending years later as Wes returned to the series with *New Nightmare*. So I sensed a responsibility to do very well by the *Elm Street* legacy. I had felt that Part 2 had treated the character of Freddy more like a crazed killer than the dream demon that I thought had so much potential from the original film; I thought if we are going to do Part 3, then let's explore the dream world more deeply, and how the dream world can empower us, which I thought would be the great potential strength of a young cast. I treated it more like a superhero movie, honestly, and I wanted to get into the sense of teamwork in the characters empowerment. That and an emphasis on the surreality of going in and out of our dreams and how they affect our waking life. My friend of many years, Frank Darabont, was my co-writer and collaborator; I dragged Frank into it, but he loves horror, as you can see from *The Walking Dead* and *The Mist*, and was delighted. I wanted to make the wildest nightmare scenes ever done. Yet *A Nightmare on Elm Street 3* was made on a typically limited budget, pre–CGI, so the innovations with physical on-set effects were a requirement. I am happy that those are the things that the audience responded to, but I knew from the beginning they wouldn't respond to the effects if they didn't love the characters. Thus it's all about the screenplay."[1]

Indeed, *A Nightmare on Elm Street 3: Dream Warriors* represents a significant step forward for the franchise to becoming a more polished and extravagant horror product for the 1980s, the result of some particularly well-chosen collaborators for the film. One major boon to the picture is its cinematographer Roy H. Wagner, who had previously shot the low-budget horrors *Witchboard* (Kevin S. Tenney, 1986) and *Return to Horror High* (Bill Froehlich, 1987). Having not only the relevant experience of working under the intense pressures of independent filmmaking within the horror genre, Wagner also brings a distinctly artistic and masterful eye for unique composition to the film, resulting in this sequel being one of the most visually impressive films in the franchise. Wagner recalls the connections made on a previous film which led him down this memorable sojourn to Elm Street:

"I had met the producer, Rachel Talalay, when she was the assistant director on another project, *Return to Horror High*. That film had been very ambitious and challenging for her. I knew nothing of her history and had no idea that she was really a producer and had been involved with New Line on the previous *Nightmare on Elm Street* films. But based upon her experience with me she knew that I would be highly qualified for her next project, so she arranged for me to meet the director, Chuck Russell, at New Line Cinema's headquarters in Beverly Hills. The meeting seemed to go very well. I phoned Rachel afterwards and told her so, believing that Chuck and I had such a great conversation that I would be getting a call to my agent soon."[2]

Unfortunately, the job was offered to another cinematographer and neither

Wagner nor his agent received the call. "It often happens in Hollywood," Wagner says, "they never have the courtesy to let you know that they have moved on to another cinematographer. I had to find it out from friends and others in the industry. This is always a drag and it is humiliating. I never got a call from Rachel or the production company. You never learn in Hollywood. I was bitter." Despite this setback, it wasn't long before the producers would ultimately come crawling back to Wagner, having seen the film almost derail and end up behind schedule with their ill-chosen initial cinematographer. One particularly difficult scene proved to all involved that perhaps it was time to call Wagner to help get the show back on track. "This was the era of beepers and phone booths," Wagner says, "a friend and I were having lunch at a restaurant on Sunset Blvd and I kept getting urgent beeps and I didn't know the number so I ignored it until the number was followed by a '911.' Then I went to a phone booth on Sunset. 'When can you meet with Chuck?' the voice said. I didn't know who was calling initially but soon discovered it was Rachel. 'We're in trouble. I'd like for you to meet with Chuck tonight so that we can discuss your taking over.' As I said, I was somewhat bitter but fortunately I was wise enough to swallow my pride and agree to take the meeting. It would occur that night at UCLA. I arrived to find the shooting company actively working on the next set-up. Rachel swiftly took me into Chuck's trailer. 'We're three days in and already way behind schedule. We'd like for you to take it over tomorrow.' They had attempted to photograph a scene and it had not gone well."[3]

The scene in question begins with Kristen asleep in her bedroom before elliptically segueing into a surreal dreamscape where she awakens and realizes that she is in a haunting, hellish vision of Elm Street. Kristen looks out over her headboard to the eerie sounds of Freddy's lullaby sung by the ethereal figures of innocent children resplendent in white, slowly skipping rope in the dead of night in front of Nancy Thompson's derelict and decrepit house.

"They had major technical issues with that scene that would require a re-shoot. In those days we had no video playback and the company had no video monitors. It was a complicated shot. The trick was to ramp the camera's speed into slow motion as the Elm Street house is revealed and the camera moves toward the house with Patricia before she steps into the house as the door slams. Our budget didn't allow for Steadicam thus we had to build a dolly track across the street and up to the door. When I operated I had to tilt up slightly so that I wouldn't see the track. Where the original crew had failed was when the camera changed speed from 24 frames to 90 frames they attempted to use HMI lights which would flicker if the camera speed didn't fit within a narrow window. That's a problem with shooting in slow motion. Just a few years later HMI's were developed with square wave ballasts thus eliminating this problem. But my crew was accustomed to using the old carbon arc lights, which had no problems with flicker at any speed. They were huge, but they provided a great deal of light and that's why it doesn't look like a milky night scene, rather it looks rich and it's because we used the arc lights. We also had an exceptional grip crew who could lay track evenly so that a high-speed move would not bounce. I knew that Chuck wanted a very high-speed move, what we used to call a speed ramp, which makes the audience feel as if they are moving quicker than the speed of light. As soon as we got to the door the camera would go back to 24 frames per second. The previous crew had attempted to race towards the door at high speed, but the shot was very bouncy and hard to come to a sharp stop; it felt as if the audience was shoved into the house, a place they did not want to go. But with our animation style shot we could overcome the bumps in the track because we were dollying very slowly. Chuck wanted it to feel like a dream state, and so how I interpreted that was it became slow motion and that's the way it is in the film. We had a device for the camera which can manipulate the speed without affecting the stop; normally when you'd go from regular speed to slow motion there would be a flash of one or two frames where it would get brighter and this device didn't do that. The biggest mandate from Chuck was he didn't want to tip our hand that she was no longer in her bedroom, he wanted to make it appear that she was still at home. Unfortunately one of hardest things we had was ambient light on that street that we just couldn't control, so the image does get a bit bluer; when I look back on it nowadays I wish I could have color timed and fixed it so it wouldn't be so blue. I couldn't because it was all photochemical and you just couldn't change that."[4]

Prior to taking over from the exiting cinematographer, Wagner had not read the script, discussed special effects, seen any of the locations, nor had he seen either of the previous *Nightmare on Elm Street* films. But now with the production facing potential disaster, he agreed to take the job under the condition that he could have his own crew: camera, grip and electric.

"I knew that we would be very critically judged on our first night," Wagner says, "I've always said, 'It's their problem until you say yes.' Well I had said 'yes' and thus they were not going to listen to any excuses about prep. Upon my meeting with the producers I was told that they had been very unhappy with *A Nightmare on Elm Street 2*. They felt that the audience could see too much of Freddy and that overall the images had to be dark."[5]

"*A Nightmare on Elm Street 3* is a very dark fantasy," Russell says, "but I didn't want it to be one of these films that is actually hard to see, I wanted it to be grim and naturalistic, but then have a distinctly different, more vibrant look within the dreams. One of the really key things for me, cinematically, were the transitions. I wanted to come in and out of these dreams as an important and sometimes unexpected part of the story. I carefully storyboarded these transitions and chose to hide them or present them boldly in each case. My challenge in dream sequences was 'have we seen it before?' I tried to personalize concepts that had the eerie dream logic we've all experienced. Roy Wagner, my cinematographer, helped me achieve that. I used to make puppets as a kid and so that played into Bradley's character who makes puppets, then Freddy turns him into one, which is a really bizarre thing on paper. Some people didn't think it would work. But it ended up being the most memorable kill. That and the bizarre 'TV Freddy' are my favorites: 'Welcome to primetime, bitch!'"[6]

"Photographically, I wanted the film to be a thrill ride," Wagner says, "I had already shot some horror films and I knew how they work. Audiences want a thrill ride. I usually tend to shoot through character but I think the fact that I didn't have any time to prep meant that Chuck and I didn't have any time to talk about the movie in a thematic or highbrow context. I approached it thinking that the audience has to believe that we weren't taking this seriously, that we have our tongue in our cheek and are in on the fun as much as they should be. Working next to Chuck and seeing how absurd everything was, I had to have a sense of humor about it. I wanted the outside world seemingly safe, real and not dreamlike, because you can play with that; if the tone of the image becomes cold it's a psychological trick that prepares the audience for something that's about to happen, it lets them in on the changing mood of the film."

Wagner continues: "It was much tougher for Jacques Haitkin, who was the cinematographer on those first two films, because he had to invent things that would become part of the *Nightmare on Elm Street* language; it was easier for me, I had no expectations. I didn't see the first two films until I got the job. I didn't want to shoot it like the first film, and I thought that *A Nightmare on Elm Street 2* looked much flatter and more conventional and I only watched it because I knew New Line wasn't happy with it, so I wanted to know what not to do. I wouldn't normally watch what other people have done because part of being an artist is that you respond to other people's work, and you begin to take a little from them, but I was a bit reluctant to go in and be influenced by how others had done it. I stay as far away from other people's work as I can."[7]

"Roy Wagner did a lot of his color field stuff on *A Nightmare on Elm Street 3*," Robert Englund says, "he was also the house cinematographer on *CSI* and his work on that is so influential. People talk about *Hill Street Blues*, or *The West Wing*, or *L.A. Law* as being 'the shows that changed television' but what *really* changed network and cable television shows is *CSI* and that is because of Roy's use of deep focus and the

Cinematographer Roy H. Wagner and actor Robert Englund on set (courtesy Roy H. Wagner Collection).

absence of space with his use of color. But before all of that, Roy brought that skill to *A Nightmare on Elm Street 3*."[8]

Just as Wagner was brought in to help save the troubled production, so too was assistant director, Dennis Maguire, the son of veteran Hollywood producer and assistant director, Charles H. Maguire (*On the Waterfront*, *The Sand Pebbles*, *The Friends of Eddie Coyle*). *A Nightmare on Elm Street 3: Dream Warriors* was New Line Cinema's first DGA (Director's Guild of America) production, meaning that the young, largely non-union crew would be working alongside card-carrying veteran DGA members, one of whom was Maguire. The assistant director remembers receiving the call to join the tense shoot:

"I was never a horror fan, even as a kid it never interested me. I was more into European art films and grew up being into more serious kinds of things rather than shlock, but I took the job on *A Nightmare on Elm Street 3* because a friend of mine asked me if I could come on and help out as they were in trouble. I was on the last few days of filming a picture in Arkansas when I got a call from my friend, Rebecca Greeley, who was the UPM [unit production manager] on *A Nightmare on Elm Street 3* and she was asking me to urgently come and A.D. on that film. She called me on a Wednesday night and told me what was going on and I explained that I don't finish shooting in Arkansas until Friday at sunrise. So we agreed that we would speak again on Thursday night and she said that there would be some other people on the line, including executives from New Line and the producers of the film: Rachel Talalay and so on. Rachel started out as a PA on the first film, she was the accountant on the second one, and she was the line producer on the third one, and then she was directing them by the time it got to the sixth one. That was the kind of thing that you could do at New Line, but I ended up making more money as the assistant director than Rachel did as a producer, probably twice as much, because I was DGA, and that woman worked her fanny off! But New Line was a small company at the time and they hadn't dealt with the Director's Guild before; the reason they went DGA on this film is because the director, Chuck Russell, had writing and producing credits to his name and so he was a DGA member and forced them to go Guild. However, Rebecca wasn't a member of the DGA on paper, so even though she was the UPM on the film she didn't receive that credit, the Vice President of New Line put himself down as the UPM because he did have a DGA card; but he wasn't doing that job at all, it was Rebecca. So after the phone call I ended up not going to bed, I just drove straight from our set, which was an hour south of Little Rock, Arkansas, to the airport and flew to LAX. They put me up in a hotel in Beverly Hills and I met with New Line on the Friday afternoon; I was so exhausted, I had been gone on location for fifteen weeks, hadn't seen my wife in all that time, I hadn't slept and probably looked like hell when I was sitting there at the meeting with these guys. Then I met with Chuck Russell at his place in Beverly Hills on the Saturday afternoon and after that I got the call from Rachel to say I got the job and was to start work that Monday. I hadn't even read the script yet, I simply didn't have time."[9]

And so Maguire joined the crew, by which time Wagner was also in place as the new cinematographer and someone with whom Maguire clicked immediately. "We were straight into the shit together," Maguire recalls, "not knowing what was happening and on top of that we didn't really know anybody. Roy has his own crew with him and I had my own crew of about three people. It was Roy's job to make that film look beautiful and he did; there are layers to his lighting and there is a great depth to his photography. He can achieve an amazing look so quickly and efficiently, getting done in twenty minutes what would take other DPs two hours to light. With his knowledge and with his respect for me we were able to set an order on how to do stuff. It was Roy who really pulled that movie together; the previous DP that got let go obviously didn't have the talent or the experience that Roy had and that's probably why New Line was unhappy and why they weren't making their days. They were five days into shooting and way behind schedule, they were lost. It was partly due to Chuck Russell's inexperience as a director and the original First A.D. not being forceful enough; some A.D.'s are like that, but I'm a forceful, active A.D., I don't just sit there and yell 'roll!' and I think New Line appreciated that."[10]

On board to create the film's memorable sets—from the cold corridors of the clinic to the red-hot hellish dreamscapes—was production designer Mick Strawn, who would become an integral figure in crafting the surreal diegetic world of various Elm Street films, as well as the television series, *Freddy's Nightmares*. Strawn had already been working on another film for New Line Cinema when he managed to obtain a seat on the rollercoaster that was the *Nightmare on Elm Street* series.

"I had met Peter Chesney, who was the mechanical effects guy, on a previous New Line film called *Quiet Cool* and we got along really well while I was working construction and art direction on that production. It always takes a while to set those jobs up, so you're looking for stuff to do in-between. I had a lot of experience in effects as well as construction and art direction, meaning I was a triple threat! So I ended up working with Peter setting up some of the stuff for *Dream Warriors* like the skateboard tracks that we used for the Freddy snake going up the wall and across the floor, a lot of the mechanical stuff. It had gotten to the point where they didn't have an art director yet and my current job was coming to an end, so I went over to the office to drop off the final billing for Peter and while I'm standing there waiting on the elevator to take me to the eighth floor, up steps a friend of mine, Gerry Olson. I said, 'what are you doing down here?' and he replied, 'well, I got a job producing *A Nightmare on Elm Street 3*' and I was like 'really?! I'm just putting in the billing for the effects!' And so we got to talking, and Gerry knew me more from the art department than the special effects department, but as we're riding up in the elevator I said, 'Gerry, you need an art director on this, and I already know the whole show, I've been working on it for four months! You need someone who can deal with the effects work and the art department with the sets.... Gerry, I'm your guy!' And before we reached the eighth floor he agreed and I got the job. It was a very successful elevator pitch."[11]

Strawn continues, "I wasn't overly familiar with the *Nightmare* films because I was too busy working, but they had a screening at one of the labs and I got to see the previous two. Then we went into concept meetings and what came out of that was we weren't going to do the usual thing where you put out a great horror film and then for the sequel you throw less money at it and put less care into it and the numbers go down; with *A Nightmare on Elm Street 3* Bob Shaye said, 'this time we're going to spend four or five times as much money on the film, but we need a guide on how to make this not just another routine sequel.' So over the course of these meetings we came up with three different concepts. The first concept was to let Freddy off the chain, because we have Robert Englund, who is this amazingly smart, funny, visceral person; he's got style and swagger, and it's what he does best, so the first thing for us to do was to put some humor into it, to let Robert bring some of his personality to it and allow the character of Freddy to really come to the fore. The second concept addressed the problem I found with the first two films, which is that it had a 'Superman Problem,' which is to say Superman can do anything, or in our case, Freddy can do anything, so what's the point? Where's the tension? The characters eventually have to go to sleep and then Freddy wins. The solution to that was to be able to suck other characters into the dreams. In this case it was Kristen who can bring everybody else into her dream and that makes it so that you have a group who can gang up against Freddy; so now you don't have as much of the Superman Problem. That in itself was a game-changer. And concept number three was mine: I said that I see this as more of an adventure film, we can go more elaborate with the dreams and so I'm going to take us to some weird places. The way I looked at it was, we're not on location much, a lot of this will be on a stage and I can really work with that, although when I say 'a stage' what I mean is a big warehouse across the street from the county jail! They used to have this thing, weekend jail, which would be for drug cases and stuff like that and there was this taco truck that used to sit out front for twenty-four hours a day and it serviced the jail for the most part. It was strange to be standing there at some ungodly hour, like 5 or 6 a.m. on a Monday morning eating a taco and watching the grips come right out of the jail and across the street to the warehouse to start work. But that's what I did. Those are the three things that made this a different film. I think I spent about $40,000 more than I was supposed to and I'd end up firing everybody, but then I'd have to hire everybody back again to get the work done."[12]

Thankfully, one of those that Strawn didn't fire, but rather took a chance on hiring, was Andre Ellingson, another intrepid young soul who would benefit from the New Line Cinema style of career advancement. Arriving in Hollywood in 1986 at the age of 23, it didn't take Ellingson long to find work as a PA on rock videos for the likes of Michael Jackson, Cheap Trick, ZZ Top, and KISS. Soon enough Ellingson met Mick Strawn and his sister (fellow Elm Street production designer) C.J. Strawn, and being that the siblings Strawn were already working for New Line Cinema at this point, they soon offered their new friend a job as an apprentice carpenter on their current project, *A Nightmare on Elm Street 3*. It wouldn't take long for Ellingson to rise through the ranks and graduate from assistant carpenter to construction foreman on *A Nightmare on Elm Street 4: The Dream Master* and special effects coordinator on *A Nightmare on Elm Street 5: The Dream Child*, and the television series, *Freddy's Nightmares*.

"New Line Cinema was extremely busy at the time," Ellingson recalls, "They had the Elm Street franchise going on and a lot of other stuff. They were one of the first non-union companies to break out of the union mold in the mid-eighties in Hollywood and it was good to get a job with them because they had so much in production. Back then there were music videos being shot on every street corner in Hollywood because MTV was so huge, so I got a lot of work as a PA on those and after about nine months of doing that I met Mick and C.J. and they gave me a job on a movie they were working on. That was the first moment I walked on to a movie set and it was *A Nightmare on Elm Street 3*. I will never forget it: this huge stage, just massive, and there were all these cool sets and the Freddy Snake was sitting right in front of me; I had never seen anything like that before. Mick hired me as an apprentice carpenter but I didn't know anything, I was just out of film school where we were taught about cinematography, writing, editing, all that stuff; I didn't know how to build anything, but I learned right there on the set. It was an amazing experience because Freddy Krueger and the Elm Street franchise were becoming huge! I was telling all my friends back in Montana that I'm working with Freddy Krueger and they're like, 'Jesus Christ, you've hit the jackpot!'"[13]

With the cast and crew now in place, production resumed in earnest. Wagner recalls his first night on the set, shooting the pivotal scene in which Dr. Gordon and Donald Thompson visit the grim site at which the Elm Street parents buried the bones of Freddy Krueger: "My first shot was an angle of John Saxon's truck driving up to a salvage car graveyard. The camera would rise and reveal a frightening monolith of demolished vehicles as far as the eye could see. But none of the electrical cable had been laid. As any cinematographer will tell you that's the most costly and time consuming portion of a production's below-the-line cost. Chuck had decided at the last minute that we should have a symphony of automobile headlights that would flash on and off as John Saxon and Craig Wasson called up the dead. All of the stacks of cars were in a rubble of crashed metal. The crew would have to climb amidst the wrecks to wire individual headlight cues to respond to an ambient cue that none of us had heard. All of this had to be done before we got our first shot. Usually you can expect at least an hour of lighting if the lights have been placed and the cable laid. I knew they were expecting me to be fast thus I revealed to my crew our expectations and we chose to focus on the easier and yet still quite complicated opening shot of Craig and John driving up to the gate. Within a half hour we completed the first shot and coverage as the crew was quickly rigging the amphitheater of cars surrounding Freddy's grave. We had lifted the immediate burden of speed from our shoulders so that we could focus on that very complicated scene where Craig and John find Freddy's grave, dig, and discover his bones. There's an image of me in the grave looking back with a sardonic smile at the still photographer as if saying, 'Are you kidding me? And this is the first night!'"[14]

Maguire recalls being thrown in at the deep end that same night: "One of the things I remember most vividly of being on that huge demolition graveyard was John Saxon being an absolute pro. He just arrived, did his thing, didn't act like a prima donna, and was totally game for it. I mean he had to do that gag where he is stabbed through the chest with the fin of the car in this cold, damp location in the middle of the night, and he was just all for it. At one point that night we were waiting for Robert Englund to come out of makeup and I was like, 'Jesus, just put the hockey mask on him already and get him out here!' Well, some of the crew members looked at me aghast, like, 'Are you kidding?! That's Jason! That's *Friday the 13th*!' I hadn't even met Robert at this point so I hadn't seen him in character. Eventually I recognized Freddy from the posters of the older films and I thought, 'oh yeah, the burnt guy!' There are some people who would kill to be working on those films, but

Roy H. Wagner is deep in the Elm Street trenches on his first night of filming (courtesy Roy H. Wagner Collection).

I didn't know anything at all about *A Nightmare on Elm Street* or Freddy Krueger, I was only there as a favor to my friend Rebecca. Had it been Jo Somebody calling me after being gone on location for fifteen weeks I wouldn't have taken a movie like this. I have only taken over movies three times in my career and it's always tough because you're not the guy who prepped it, you don't know everybody, and what happened is that me and Roy came in as the new guys after the other group who prepped the movie were gone after five days; the cameraman, the camera crew, the grip, and assistant director all got fired."[15]

When we look back at the box office success and pop-culture omnipresence of Freddy Krueger and the Elm Street series in the mid–80s, it is easy to forget that these films were still produced in the context of low-budget independent filmmaking and were achieved with cast and crew enduring all the attendant issues of such. However, the production of *A Nightmare on Elm Street 3: Dream Warriors* signaled a shift in the way horror had become big business, and New Line Cinema knew their fortunes rested on the success of this film. The shooting schedule was planned for forty days, an unusually generous time for a New Line film as up to that point a standard production schedule would rarely go beyond eighteen days, twenty at the most. Taking into consideration the re-shoots that were to replace the unusable footage already filmed by the previous crew, the film wrapped after forty-two long, busy, eventful days, brought to completion with the resolve and attitude of those that persevered with the spirit of independence and collaboration.

"Being a cinematographer on an independent/low budget feature has problems that seldom if ever arise in any other form of filmmaking," Wagner says. "We didn't have monitors, so Chuck couldn't look at a monitor and say, 'oh, you didn't pan far enough!' The only time we had a monitor on set was when we had the Louma crane in Freddy Hell because the set had been built in such a way that you literally couldn't get a camera inside of it, but with the Louma crane we could get the arm into the set and have it move around. With a studio production you can run over schedule and budget, and it might mean you may never work for that group again but at least the parent company will protect their asset. *A Nightmare on Elm Street 3* could not be fully funded by New Line Cinema. It required additional investors. None of them with deep pockets. New Line was a very small independent company that relied heavily upon the success of its past productions. Even though the first *Nightmare* had been successful New Line had made some disastrous films. Warner Bros. was still in their future. They couldn't afford something very ambitious like *Nightmare on Elm Street 3*. If New Line failed with this film they were finished. This was a heavily-ladened special effects film and if you cannot accomplish effects within the bids provided by the effects teams, production must be compromised in other ways. Either the schedule is diminished or the effects become compromised."[16]

Having brought much-needed skill and economy to the production which had been running behind schedule, Wagner set about the difficult task of realizing the myriad scenes involving complicated physical gags and intricate setups. One of the

Hell on set (courtesy Roy H. Wagner Collection).

most elaborate and difficult-to-execute effects sequences in the film features Freddy taking the form of a giant serpent. In the scene, Kristen wanders through the Thompson house before being frozen in terror as the lights flicker and Freddy, in an undulating snake-like form, crashes through the walls and runs under the carpet before emerging from beneath to swallow her.

Maguire recalls the difficult staging of the scene: "The Freddy Snake scene was very complicated and of course things went wrong, and when something like that would happen I would just turn to Roy and say, 'okay, we're going to go over here and shoot this while they fix that and by the time they re-rig everything we'll be ready to come back and shoot it again.' So I would find out from Mick or one of the effects guys how long it was going to re-rig one of their failures, which was quite often to tell you the truth; not a lot of stuff went off on the first take, whether it was the TV gag or the snake in the walls. Eventually it all cut together and looked great, especially for the time and the period, but while we were shooting there was a lot of research and development going on right then and there."[17]

"In pre-production everyone felt this would be a very simple trick to pull off," Wagner recalls. "They had built this living room set so that the floor was made out of balsa wood and a miniature rollercoaster track was built under the carpet and a special elongated series of skateboards with army combat helmets would ride along the rails pulled by a team of grips. They had experimented with this gag for weeks and when they felt ready the production team was assembled to shoot this plus an additional portion of the snake racing across the back wall tearing through balsa wood and plaster. Never believe the very best effects team that assures production that their gags will be fool-proof or stay on budget. I've always said, 'Anything is possible in pre-production' because we all are hoping to assure production that we can accomplish the work according to their budget. And the effects team felt that they would accomplish it all in one shot. After all, production was breathing down their neck for the heavy cost overruns.

The Freddy Snake room had to be at least four different sets also and was extremely difficult to get right. There were so many articulated puppets and they were amazing, they looked as good standing next to them as they did on film; it was the best puppetry I'd ever seen and that was Phil Tippett's work. Had it been a more expensive movie there would have been more elegant ways of doing things but we were running by the seat of our pants, and most of our budget was going to the effects and set construction. But being a low-budget film we could only afford two cameras. I was operating one and I believe that Academy Award winner, Russell Carpenter ASC, was operating the other. One was high speed and the other was normal speed. The set was incredibly tense for this was to be one of our biggest stunts to date. Of course the setup with effects took much longer than expected. All of the production executives were on the set making none of us work any faster, only more frightened. We were ready. All barricaded and protected from any disaster. Our A.D., Dennis Maguire, checked with the effects team and the grips prepared to play tug of war with the Freddy Snake, Chuck and the camera team. Roll Camera! Dennis shouted above the noise to call 'action!'

The set shook. There was a noise as loud as an explosion. I missed it! I turned to Russell. 'Did you get it?' 'I didn't see a thing!' he replied. We turned our gaze towards

2. The Monster Goes Mainstream

SUDDENLY "FREDDY-SNAKE" BURSTS UP THRU FLOOR & GRABS HER! (TEARS THRU CARPET TO:)

Nerf Snake
(Snake #1a)

Manual 1 ft. rise Actress
2 ft. snake swallow
One foot loose - one tied in
Pre-broken carpet
Swallow to knee

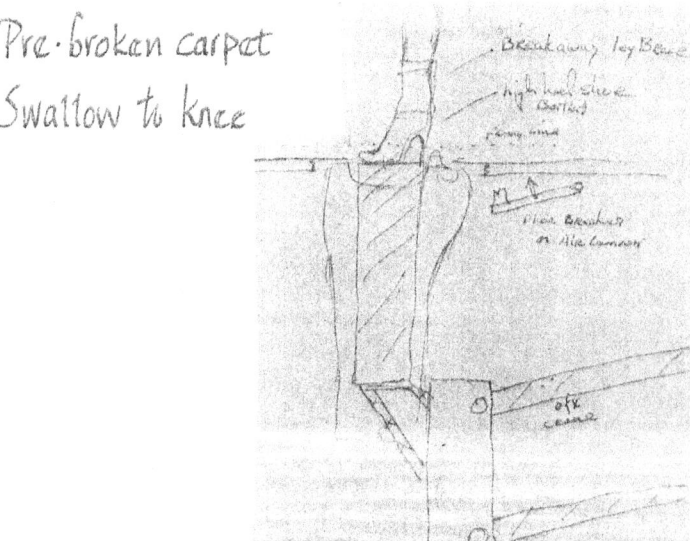

Above and following 10 pages: Roy Wagner Freddy snake scene storyboard (storyboard courtesy of Roy H. Wagner Collection).

LOW ANGLE - KIRSTEN GRIPPED BY TRESN-SNAKE

Snake #1b
(Rise and Fall Snake)

Fall-over controlled by stunt girl weight shift. One ft. movement overlap with 1a.

Snake starts 2 ft. above floor. Capable of 5 ft. rise.

Same nerf head as 1a.

Two hour (mechanical only) structure changeover time.

Kevin Yagher to splice on 4 ft. extension & touch up Glen

2. The Monster Goes Mainstream

Rise and Fall Snake
(Snake #1b.)

stunt pad below ground

SHOOT IN REVERSE

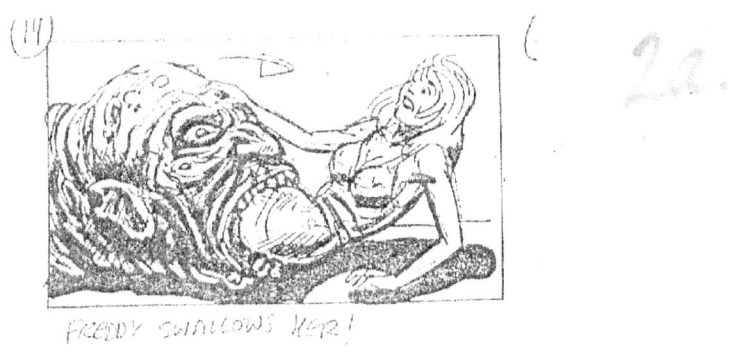

FREDDY SWALLOWS HER!

Snake #2a.
Swallow Snake

To be filmed in reverse.

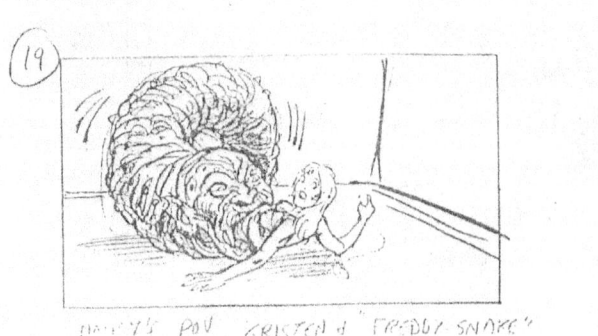

Snake #2 b.
Swallow Snake

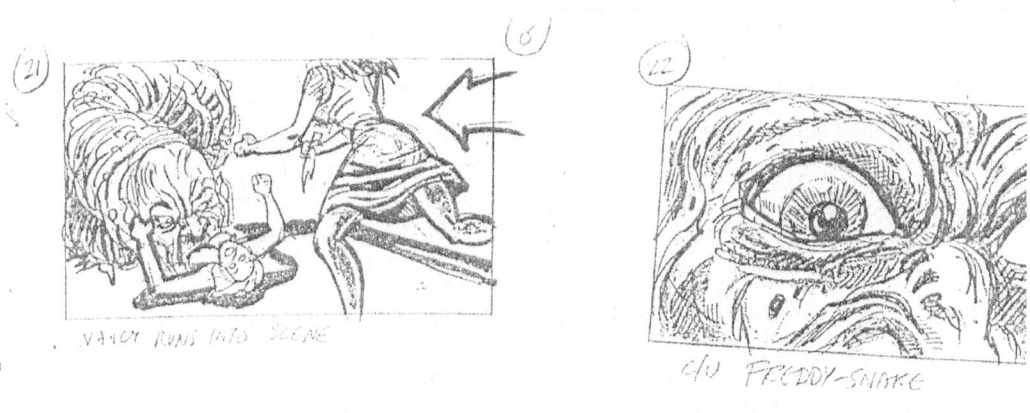

All same as snake 2a. With solid foam body.
Body manipulation help (rig to camera)

and/or
1.) rods manned from below floor & behind holding up arc
2.) crane overarm rig above frame to piano wires into arch.

the Fullers Earth-filled set. Nothing had moved. Nothing! What was all of the noise? None of the onset gag had worked. The entire back of the set was ripped apart. Somehow the opposite had occurred. Had the carpet held our side together while forcing the bottom and the back of the set to disintegrate? After the shock, yelling, and dismay it was determined that we would have to come back in a week to reshoot a completely rebuilt set. Another costly delay. Where was the money going to come from?

There were further issues with the Freddy Snake. The puppeteers were exceptional, but they just couldn't get the snake to realistically gobble up Patricia Arquette. Gravity always forced the movement to look unnatural, so we decided to film the snake gobbling Patricia in reverse. It worked perfectly. Initially the snake almost completely covered Patricia. She writhed in terror and the snake chomped and was pulled away. Perfect! A simple solution. The entire sequence required that same living room to be built upon a platform. In another portion of the sequence Freddy Snake would rise from the floor, his mouth capturing Patricia. The snake would drop to the floor and proceed to 'gobble' her up. That's way more than one shot. The stunt team worked with effects for the lift. It required the snake to crash through the floor and partially swallow Patricia's stunt person, I believe Debbie Evans. That was done with the stunt person standing on a concealed platform on a Nike Chapman camera crane. It would lift her and then the snake to the top of the set. An additional angle would show the stunt person and snake falling to the floor. Both of these setups were fairly simple. Old time stunt work."[18]

#4.

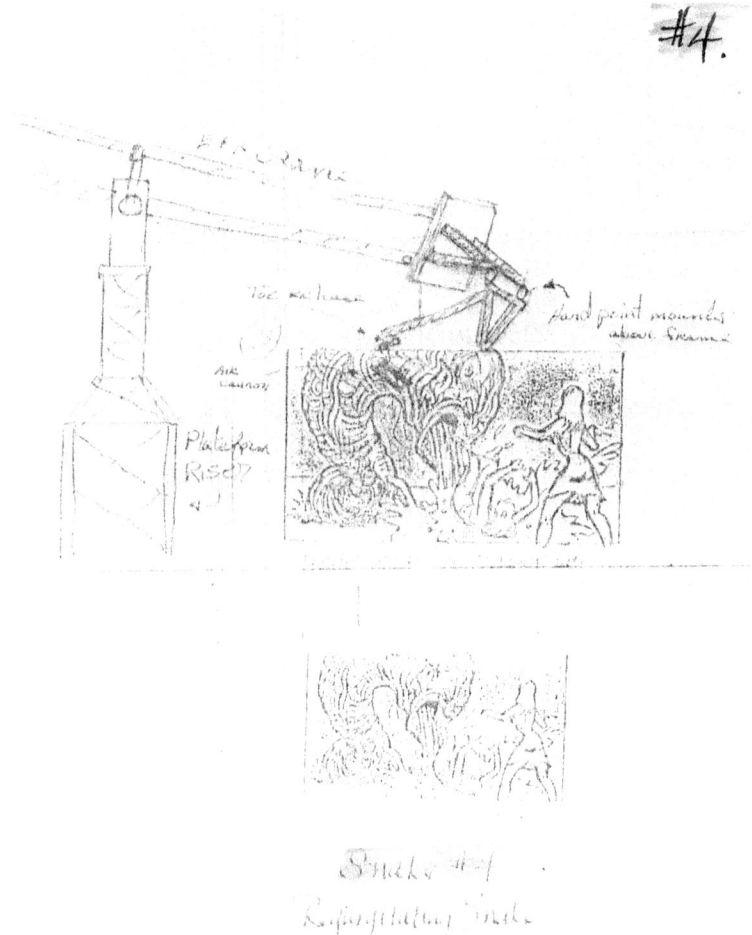

Skin & head - Kevin Y.
Mechanical Eyes - Kevin Y.

Body armature set to overarm (above frame) EFX crane with semi-rigid mounting into top of snake head. Stunt girl has toe-hold self release bars. At her release snake to have a 10-12 gallon rancid vomit dump tank with plastic seal ruptured and initiated by a directional air cannon.

Blocking Rehearsal Necessary Minimum 1½ days prior to shooting.
Camera Platform height
EFX Crane Angular position to Snake
Below floor manipulation requirements

2. The Monster Goes Mainstream

5a.

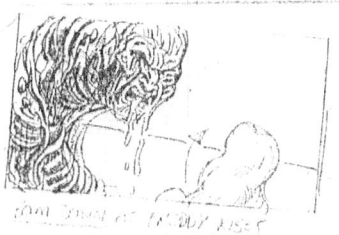

Talking Snake

Snake 5a.

Face & Head articulation - Kevin Y.
Solid foam body articulated from EFX
crane extension from low + behind
base of snake. captive & moved
manually beneath frame.

Snake #5b
Talking snake

Same mounting rig of same skin + head as 5a but possibly mounting point reset to make room for camera.

2. The Monster Goes Mainstream

FREDDY TRANSFORMATION BEGINS...
(1 QUICK CUT — TRANSFORMATION IS ALMOST INSTANTANEOUS)

Snake #5c (possible a.)
Talking Snake

Same Snake & rig as 5a but Possible extension of mounting points will be required to clear frame.

(CONT)
THEY DIVE AWAY DS AS THE FREDDY MONSTER LUNGES (AIR)

Snake #5d

Same snake & rig as 5a but Efx crane needs to be mounted on a dolly and mounting points shifted to suit frame.

✳ Head needs protection — No double.

CRASH! THE DOOR EXPLODES IN A STORM OF WOOD & SPLINTERS!

Peeler Log
(Non) Snake #6

No Snake - Peeler Log

Swung in from ceiling on cables into breakaway door with dust & debris filled air cannons.

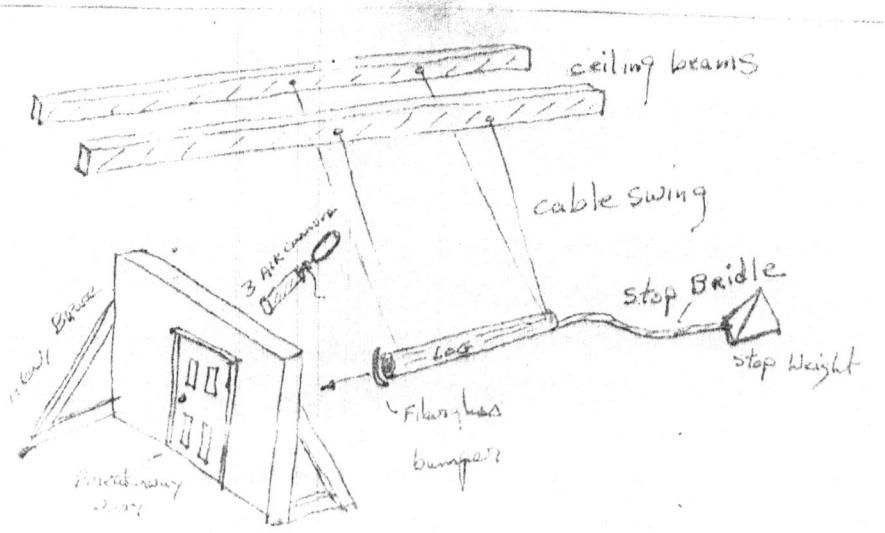

Director Chuck Russell recalls that "when Patricia Arquette had to be gobbled up by the Freddy Snake, it was a full scale animatronic, quite a large prop. We called it 'The Nerf Freddy' because the parts were soft and flexible for safety. But we had made the head so soft that the face just collapsed as it gobbled her. The simple solution was reverse photography, so we pulled the Freddy Snake off of her but when we printed the shot in reverse it appears to consume her. What you see is actually an 'un-gobbling,' so there would be no harm to Patricia and the face did not collapse."[19]

Wagner continues, "The other difficulty came when the effects team brought the Freddy Snake onto the set. I was there early making sure that we were matching the lighting setup from the other living room set but when they proudly revealed the snake all of the color left my face. It was beautifully sculpted. My issue was its color. It was flesh colored. There was no doubt it looked exactly like a giant penis. Remember, this was the early '80s. Today we would have relished in that but New Line was very concerned with their Producers Association rating. I immediately asked for Chuck to come on the set. We both looked at each other and started laughing. No prude was Chuck but initially he suggested that it had to be rebuilt. With production at our heels it was decided that removing the flesh color would take away the greatest curse. Again, more waiting until the proper color was stroked upon the shaft of the snake. Another time things didn't go to plan was in the tricycle scene in the hospital, the tricycle would not stand up on its own. It was built to melt. There was no structure to maintain its form until it melts thus effects had to construct a form on which they could use a squib, this little explosive device that would trigger its deconstruction. Even still they needed heat guns to try to make it melt. I think we only had one tricycle due to the budget. Mechanical effects are almost always more realistic than optical effects and Peter Chesney had a lot of complicated physical effects to pull off; that scene where Freddy lifts the kid was supposed to be done on a crane, but the set was so small they had to build a smaller crane to get in there and lift him. We had no CGI, but that is one of the great things about *A Nightmare on Elm Street 3*, that we achieved all of those effects in-camera, meaning you have real reactions from the actors."[20]

"Story and character are key, the action and the effects are the icing on the cake," Russell says. "It's a little like your side job is to be David Copperfield, working out these illusions which on *A Nightmare on Elm Street 3* were mostly practical effects. But honestly, if I was to make the film again today, I would still do it using mostly practical effects and just enhance them with CGI, which is a remarkable tool that has changed filmmaking forever, but it's not necessarily the best approach for horror. Some of the heavy CGI that you see in some sci-fi films make you go 'wow, those are great effects!' but it doesn't affect you emotionally if it overwhelms story and character. If the audience cares about the characters then even a cheap practical effect can be terrifying. For *A Nightmare on Elm Street 3* we had no CGI effects available, but being forced to execute things with primarily physical effects actually makes it more frightening in a visceral way. A tangible physical on-set gag can also help the actor's performance. The craft comes in the design of a sequence, shot-by-shot to make a physical gag look imposing, but in reality making sure it's absolutely safe."[21]

"The special effects used in the Elm Street films were perfect for their time," Robert Englund says, "and practical effects will always hold up, all you have to do is look

NIGHTMARE ON ELM STREET – ELEMENT BREAKDOWN

DQ 2   TRICYCLE GLOWS RED-HOT AND MELTS

ON SET
2x BICYCLE – PNEUMATIC BIKE
HEAT BELT BIKE

ELEMENTS:

1. Producer provides background plate.

2. Articulate Roto Matte

3. Animation glow.

Roy Wagner storyboard of the melting tricycle (storyboard courtesy of Roy H. Wagner Collection).

at something like John Carpenter's *The Thing* to see how it will never be outdated when used so brilliantly. I think we have become too sophisticated with new CGI but there are times when it works. We saw Chuck work really well with computer effects on *The Mask*, and it was perfect for that film at that moment in time. He blew people's minds with this incredible hybrid effects movie and it really holds up; I don't think people really appreciate that these days because it is just remembered more as a Jim Carrey movie or a Cameron Diaz movie."[22]

"It was an exhausting shoot," Wagner reveals, "most of us were on flat salaries, and we worked no matter how many hours it required to complete the scheduled day's work. Often we would shoot around Freddy, whose makeup required many hours. By the time Robert Englund was starting his day on set we had already been filming at least three hours. No wonder the first cinematographer fell behind. Like is often the case, either the schedule or the director is too ambitious. The producers weren't complaining though, we had an obsessed filmmaking team that was young and desperate to make a great new Freddy movie."[23]

"That was the kind of chaotic resolve we were working with," Andre Ellingson recalls, "one day there were five units working all at the same time, hundreds of people all over the place shooting inserts, big effects shots, smaller effects shots, building sets, it was a fucking madhouse! But on this particular day the producers came in and went up to Chuck Russell and they're like, 'what's going on here? You've got five units running!' and Chuck just says, 'I have no idea!' I'll never forget that. We were just getting as much stuff on film, knowing it will become something."[24]

"We were in a warehouse in downtown LA and we had a 40 × 60 foot green screen," Dennis Maguire says, "which was massive for a little horror movie. We would constantly have sets up against that; we would shoot some regular footage, then go over and shoot some big effects shot, then go back again to the regular stuff. Sometimes I would shoot two of those green screen shots a day just to help the effects guys out because they needed to get those shots."[25]

"Mick Strawn, our Production Designer, had the most impossible job of all," Wagner recalls, "which was building all of these sets, virtually the whole film is on a set. He was constantly forced to build additional sets, and sometimes there could be three versions of the same set, such as the scene where Joey is tied to the bed. You have the regular flat bed, then we had a version of it standing upright so we could have the bed breakaway with a green screen behind him for adding effects in later. And then you have the part where the nurse enters and becomes a female Freddy. These duplicate sets are built to manage different effects. We would film the first unit work, the setup of the scene, the dialogue and completion. The second unit would be required to complete all effects work. For example when the young boy is visited by a nurse who proceeds to take off her clothes then suddenly appear as Freddy we would film the sequence without the 'puppet tongues' which were brilliantly executed by Phil Tippet. The tongues were so realistic that I could stand right next to them and they looked real. That sequence required several identical sets. The entry of the nurse was done on location at the abandoned Westwood Veteran's Hospital. When she entered the room that was a separate small set photographed during post-production. The close ups of the boy on the bed were also done at that time. The full set was used for the masters knowing that we did not have time in the original schedule to gather all of the coverage.

"When the bed mattress falls away revealing Freddy Hell the production designer had to build an exact duplicate of the set on its side. In other words the floor and the bed were mounted on a side wall so that we could get a blue screen (for Freddy Hell) in the background. That required the actor to be tied standing instead of lying. The camera was mounted on a crane with a 360° camera head. All of this was time consuming and required complex rescheduling of actors. Mick pulled off a lot of complicated tricks, such as when they are spiraling down the staircase into Freddy Hell; that shot lasts as long as it can last because if they got one more step down you would see that it was a forced perspective. I walked into where they would climb into that spiral and it looked horrible, until you put the camera up on top and looked straight down into it, then it looked like it went on forever. But for that to happen the camera had to be in exactly the right spot. One of the shots they wanted to have was Patricia getting up out of bed and going to the door and when she gets to the door it suddenly closes and she's in the Elm Street house. Construction built a magic trick, which was the

Welcome to Elm Street

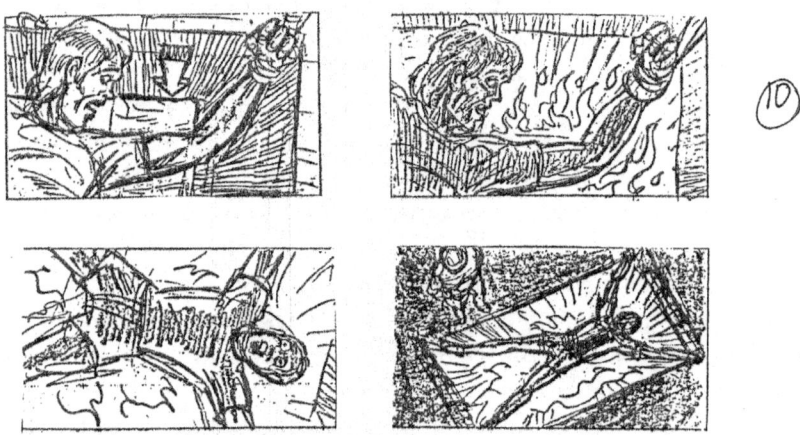

NIGHTMARE ON ELM STREET – ELEMENT BREAKDOWN

DQ 14   MATTRESS FALLS AWAY BENEATH JOEY TO REVEAL FIREY PIT

ELEMENTS:

1. Bluescreen photography on tilted set
2. Motion control of Mattress miniature
3. Motion control of Pit miniature
4. Motion control of Rear Projected Fire
5. Garbage Matte for Blue Screen

[handwritten notes:] FIRE SLOW MO PLATE. ROOM BUILT TWICE 1- NORMAL 2- ROOM ON SIDE (BED IS ACTUALLY WALL THIS ALLOWS JOEY TO STAND IN BED FRAME MATTRESS PULL AWAY WITH DOLLY BLUE SCREEN BG

NOTE: Joey & room to be rigged vertically with bluescreen visible where mattress should be. DQ will supervise shoot & composite miniature mattress falling into firey pit, then composite into shot.

Optical composite — SUPER 1:85 reduced to Academy during optical comp.

Above and following page: Roy Wagner storyboard of Joey fire pit scene (storyboard courtesy of Roy H. Wagner Collection).

2. The Monster Goes Mainstream 71

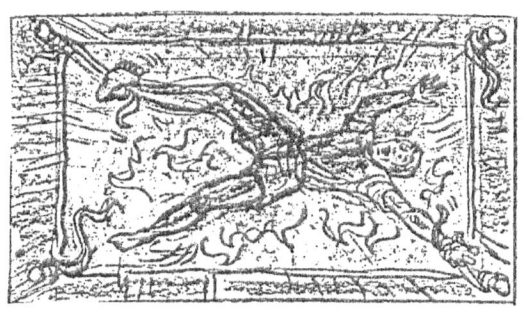

NIGHTMARE ON ELM STREET - ELEMENT BREAKDOWN

DQ 22   JOEY SUSPENDED OVER FIREY PIT--THE TONGUES LOOSEN AND HE SLIPS LOWER, TOWARD THE FLAMES

ELEMENTS

1. Bluescreen photography on tilted set
2. Miniature Pit (from DQ14)
3. Fire element

NIGHTMARE ON ELM STREET - ELEMENT BREAKDOWN

DQ 23   JOEY CLINGS DESPERATELY TO NANCY OVER FIREY PIT

ELEMENTS

1. Bluescreen photography on tilted set
2. Miniature Pit (from DQ14)
3. Fire Element

hospital set on one side and the house interior on the other side, and we had to make the switch for the audience in-camera so that it was happening in real time in front of you. Our use of objective-to-subjective camera movement was a critical ingredient that had frightened me as a young boy watching early horror films. That's the kind of thing I thought Roger Corman would have done. I loved changing the point of view in the midst of the shot—we look at her, then the camera becomes her point of view. You're no longer safe for you are the character's eyes. There's no proscenium for you to hide behind. My favorite effect in the entire film is where Nancy falls into a trance and falls through her chair into the dream world. We built the chair up on a platform with a pad underneath that Heather could fall into. The camera was angled so that we did not see the platform and so that the raised chair did not affect the perspective of the rest of the room. The property master slit the chair seat. The camera was on the exact plane as the seat so that we could not see the slit. We locked the camera down and shot a 'plate' without Heather so that we would be able to erase her when she fell into the bottom of our frame. In effect we had a hard matte line at the seat position. Without touching the camera we rolled on Heather falling through the seat. When the effects team combined those two shots she disappeared as she passed the chair seat, falling into another shot. Simple. In-camera effects are almost always better. However, not every physical effect shot is such a great gift, such as when we filmed the dining room pig scene. I don't recall if it was scripted or not but when Patricia enters the dark Elm Street house she randomly goes in to the dining room where a full meal has been prepared on the table. In the middle is an entire pig on a platter. The camera wraps around the table as she enters. Suddenly the pig leaps at her from the platter. I recall a major battle between props and production. There was no pig. Surely they had built a fake pig! Alas there was no fake pig. They were going to purchase a pig, pull out its innards, and drill a hole in the table. A puppeteer would slide his hand inside the pig and force it to leap forward at the proper cue. Of course we didn't get to the pig scene for several days. By that time the horror was not in the gag but the stench coming from the pig. It's in the movie. It took a number of takes to get the dolly move and to get Patricia's performance to Chuck's approval. That was one of the worst days on the set."[26]

"There were many trying times on that set," Maguire states, "When we were shooting the marionette sequence out there we set up a fairly wide shot looking down the corridor at Brad Gregg, he is like ten meters away from the camera. Just as we were about to roll I realized the makeup guys are down there with little makeup brushes hand-painting the tendons, and I'm like, 'guys, what are you doing?' and they're saying, 'we're just adding some more blood!' I told them that we're never going to see that, it doesn't matter, we've got to shoot. It's in the middle of the night, we're running out of time, we've got to go, and they are looking at me all flustered. Sometimes we butted heads with the art department and special effects department because they were under the assumption we would be working similarly to the previous crew and there was a little friction because we were making changes and moving a lot faster. It was unfortunate to the point where they were writing stuff on the bathroom walls about Roy and me, which was disheartening in the long run. The guy that did the Freddy makeup, Kevin Yagher, kept showing up late, it was just pathetic.

He was a prima donna and I always had my Second A.D. marking it on the production report whenever he would be late. I knew I would need to start recording his arrival because if it was ever said to me that we are running behind then at least I had documentation as to why, because whenever he was late that would delay the rest of us. I always had to have something in my back pocket to shoot while we were waiting for him to show up and have Freddy ready for us. There was one day that Freddy was particularly late to the set and it was holding us up; I was upset and eventually Rachel found out because I had been stalling and trying to shoot around him. So I explained to Rachel that this isn't the first time, it's on all of the production reports as to why we're running late, I said 'Kevin has been consistently late and my Second A.D., Robin, has been logging his times. He is supposed to be here at 7 a.m. and he's not coming in until 7.30 or 7.45, he has been doing this for weeks!' So that's the kind of situation where I needed that log. Rachel had to read Kevin the riot act and after that he was never late."[27]

"The crews on these films were really experienced with New Line Cinema," Mick Strawn says, "and you've got to understand that these films were built on the basis of a non-union crew that was coming of age. We had an over-experienced First A.D., Dennis Maguire, who came from the union world and we were just stepping all over the goddamned guy. We were all bluster, he would tell us how to do it his way and we'd be like, 'yeah, yeah, well we're gonna do it better,' and within the next ten years it was us who were the established bunch in Hollywood because this is where everybody had cut their teeth. This was like graduating from the Roger Corman movies or from Full Moon Features, it's where you worked your ass off before you moved up to bigger things and made a name for yourself; this was a step up for a lot of talent. It was pretty interesting because I don't think that Dennis had any idea that we were just going to make it happen, he would look at something and say 'oh, this seems like too much' and we would just blast over the guy. You had people like me, Peter Chesney, and others who were just going to do it and do it right; we had been set challenges before and we just went out and did it, and I don't think they were quite ready for that. Some days on that set it was basically a confrontation of the Old Guard versus the New Blood and it didn't help that there was always a bit of a rub between Chuck Russell and everybody else, because Chuck wanted it done his way or the highway. He was not a very compromising person. A lot of decisions hadn't been made on how we were going to do things and so we went over-budget on the film because Chuck forced the issue with producers."[28]

"Chuck was wonderful in his vision," Maguire states, "but if he didn't have the partners that he had it would never have been as successful as it is. Look at the 'Welcome to Primetime, Bitch!' scene, that was Robert, he didn't like the line of dialogue he was supposed to say so he just said, 'hey, what do you think if I say this: 'welcome to primetime, bitch!' and I thought that was fantastic and of course Chuck loved it and it ended up in the movie. That was just one of those spontaneous things, perhaps he thought about it while he was in makeup.

But there were always combustible things like that happening which made it remarkable. At one point we were shooting at the Veterans Administration complex in Westwood, California, next to UCLA, and as we were filming Chuck was running

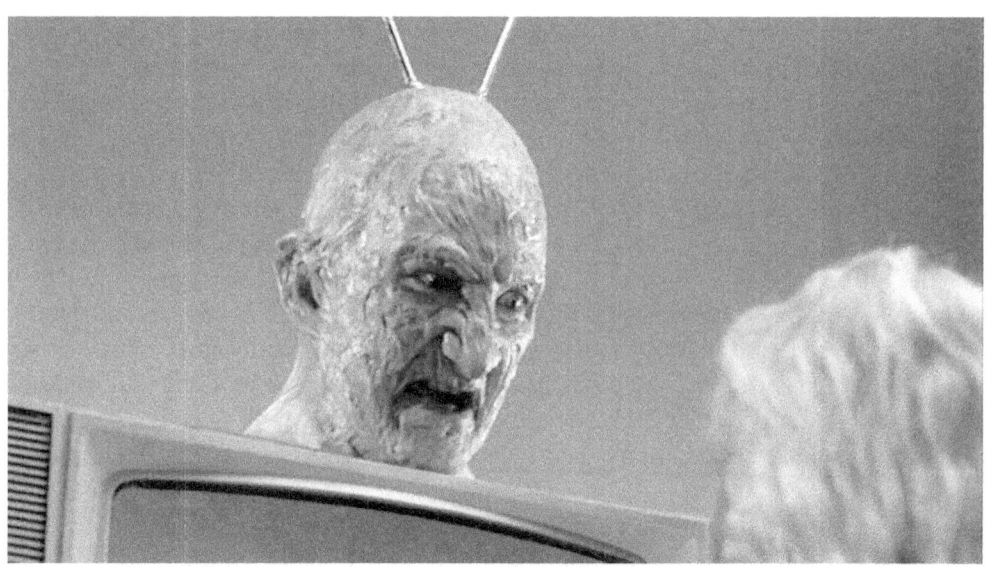

"Welcome to Primetime, Bitch!"

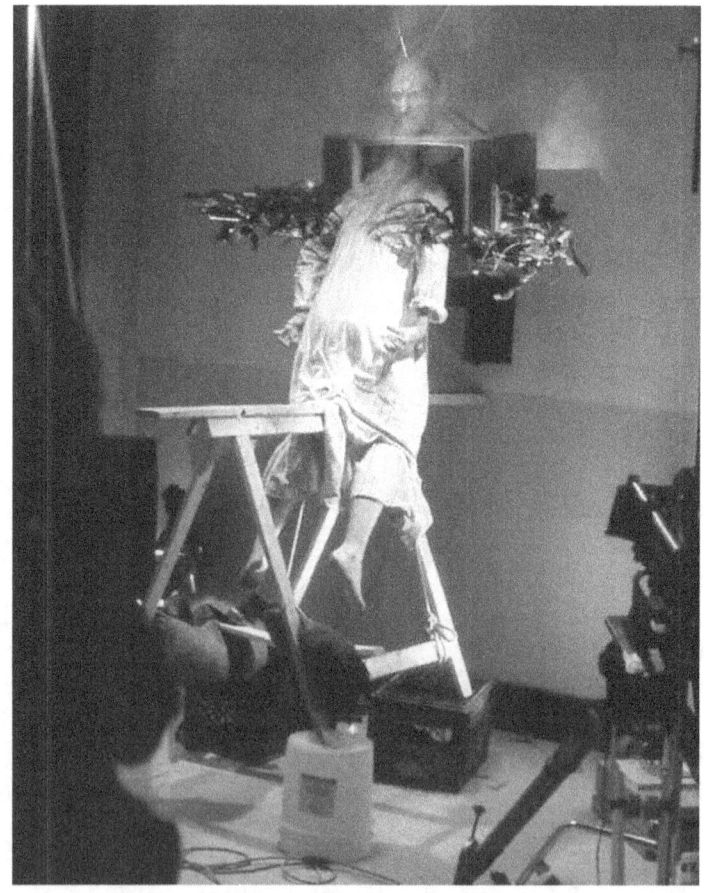

On set of the classic Freddy Television scene (courtesy Roy H. Wagner Collection).

over time and our producers were freaking out. We were supposed to finish that day and I said to Chuck that we can't come back tomorrow. Roy and I were wondering, 'what else does he need, what more does he want?' We had completely covered it, but Chuck goes, 'I need this, this, and this' so we asked for an hour more to finish it. It was two or three shots, Roy worked really fast and got them done, that's a wrap, and I tell the crew we're opening on another building tomorrow, and then all of a sudden Chuck stops me and says, 'No, we're not done here!' And I said, 'You told me we would be done when we get 'this, this, and this,' and we shot 'this, this, and this.' We're done! We're not coming back here, Chuck, we can't afford to!' I could see the two producers were getting very anxious, they had already given us an hour extra and overtime was a big deal with New Line, it's a lot of money once you go into overtime. So we went off to dailies in some screening room in West LA not far from that veterans' complex and after we looked at the footage Chuck said he wanted to talk to me and he started giving me a load of shit and I just put up my hands and said, 'okay, Chuck. I'll call the producers and tell them to find somebody else to take over from me.' I told him 'I'm here to help and if you don't feel I'm helping you then I'm done, I don't need this.' And then he began backing off. I told him how we will get through it and that's the way we did it; had we done it any differently they would have went weeks over schedule and New Line would have been very unhappy. I protected the producers as best I could and after that first sparring match between Chuck and I we were shooting on-schedule and everybody was happy with the footage that was being shot. Chuck is an interesting guy, very dedicated to his work."[29]

"The very first time I met Chuck I liked him," Wagner says, "I believed we would be friends for life. Remember, I didn't get the job! Chuck is really a passionate filmmaker. Being this was one of his first big breaks he had the good sense to fight for extra time, which the production budget didn't have, and he never accepted anything but the best in performance from all of us. By the end of the first week Chuck and I had built a wonderful working relationship. I wanted to ask him a question that few of us ever get the chance to ask: 'Why did you hire the other guy?!' Chuck was very honest. He said that although he felt I was a nice guy I didn't come off as an artist. The other guy had this lovely foreign accent and presented himself as a very artistic cinematographer. He assured me that he was incredibly grateful for my accepting the job. On the set, in action, I revealed a knowledge and passion he just didn't see in that first meeting with me. The partnership between a director and their cinematographer must be honest and collaborative. Often you are the only person standing between him and the ire of production. It's your job to execute his plan, no matter how it might change, without costing production any additional time or money. This partnership is critical and it's why great filmmakers tend to keep the same director of photography, operator, production designer, editor and assistant director. I'm still incredibly grateful for Chuck's honesty. As the weeks passed and I continued the extremely long days I began observing a characteristic I've noted in some of the best directors I've worked for: Chuck didn't give up. No matter what production said or the schedule dictated, if Chuck saw a better way to do something he never gave in. From him I came up with a statement that I've used throughout the rest of my career. 'It's their problem until you say yes.' It's true. No matter how unrealistic their production budget or schedule is, and it's almost always unrealistic, it's the studio or producer's problem until the cinematographer, production designer, editor and/or the director promise or agree to meet their demands. As simple as that seems, as soon as you say 'yes' their problem is no longer theirs but yours. For Chuck it always had to be better!"[30]

Maguire concurs with Wagner's observation of his tireless director: "When we would wrap the First Unit, Chuck would move over to the Second Unit and I felt compelled to support him. One night I was so exhausted but I looked over at Chuck and noticed that he was as happy as a lark with the same energy he'd started with, so I asked him, 'Chuck, how do you define the director's position?' 'Last man standing,' he said. 'You can never give up!' I was supposed to do *The Blob* with Chuck, but I was delayed on another picture and missed the two-week prep for it and I told Chuck I didn't think I would be able to do it, and he was like, 'oh come on, you can do it!' But I told him I wouldn't be able to do it justice because he would need someone who is there from the beginning."[31]

"Our assistant director, Dennis Maguire, is one of the best A.D.'s I've ever worked with," Wagner says, "he would relay to Chuck the schedule and demands of production throughout the day for we were never on schedule. Chuck would seem to agree and just continue on the alternate path he had chosen and some of these paths would have subverted the schedule and the budget. Poor Rachel Talalay was always trying to pick up the pieces and finding money to make it better because we were always going over-budget. I asked Chuck how he could get away with this. 'They'll forgive you if the finished film is a huge success but if you follow the schedule and budget and deliver a dud they'll never forgive you.' That was a life lesson I've never forgotten."[32]

"They needed Roy Wagner to come in and set everything right," Maguire insists, "he would ask me how much time he can have to do something and I'd tell him we have six more shots to go and then we wrap, and he'll go, 'okay, that means we have ten minutes; got it,' and he'd go off and, boom, he'd be ready! Roy knew Film, he knew what he needed to get the look he wanted within budget and schedule. I saw him showing some stuff to the visual effects guy, he even brought in some photographs from *Mary Poppins* to illustrate to us what he was talking about. He was able to get the best from people. Throughout my career I found that you meet the best people and the nicest people when you're working on a film where there is no expectation to be successful, when you're on a film with huge expectations everybody is panicking that what they're doing isn't going to work, and when it does come out successful suddenly everybody is responsible for having made it successful and everybody has a different story for why it became successful and it usually revolves around them, but in truth it was the collaborative partnership that allowed it to happen."[33]

"I believe in partnership and collaboration," Wagner says, "and whatever is good about *A Nightmare on Street 3* is because of my collaboration with Chuck, Frank, Bruce, and with Robert Englund; it was remarkable. You like to think that all the great ideas are your ideas but they are never just all your ideas, it's a conglomeration of everybody's ideas. You have to serve the story, the characters, the director, and in the middle of all that you hope you can serve your own art. On *A Nightmare on Elm Street 3* there were lots of different versions of what I 'should' be doing, but you can't listen to all of those voices because it will destroy everything. But you can only serve one master. New Line believed they knew what made the franchise work. They didn't. I don't think Wes Craven even knew what made his film work. I had a director who wanted me to shoot Freddy one way and a studio who wanted me to shoot him another way. The big giant mandate from the studio was 'we don't want to see Freddy, we want very little of Freddy' and I didn't get to shoot any tests of Freddy at all. They told me they didn't want Freddy to look like he did in *A Nightmare on Elm Street 2*, so I had to go back and see what that looked like. On *A Nightmare on Elm Street 3* his makeup was so beautifully done and yet they hated the makeup, they thought it stole from Freddy and I agree with that to some degree. If you can see your antagonist it's not as effective, but the way the script was written had Freddy being present and with much more emotion, he was much more of a person and a character. In the first film you're not sure if he's a manifestation, if he's real or not, but in *A Nightmare on Elm Street 3* he is real. If you look at the scene where he plunges the syringes into the girl—'what a rush'—and he gets an almost sexual thrill from it, well you've got to have him there and be able to see him. To have him shrouded in silhouette there wouldn't work, he now has a personality and we are seeing another side to his character, which is playful and humorous as well as all the horrific things. Once they realized the rest of the film was working with Freddy out in the open we could work with that more; so that was one of the first mandates: that the Freddy photography has got to be dark. I had to be careful to get it right, and there's a couple of times where I felt I went too far because I was trying to give the studio what they wanted. I tend to provide the studio with a thick negative. In that way the negative can survive more passes through the printer plus it allows for more printing range for the release print without becoming 'milky' or washed out in the shadows. After dailies every day the producers would come to me and demand that I stop down, 'make it darker.' I think *A Nightmare on Elm Street 3* could have looked a lot better if I had been allowed to protect the detail in the shadows, making them dark but rich. There are several scenes that really reveal the thin negative. The hall of mirrors is the worst. That set had a ceiling and no place to put any lights. I ultimately removed some of the mirror panes and brought some light in but, to me, that's the most unsuccessful photography in the entire film, that sequence looks ugly, I'm not really happy with how that part of the film looks because I was trying to print down"[34]

"Shooting the hall of mirrors scene was so intense," Maguire confirms, "it was such a big deal for New Line, it was a big production shot, and from a safety point-of-view with all the glass, there was no Take Two or anything."[35]

"I never had any prep before I started filming," Wagner reiterates, "but, as I said, once you say 'yes' it's your problem. The schedule was one of the most difficult I've ever experienced. New Line Cinema allowed me one pass on the final color timing and then kicked me out of the lab. I was never happy with the release prints. I found them milky and inconsistent but Bob Shaye knew everything about *A Nightmare on Elm Street* and so I had my one pass and that was that. It was the first and last time I've ever experienced that lack of collaboration from a studio, especially one which was in dire financial shape before I took the project over."[36]

However, Wagner's work would not go unnoticed by the right people. Several

NIGHTMARE ON ELM STREET – ELEMENT BREAKDOWN

DQ 25A   FREDDY AT END OF HALLWAY TURNS & JUMPS INTO MIRROR   GLASS IN MIRROR FRAME
BLACK DUVOTINE BEHIND GLASS

ELEMENTS

1. Plate of hallway <u>with</u> Freddy – one angle
2. Plate of hallway <u>without</u> Freddy – one angle
3. Bluescreen in place of mirror <u>with</u> Freddy – reverse angle
4. Bluescreen in place of mirror <u>without</u> Freddy – reverse angle
5. Garbage matte for bluescreen with Freddy
6. Garbage matte for bluescreen without Freddy

NOTE: Optical composite – SUPER 1:85 reduced to Academy during optical comp.

Above and following 6 pages: Roy Wagner storyboards of hall of mirrors scene (storyboards courtesy of Roy H. Wagner Collection).

2. The Monster Goes Mainstream

NIGHTMARE ON ELM STREET - ELEMENT BREAKDOWN

DQ 25B   MASTER SHOT AS FREDDIES APPEAR IN ALL MIRRORS

ELEMENTS

1. Plate of hallway - (Bluescreen at back wall)
2. Plate #1 of Freddy to insert in mirror
3. Plate #2 of Freddy to insert in mirror
4. Plate #3 of Freddy to insert in mirror
5. Plate #4 of Freddy to insert in mirror
6. Plate #5 of Freddy to insert in mirror
7. Plate #6 of Freddy to insert in mirror
8. Plate #7 of Freddy to insert in mirror
9. Articulate Matte of Mirror area

NOTES: Optical Composite - SUPER 1:85 reduced to Academy during optical comp.

Optical reposition to "flatten" Freddy image to 2-D appearance, and optical composite including staggered "pop-ons" of Freddys

NIGHTMARE ON ELM STREET - ELEMENT BREAKDOWN

DQ 26A   FREDDY IMAGE IN MIRROR GRABS KINCAID

ELEMENTS

1. Plate of hallway (no mirror) with Freddy standing where mirror image should be, actually grabbing Kincaid

2. Separate plate with black plexiglass mounted in mirror frame

3. Plate of Freddy for insertion into mirror. Optical reposition to "flatten" Freddy image to 2-D appearance

4. Roto of junction of 3-D and 2-D arms

5. Animation at junction area

NOTE: Optical Composite - SUPER 1:85 reduced to Academy during optical comp.

2. The Monster Goes Mainstream

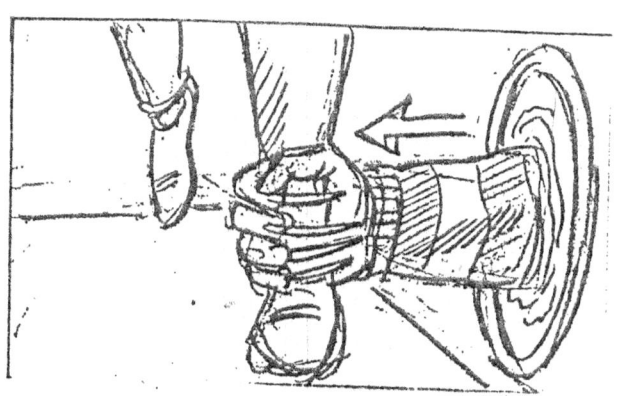

NIGHTMARE ON ELM STREET - ELEMENT BREAKDOWN

DQ 26B   CLOSE-UP OF FREDDY'S HAND GRABBING ANKLE

ELEMENTS

1. Plate of hallway with Freddy reaching from false mirror area

2. Separate plate of black plexiglass mounted in mirror frame

3. Articulate Roto Matte

4. Animation element

NOTE: Optical Composite - SUPER 1:85 reduced to Academy during optical comp.

This shot appears to be at an angle from which you would not need the 2-D in the mirror effect

NIGHTMARE ON ELM STREET - ELEMENT BREAKDOWN

DQ 27A   FREDDY GRABS NANCY INTO MIRROR
            (Composed like DQ 26A)

ELEMENTS

1. Plate of hallway (no mirror) with Freddy standing where mirror image should be, actually grabbing Nancy

2. Separate plate with black plexiglass mounted in mirror frame

3. Plate of Freddy for insertion into mirror

4. Roto of junction of 3-D and 2-D arms

5. Animation element

NOTES: Optical Composite - SUPER 1:85 reduced to Academy during optical comp.

Optical reposition to "flatten" Freddy image to 2-D appearance.

2. The Monster Goes Mainstream

NIGHTMARE ON ELM STREET – ELEMENT BREAKDOWN

DQ 27B   KRISTEN BEING "ABSORBED" INTO MIRROR

ELEMENTS

1. Plate of hallway (no mirror) with Freddy where mirror image should be, actually grabbing Kristen
2. Separate plate with black plexiglass mounted in mirror frame
3. Plate of Freddy & Kristen for insertion into mirror
4. Roto of junction of 3-D and 2-D arms
5. Animation element

NOTES: Optical Composite – SUPER 1:85 reduced to Academy during optical comp.

Optical reposition to "flatten" Freddy & Kristen image to 2-D appearance

NIGHTMARE ON ELM STREET ELEMENT BREAKDOWN

DQ 27C   NANCY BEING PARTIALLY YANKED INTO MIRROR

ELEMENTS

1. Plate of hallway (no mirror) with Freddy where mirror image should be, actually grabbing Nancy

2. Separate plate with black plexiglass mounted in mirror frame

3. Plate of Freddy & Nancy for insertion into mirror

4. Roto of junction of 3-D and 2-D arms

5. Animation element

NOTE: Optical composite – SUPER 1:85 reduced to Academy during optical comp.

Optical reposition to "flatten" Freddy & Kristen image to 2-D appearance weeks after *A Nightmare on Elm Street 3* was released, he received a phone call from special effects maestro Stan Winston, who was preparing to make his directorial debut with the surreal creature feature, *Pumpkinhead*. That film would ultimately be stylishly shot by Montenegrin cinematographer Bojan Bazelli after Wagner passed on the project, as he recalls: "My agent received a call from Stan. He loved what I had done on *A Nightmare on Elm Street 3* and wanted me to do *Pumpkinhead*. But I read the script and couldn't figure out how they would ever get that monster to seem real. Then I had sought to work on Chuck's next feature, *The Blob*, but the producer turned me down. He wanted a cinematographer who was capable of winning awards. I showed him. I won my first Emmy soon after that."[37]

And the success continued for Wagner as, following this trip down Elm Street, his career would flourish shooting major studio pictures such as *Another Stakeout*, *Drop Zone*, and *Nick of Time*, as well as some of the biggest shows on television: *Quantum Leap*, *Party of Five*, *CSI: Crime Scene Investigation*, *House*, *The Beast*, and *Ray Donovan*.

"Alas, I've had a remarkable career since *A Nightmare on Elm Street 3*. I'm astonished that the film is as well received as it is photographically. What would have happened if I'd not returned the emergency phone call or if I had turned the project down? I know that New Line Cinema got the perfect partner in me for I had been trained by one of the fastest and best cinematographers in Hollywood. Harry Stradling Sr. ASC won Oscars for *A Streetcar Named Desire* and *My Fair Lady* plus he was nominated ten other times. The rule he often told me was, 'don't draw attention to yourself. If a director asks you to do something that's impossible it's your job to find a solution. They don't pay you to say 'no.' As a cinematographer you must make the director feel that his power is limitless. If they come up with something impossible just say 'yes.' And that is what I did with Chuck and Rachel every day. I believe we came in on schedule. In spite of the additional equipment we had to maintain to support all of the different units I believe we were right on budget. Would I do it again? I'm a Hollywood studio cameraman. Some of my projects I'm very proud of. Some not so much, but I'm very proud of the longevity of my career. Fifty years. Very few people get to follow their dream for their entire life. For a dreamer from a tiny little town in the Midwest where I was told it's impossible to become a director of photography I guess I've done ok."[38]

Aside from the myriad aesthetic qualities of the film, *A Nightmare on Elm Street 3: Dream Warriors* is one of the best entries in the franchise because of the skillful manner in which it establishes the backstory and the myth of Freddy Krueger. It is an origin story of sorts, bringing greater depth to the series and its villain by introducing a religious element as well as the notion of Freddy being the result of genetic evil. Dr. Gordon repeatedly comes across an ominous nun who introduces herself as Sister Mary Helena (Nan Martin), whose real name is later revealed to be Amanda Krueger, the mother of Freddy Krueger. Dr. Gordon is informed of the blasphemous conception that occurred in Westin Hills in the early 1940s, after Amanda was accidentally locked inside the hospital for several days over one Christmas. Throughout the course of that torturous time the young nun was subjected to rape and defilement by the psychopathic inmates of the asylum, and thus Freddy was born the bastard son of a hundred maniacs. The "sins of the father" theme is a recurrent idea that permeates the Elm Street films, and the bombshell revelation that Freddy himself is the aberrant result of a corrupted lineage is a most fascinating subtext for the writers to elaborate upon.

"We invented the whole backstory with the nun," Russell says, "we created her to be Freddy's mother because I wanted to take the mythology that Wes introduced to the next level or it wouldn't have been fun for me or the audience. And I think one of the great themes of the series is Wes' concept of the 'sins of the fathers' being visited upon the children. I wanted to take the ball further down the court here."[39]

The film also serves fans of the original by providing continuity and developing several characters from that first entry, including Nancy and Donald Thompson. Their father-daughter relationship is strained, with Donald now a burnt-out alcoholic security guard after having been unable to continue his work as a police lieutenant following the events of the first film. But one of the film's greatest narrative strengths is the newly introduced ensemble of teen characters, who also happen to be the most socially diverse group of the series. To date, Freddy's victims have been largely of a comfortable and complacent middle-class milieu. Only Rod Lane, with his Latino ethnicity as well as his delinquent dress and demeanor signifies anything outside of the traditional Springwood socio-economic milieu. Conversely, the introduction of Kristen Parker in this film introduces another social stratum: the upper class. As we see, Kristen is the troubled child of a broken but decadent bourgeois home. Her mother, Elaine, is recurrently seen admonishing her daughter while preparing for her dates, dressing in the finest furs as her suitors help themselves to the liquor cabinet. By *A Nightmare on Elm Street 4: The Dream Master*, Elaine is shoving pills down her daughter's throat to keep her oblivious to any of her own failings as a mother. We aren't privy to the other teens' social background on screen, though as they relate their respective troubles and neuroses in the group therapy sessions, we

Nan Martin as Sister Mary Helena (aka Amanda Krueger).

are able to fill in the blanks and bring our own interpretation to the characters' histories. Taryn and Kincaid are tough, streetwise kids who have evidently experienced violence and aggression in their lives, while Jennifer, Joey, Phillip, and Will are seemingly more traditional suburban kids with more benign interests: women, art, and celebrity. One thing they share for sure is the burden and the unfortunate legacy their parents have left behind for them to endure.

"Some of these things you do on a gut level," Russell affirms, "but that was a goal of mine, to get a range of why it's hard to be a teen. Whether it's divorced or alcoholic parents, drug addiction or whatever other challenges hits kids at that age. The Wizard Master character, Will, is disabled and doesn't really connect with others except through fantasy. Of course he is in a wheelchair and that's the idea of being different and not being able to make friends easily. This alienation was a central theme in Wes' original, the banding together of kids at that age, because no one else believes them. The physical production side of directing a horror film is, of course, quite a different job from developing the themes in the screenplay, but the visuals should reflect that theme. One of my favorite examples of this in *A Nightmare on Elm Street*

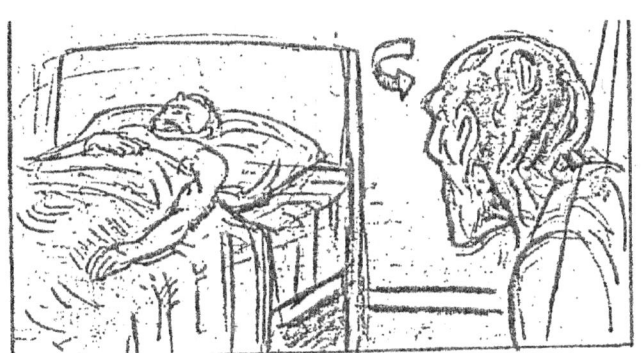

NIGHTMARE ON ELM STREET - ELEMENT BREAKDOWN

DQ 5   MARIONETTE CHANGES INTO FREDDY, PHILLIP IN BED IN F.G.

ELEMENTS:

1. DQ plate photography.

2. Bluescreen stop-motion/puppet animation (Beswick)

3. Garbage Matte for blue screen

Above and following 2 pages: Roy Wagner storyboard for Phillip Marionette scene (storyboard courtesy of Roy H. Wagner Collection).

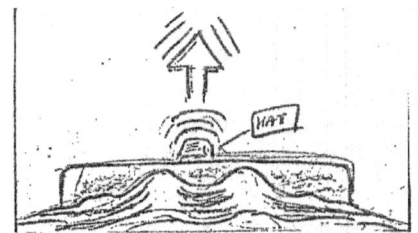 

NIGHTMARE ON ELM STREET – ELEMENT BREAKDOWN

DQ 6   FREDDY/MARIONETTE GROWS INTO FREDDY

ELEMENTS:

1. DQ plate photography of background.

2. Bluescreen photography of Freddy.

3. Garbage Matte for blue screen.

4. DQ photography of marionette.

 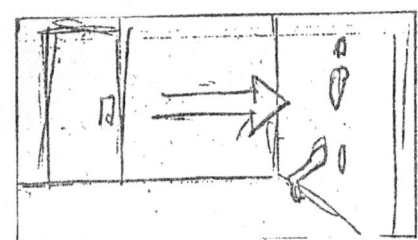

NIGHTMARE ON ELM STREET – ELEMENT BREAKDOWN

DQ7   PHILLIP WALKS THROUGH WALL

1. DQ motion control plate photography of b.g.

2. DQ motion control bluescreen photography of Phillip.

3. Garbage Matte for blue screen.

4. Animation to wipe off Phillip as he goes behind wall.

2. The Monster Goes Mainstream

NIGHTMARE ON ELM STREET – ELEMENT BREAKDOWN

DQ 9   DOWN SHOT: MOVING SHOT, PHILLIP ON TOWER ('VERTIGO')

ELEMENTS:

1. DQ plate photography on stage or location
2. Matte painting/matte scan composite.

NIGHTMARE ON ELM STREET – ELEMENT BREAKDOWN

BACKGROUND PLATE AT UCLA
FOREGROUND BLUE SCREEN W/ FREDDY

DQ 10   UP SHOT: TRANSPARENT FREDDY AGAINST NIGHT SKY

ELEMENTS:

1. DQ photography of Freddy against black BG.
2. DQ plate photography on stage or location.
3. Animation Starfield element.

3 is the hypodermic-fingered Freddy, which became a well-known image. It works because it's unexpected, yet plays off that victim's greatest weakness. My intention was to hit a nerve regarding drugs and addiction through Jennifer Rubin's character, Taryn. The sequence is a metaphor for the seduction of addiction and suicide, of self-destruction, and for me that's the deepest chord that Freddy can represent in these films: that he is inside your dreams creating your self-destruction.

Freddy starts with his illusions on Patricia Arquette's character at the beginning of the film. He slashes her wrists in the middle of a bad dream and in reality it looks like a sleepwalking suicide. Thanks to Patricia's performance and solid FX, it is pretty disturbing imagery. After the release of the film, one way I knew that the themes of the film were working was that they wanted to ban it in England! Apparently the issue was the teen suicide. I talked to some reporters in defense of it, and I said, 'Look, we address suicide as an evil to be overcome, we've made Freddy a metaphor for suicide and he is defeated by our heroes banding together and empowering themselves. It is an empowering story!' I told them that the real problem is this English writer, Bill Shakespeare, and his play *Romeo and Juliet* which glamorizes suicide. Obviously, I was kidding, but it didn't go over very well at the time. I was trying to make a valid point, that there's a difference between glamorizing suicide and addressing it."[40]

"If you look at older horror films," Wagner suggests, "like Roger Corman's *The Pit and the Pendulum*, or William Castle's *The Tingler*, those were terrifying films in their time because they dealt with themes and ideas we hadn't seen before. Corman is very into the psychology of images, particularly Freudian concepts and he would use camera movement as a tool and often put people on the wrong side of the frame so as to misdirect the audience, or he puts you in the subjective viewpoint of the character. We tried to do that in *A Nightmare on Elm Street 3* but I don't think we did that as well as Roger did. One thing I wanted to do but New Line wouldn't spend the money on the optical, is when Patricia is running down the hallway and suddenly she goes into slow-motion but Freddy is still coming after her at the normal speed; every one

"What a rush!"

NIGHTMARE ON ELM STREET – ELEMENT BREAKDOWN

DQ 1   A HUNDRED TEENAGE BODIES HANG FROM THE CEILING

ELEMENTS:

1.   DQ plate photography of Kristen, w/approx. 6 hanging bodies.

2.   Matte Painting – Original Neg of Kristen – comp w/painting

3.   Bluescreen photography w/hanging bodies

4.   Garbage Matte for blue screen

NOTE: Matte Camera and Optical Composite
SUPER 1:85 reduced to Academy – during optical comp.

This shot will be a combination original negative matte painting and bluescreen.

Roy Wagner storyboard depicting hanging teenagers, reflecting the suicide theme of the film (storyboard courtesy of Roy H. Wagner Collection).

of us has had that dream where we're running away from something and the farther we run the slower we get and the menace gets closer and closer. It plays into the idea that you can't escape your dreams. But it doesn't quite make as much sense as we had hoped; had it been done digitally we would have achieved it a lot more effectively. I'm fascinated by metaphysics, I grew up along the Mississippi River and I've seen ghosts and experienced the metaphysical thing of having orbs of light come into my room in the middle of the night and being terrified by it; so I've experienced some metaphysical events which have fascinated me to where it feels like an interesting puzzle. It's all to do with our psyche and how we perceive things; you and I could experience the same event but perceive it entirely differently from one another. It is the same with film, we might watch the same film and take away two completely different interpretations of it."[41]

A Nightmare on Elm Street 3 would be the first film of the franchise to take advantage of the burgeoning cultural phenomenon that was MTV and to make reference to the world of pop-culture that exists externally to the Elm Street diegetic world. Zsa Zsa Gabor appears as a guest of Dick Cavett on his talk show before he turns into Freddy, who then slaughters the preening celebrity. The soundtrack for the film also makes use of popular acts such as Dokken, who contributed the excellent theme song, "Dream Warriors." In an inspired moment of cross-promotion, the music video for the song, which features Patricia Arquette and the band members being terrorized by Freddy, would be the first to be placed on a VHS tape to tie in with a film's soundtrack.

"Look at how they crossed Freddy over into the music world," Strawn enthuses, "We had Dokken on Part 3 and then we put Freddy in a music video with The Fat Boys on Part 4! There were some memorable moments filming with Dokken; the guitar player, George Lynch, was going to be part of this gag where he comes through a wall for his guitar solo. We told him that people don't break through walls and remain standing up because your feet and your head are two completely different items. Just as you come to a wall your feet are going to come to a stop because it's a normal thing to do. So we told him we want him to do a rehearsal, to go through the wall a first time so he knows what the feeling is like and so that he wouldn't fall on his face. But he was being the macho guy, and I'm pretty sure he was as high as a kite, and he didn't want to try it out first before filming. So he's just like, 'no, I'm just gonna blast right through it,' and he takes about five steps back and starts running with his guitar towards the wall and his feet stop, because that's just human nature, and so he ended up plowing through the wall head over tail; if you look at the video you'll see how awkward he comes through it and you can tell he didn't intend to do that. In the shot he comes piling through the wall and you can see him struggling to stay on his feet, and then in the next cut he's standing up normal and playing his guitar, which was a separate take because when he came through the wall he was not able to stay standing and do his guitar solo, his face was just in shock and confusion, like 'to hell with that!'"[42]

With its witty pop-culture references and loquacious Freddy, this particular sequel is notable as the entry which introduced the verbal cleverness and humor which would become a trademark of the *Elm Street* brand. It would be around the time of this film's release that Robert Englund began appearing on television, sometimes as himself, other times in character as Freddy, in a variety of promotional situations which made it abundantly clear that the villain was indeed the star of the show. Such PR campaigns would benefit from Robert Englund's dark, inimitable brand of humor and zest for all things Elm Street. Later sequels would run wild with the comedic elements, often to detrimental effect for the franchise's horror credentials, but Chuck Russell strikes the perfect balance of horror and humor here.

"I made *A Nightmare on Elm Street 3* using a dark sense of humor that I have used in my other work," Russell states, "That can work in horror if you remain true to the central premise. In this case, exploring our fears. If humor is character-based—truthful to the character, not corny—and the suspense is legitimate and horror is the true pay-off then it can all work together in symphony. Humor and horror are strangely similar. There is a tension that exists in the setup of a punchline and the delivery which is similar to setting up and paying off a scare. I wanted to make Freddy both scarier and funnier, and in fact Robert was so effective in the role, I wanted to give him more dialogue. Our producers at New Line were originally afraid of letting Freddy do anything very different, such as not having his hat on or the red striped sweater. But I wanted to make it surprising or what's the point? Such as the scene where he appears in the tuxedo while holding Brooke Bundy's decapitated head! This all seemed very risky to my producers at the time. They were particularly concerned about that tuxedo. Afterward, because the film was very successful on its first run—it grossed more than the first two films combined—they realized they wanted to go even further in that direction."[43]

"*A Nightmare on Elm Street 3* is very much a horror film but it almost feels like a comedy," Maguire adds, "and horror and comedy are interesting genres, they are virtually the same, as they often play in threes: the comedian will tell you a joke, then he'll set you up for the next joke which doesn't play as well as the first joke (he lets you off the hook so to speak), and then it's the third joke that gets you. Horror is much the same: you get a scare and you get a laugh out of it, you've gone over the rollercoaster's first hill thinking 'That's not so bad. I'm safe now.' The next scare is minimal, making you believe you can control your emotions and then they hit you hard with a real fright. That's the way *A Nightmare on Elm Street 3* was and Chuck understood that, and we also had a great writing team; Frank Darabont was just a baby at the time, before he became very successful; Bruce Wagner was the dark side of everything and that was needed, it needed a decadent, demented element—things like teasing the junkie with the needles on Freddy's fingers—and Chuck has this very sardonic humor, he sees the funniest things in the oddest places."[44]

"What made *A Nightmare on Elm Street 3* work is the humor that the three writers brought to the script," Wagner says, "that was a major ingredient in making the film as successful as it was. After that Freddy became a cult figure and Robert became hugely successful as a result of it. By the third film he became a star."[45]

"It's a hat trick, Freddy works as horror, comedy, and adventure," Strawn affirms, "this was a sophisticated creation and it's due to what we did on *Dream Warriors* and *The Dream Master* that Freddy became that pop-culture icon. The difference between the two is that Chuck Russell wanted to tell a story and he wanted it to be a thematically serious film like *The Omen* or *The Exorcist*, he wanted it to be something very heavy; and then the way Renny Harlin approached the next film was to treat it like a rock video. The story of *Dream Warriors* is great because it brings in those kids and the idea that collectively they have some power to wield against Freddy, but I would say that whatever humor is in *Dream Warriors* is not so much Chuck's as it is Robert's, because he was really given the opportunity to bring his personality to the film and a big part of his personality is his sense of humor."[46]

In the three decades since the release of *A Nightmare on Elm Street 3: Dream Warriors*, the film has deservedly become known as a favorite among fans of the franchise. It is easy to understand why that is: there is a lot of playfulness and suggestiveness in Englund's performance of Freddy Krueger here, he brings a dark, almost sexy swagger to the villain, something which defined the character and what he would be for the remainder of the series; the film executes fantastically intricate and imaginative set pieces while populating the narrative with the most likeable and well-drawn characters of any of the films, and it provides a rich, thematically dense mythological backstory to the creation of Freddy Krueger. Crucially, it also honors Wes Craven's original film by expanding upon and bringing to a close the familial thread of his narrative in seeing the return of Nancy and Donald Thompson, providing the opportunity for Heather Langenkamp and John Saxon to reprise their iconic roles much to fans' delight. Langenkamp in particular will always remain crucial to *Elm Street* lore, being the first heroine of the series and Freddy's true, original, and ultimate nemesis, something Chuck Russell deftly utilized.

"Returning Heather's 'Nancy' to the Elm Street series was the key to a legitimate sequel," the director affirms. "She is the Yin to Freddy's Yang, two sides of a nightmarish coin, a role that Heather made so memorable. She projects a vulnerable but endlessly resourceful girl-next-door who refuses to give in to Freddy's mad world. The original 'Final Girl.' We love theorizing about Freddy, but it seems to me there would be no Freddy without his eternal rival, Nancy, and the Elm Street kids that followed after her. I was invited to a convention for the 30-year anniversary of *A Nightmare on Elm Street 3*, and fans of all ages are still thrilled to line up for Heather's autograph. Makes you realize she was a role model to a generation of fans."[47]

"I do believe *A Nightmare on Elm Street 3* is the fan favorite," Englund says, "and that is because there are so many wonderful set pieces and it plays with that large cast. The concept of the group therapy lends itself to that great ensemble acting because they are all together. It's especially wonderful because you have that friendship between Heather Langenkamp and Patricia Arquette, you have the scenes with the girl who wants to be an actress, and the scenes with the tough girl, and the one where the kid gets turned into a puppet; it's got so many great set pieces and interesting characters that it's easy to see why it is the fan favourite."[48]

"I love that it is a fan favorite," Russell admits, "and I'm not going to be the one to say it, but if that is true I'm delighted. And if it is true then it is perhaps because I love horror films, I'm a fan, I think that exploring our fears is exhilarating; only by going through the catharsis of a really terrific horror film you get to really learn more about yourself and your fears. I'm certainly proud of it, as it continues to make an impression over the years. I'm proud of our team of young actors and filmmakers. There's a bit of the eighties hairdo and fashions that makes me wince, but otherwise the film is still entertaining and has its own kind of morality. Good over evil, face your fears, that kind of thing. At the time it was a case of fighting every day to stay on budget and schedule in order to create these illusions. For the actors, horror genre is hard work, draining in fact. I was pushing my cast to go to the place of fear while maintaining the sense of love between that on-camera team. In horror you don't want to just pose nicely, you need to internalize the fear we are projecting on camera for it to be effective. I think my cast all did that, and it seems young audiences still respond to them; and younger viewers have great bullshit detectors. One thing I always try to put in my films is heart, rooting interest, a love of the characters. Just because it's the horror genre doesn't mean you can't have heart and that's another thing our cast put into it. A sense of facing our fears to protect those we love is universal. In the last decade we've seen horror become more and more nihilistic, bad guys win and there is not much hope. I'm not putting that down, *Hereditary* is an extremely powerful film in that regard. But in my world view, the horror genre is a kind of promise: Here's the most terrifying thing you can imagine, and you have, by guts and luck, a character who faces up to it. The common person rising against overwhelming odds is a powerful theme. I see the horror genre as being truly cathartic, as a way to experience the thrill of facing our worst fears, while in the safety of a movie theatre, or our own living rooms.

I was really happy to take this little *Elm Street* journey that Wes had started and take it to a further place in respect to the series. Something special must have happened in the *Elm Street* series, because Freddy still seems to live on, in the shadows beneath our beds."49

> "Sorry?! Sorry that you and your tennis pals torched this guy and now he's after me? In case you haven't been keeping score, it's his fucking banquet and I'm the last course!"—Kristen Parker

A year after the events that took place in Westin Hills Psychiatric Hospital, the surviving dream warriors Kristen Parker (Tuesday Knight), Joey Crusel (Rodney Eastman), and Roland Kincaid (Ken Sagoes) are released back into the seemingly safe suburban haven of Elm Street only for Freddy to begin haunting their dreams once again. Despite utilizing their unique powers to assist each other in their nightmares, these unfortunate teens are duly dispatched with extreme prejudice after Freddy is resurrected by the fiery urine of a demon dog from hell. Freddy is fast running out of teens to torment and so in order for his evil spirit to survive to feed on the souls of more children, he must influence Kristen to summon another Springwood teen into her nightmares, thus allowing Freddy to continue his reign of terror in the dream world. And so before Kristen succumbs to Freddy, she passes her powers to her boyfriend Rick Johnson's (Andras Jones) vulnerable and emotionally fragile sister, Alice (Lisa Wilcox). "Why don't you reach out and touch someone?" suggests Freddy, evoking the famous AT&T jingle with one of the film's many pop-culture quips. With Freddy now terrorizing Alice's subconscious, he is free to roam her dreams and those of her brother and her friends, including the handsome jock, Dan (Danny Hassel), the nerdy asthmatic, Sheila (Toy Newkirk), and the strong, athletic Debbie (Brook Theiss). But neither book smarts nor push-ups are any match for the mercurial man of their dreams, as Freddy gains a new foothold in Springwood once again, and as Alice's friends fall victim to Freddy one-by-one, she must find the strength and will to battle him on his own turf: in the dream world.

A Nightmare on Elm Street 4: The Dream Master was rushed into production after the massive success of the previous film. With a release date on the calendar but no director behind the camera, several units were ushered into production by the time Finnish filmmaker Renny Harlin came on board; though that only happened after much insisting to New Line Cinema chairman, Robert Shaye, that he was the right man for the job. Harlin was a relative newcomer, having directed one film in his native Finland (*Born American*, 1986) before heading west to find fame and fortune in Hollywood. His first American feature would be the low-budget horror, *Prison* (1988), though it wouldn't lead to much success for the eager filmmaker. But then the opportunity to ride the New Line gravy train came along and Harlin essentially pestered studio chief Shaye to give him a ride on the Elm Street Express.

"I was really down on my luck," Harlin says, recalling his first meeting with the top New Line executive, "and after fifteen minutes Bob Shaye is like 'okay, goodbye' and he pretty much throws me out of his office.... I went five times back to New Line, pretty much unannounced. I didn't call an assistant or make an appointment, I would just go and hang out in the lobby and go to Bob Shaye's office and say 'hi I'm back' and he's like, 'the Finnish guy? What's he doing here?!'"[50]

"I had seen the movie he made, I think it was called *Prison*," Shaye recalls. "We needed a director desperately and I knew it was going to be a huge amount of work and we decided he's a big guy, he probably has a lot of energy and could work really hard twenty-four hours a day for six weeks to get the film ready."[51]

Freddy hurts in the final showdown of *A Nightmare on Elm Street 4: The Dream Master*.

With a director in place, the grueling six-week schedule would ensue and prove an intense shoot, though the endurance of the youthful cast and crew paid off handsomely as the final result is perhaps the most energetic and adventurous film in the Elm Street series. Production Designer Mick Strawn was there from the very beginning of the production and confirms the chaotic rush to begin the film prior to Harlin's hiring:

"We started *The Dream Master* in February of 1988 and it was released in August of that year. We began with a forty-page outline on a film which is 99% practical effects, so that's the kind of schedule we had! I was running the art department as well as a lot of the effects work and we just had no time to go into optical houses, we only had three or four optical shots in the whole frickin' mess! And then Renny finally gets hired and is thrown into this group of young people, I mean they were so young that I was the old man of the bunch and I was only 31! *Dream Warriors* had a decent budget, but thankfully on *The Dream Master* they were just throwing money at us. Put it like this, if my concept was a huge junkyard then I was just going to go out and use a huge junkyard with actual cars, and that's what happened! On the previous film we constantly came up against it with Chuck Russell, but on *The Dream Master* we just went ahead and did whatever we wanted to. If they turned around and said, 'hey, you're spending a lot of money!' we could just say, 'well, yeah, have you got a script yet?' *The Dream Master* didn't really have a script but it had a crew!"[52]

One of those crew members was special effects artist, Nick Benson. Having just graduated high school in 1986, Benson went straight to work in the film industry and within two years had already begun building a career working on elaborately designed horror films such as *Night of the Demons* (Kevin Tunney, 1988), *Dead Heat* (Mark Goldblatt, 1988), *Society* (Brian Yuzna, 1989), and *The Blob* (Chuck Russell, 1989); along the way he met Mick Strawn, who suggested joining the *Nightmare on Elm Street 4* crew, a move which proved a fortuitous engagement for the ambitious young horror fan.

"I just immersed myself in the industry as best I could," Benson recalls, "I got some really great opportunities to learn by sticking myself into any production that I could stick myself into. And then I met Mick Strawn and it was on his suggestion that I got on *A Nightmare on Elm Street 4*, so I gave 'Screaming Mad' George and Steve Johnson a call and I wound up on both crews, the puppeteering crew for Steve and the cockroach transformation scene for George. I had been an Elm Street fan anyway, so it was like a Holy Grail kind of film for me and it turned out every effects shop in Hollywood was working on this. We had KNB, we had John Buechler, we had George, Steve, and all these other major effects guys who had a part in it. I had just come off of working on *The Blob* and a lot of people that I knew from that film were working on this as well. *The Blob* was huge, a big budget film with massive crews and we had time to get things done. *A Nightmare on Elm Street 4* also had a larger budget and larger production than I was used to working on, but we had to accomplish a lot in a shorter amount of time; it wasn't that bad though, I've worked on a lot of smaller films that had tighter schedules and were a lot more stressful. When I started on the film there was a Writers' Strike which had just begun, so the studio was dealing with that and of course script revisions were impossible to get done and the cast was just working with Renny to figure out how certain scenes would play out. Some of that had a trickle-down effect on us but not to a huge extent as most of our stuff was pretty much blocked already, but the dialogue was something they had to figure out. Despite all of that chaos we were really organized and everybody knew what they were doing, it never felt like it was a bad situation to be in because it all ran pretty smooth and we were always on the same page and headed in the same direction. Mick knows his stuff and the greatest thing about working with him is that he can see what he wants and he is clear about how to achieve it. He had built a reputation to where he could talk to Bob Shaye and the New Line people and tell them 'this is what I want to do and this is how we're going to do it' and they were like, 'okay, go do it!'"53

"Mick Strawn did a spectacular job on *A Nightmare on Elm Street 4*," Robert Englund says, "he is responsible for making it look as rich and elaborate as it does. Once you stepped onto those sets and saw the work that went into them, they were so great that it could feel like you were working on a much more expansive and expensive film, but it didn't have a significant boost in budget from the previous film, we just had great people working on it. This was the first one where I made some decent money but it was *A Nightmare on Elm Street 5* that had really more money behind the production; not a lot, but for a *Nightmare* film it certainly cost a bit more, mainly because of some of the demands that Stephen Hopkins made; we really went crazy on that one! But on *A Nightmare on Elm Street 4*, the crew were all eager and up for it, they had worked on other films together and were familiar with each other, with the exception of Renny and our cinematographer, Steven Fierberg. This was their first trip down Elm Street."54

For Fierberg, a major challenge was the prospect of being the first cinematographer to bring the once-veiled villain into daylight and to make the film as visually appealing for mainstream audiences, all while maintaining the expressionist elements which had previously kept Freddy an elusive and mysterious creature. The script called for Freddy to be far more present than in the earlier films, he was now the undisputed star of the series and that meant photographing him in such a way as to allow audiences to see the man they were paying money to be entertained by.

"In this film Freddy is out in the daylight," Fierberg says, "he's making jokes, he's the hero, he is who people are buying their tickets for, and so you have to see him. But New Line were like, 'don't show him!' They didn't want him lit, they wanted him in shadows. I said I'm going to make it really dark, but you're going to be able to see him, as dark as I could make him but still visible. I deeply believe I nailed it. But Bob Shaye, who is a great guy, had said, 'I don't know if we should show him, I think he should be silhouetted,' and I just said, 'I don't think so,' and Bob didn't force me. He gave me his opinion and then trusted me to do what I felt was best. We had the first daytime exterior shot of Freddy in the series, out on the beach; we tried to darken him as much as we could, we put black everywhere so he could get as dark as Freddy could get whilst being out in the open. Robert is such a great actor that it would be a waste if you couldn't see him, it would be tiresome and boring if you didn't capture the full extent of his performance, so I mostly under-lit him softly using a bounce or some method that meant I wasn't aiming a hard light at his face. I think I was bouncing light from below, which is a technique I used years ago on an art film called

Vortex, directed by Beth and Scott B, I was doing similar things where I would light something in the vicinity of an actor and that would be the illumination for the character. If it was impractical for us to bounce then we would diffuse the light, but the idea was you could just barely see him."[55]

Indeed, Robert Englund's presence in the film is greater than in any previous entry and here the actor delivers a villainous turn of great physicality and personality, owning and relishing the frame every second he is onscreen. The actor reveals that the time was right for Freddy to come out of the shadows and embrace the fact that he was the ruler of the nightmare landscape in which he roamed.

"There's an old expression in the theatre, which is when they need you to be in a certain area of a set and they say 'wear the furniture' or 'wear the set.' And that can mean anything from leaning on a doorframe to standing behind a chair and leaning over it, or draping your arms over the back of a couch, maybe sitting nonchalantly on the arm of the couch, or leaning on a piano, and that's what that expression means: to wear the set like you've been there before, like you own that room. I wanted to do that with these conjured, surreal images that these people were experiencing in their nightmares, because it is Freddy who is stimulating that milieu, that's Freddy's world—'welcome to *my* world!' Renny understood exactly what I was doing in that film; by that point I really wanted to dance Freddy a little bit and have him be part of the frame and be part of the image and to explore the set like an actor on the stage, I wanted him to be part of the choreography of the imagination. When I saw that these sets, which were the victims' imagination plane, where so magnificent I decided that Freddy really needs to move around that landscape because he is part of it, he created it. For example, I remember putting my feet up on the desk in the classroom scene and asking for an apple—'Can I get an apple? Can I get an apple?'—and the people on the set were like 'what the fuck is he talking about?' and I said I need an apple because

Freddy soaks up some rays.

'teacher gets an apple,' kids bring an apple to teacher and that will tell the audience that I'm the teacher and I'll put my feet up on the desk like I own the room and I will start peeling the apple skin. Renny thought that was great and he let me do all that kind of stuff; he would often have a shot set up and have it marked out for where he wanted me to be but I would try something different and climb up on something and he would say 'oh yeah, I like that better!'"[56]

In the aftermath of *A Nightmare on Elm Street 3: Dream Warriors* and given the increasingly commercial milieu of Hollywood horror filmmaking in the mid- to late 1980s, it is perhaps no surprise that this next entry in the *Nightmare on Elm Street* series would utilize everything in its arsenal to reach the widest possible audience a horror film could in 1988, and it did so with spectacular results. With action, gore, and humor in abundance, a more prominent Freddy, and a lively soundtrack overrun with pop and rock superstars of the era, *A Nightmare on Elm Street 4: The Dream Master* became the biggest financial hit of the franchise to date, ranking among the top 20 highest grossing films of the year.

"Sequels are always a scary thing to work on," Benson admits, "because there is that 50/50 gamble where you are going to roll the dice and it is either going to fail miserably or it is going to do really well; I think everybody experiences a little bit of that nervousness. I was concerned about it because *A Nightmare on Elm Street 3* was a lot to live up to as it was that very rare entity: the third film in a franchise and better than the previous films. So Part 3 was a very tough act to follow and going forward on Part 4 you did sometimes question whether it was going to be successful, and we certainly made sure that everything looked right and that it would live up to expectation after the previous film being so good and so successful. The great thing now is that many people tell me that they love Part 4 as much as they love Part 3; those are always the two films that end up the fan favourites."[57]

With a rookie filmmaker in Renny Harlin at the helm, it could have been a disaster for the tentative New Line Cinema, but evidently Harlin proved the right director at precisely the right time, bringing youthful vigor as well as the acuity of being someone in the age range of the picture's target market; this, combined with cinematographer Steven Fierberg's lively Asian-influenced framing meant the picture would be the definitive MTV horror of the era. Fierberg emerged from the New York City independent film world of Paul Morrissey (*Forty Deuce*, 1982) and Beth and Scott B (*Vortex*, 1982) before making his mark on mainstream Hollywood with *A Nightmare on Elm Street 4*. Since then, he has gone on to shoot films for the likes of Steven Soderbergh, Alex Cox, and Edward Zwick, but it was his dalliance with Freddy Krueger which proved a cathartic and memorable experience for the horror-shy cinematographer.

"*A Nightmare on Elm Street 4* was one of the highlights of my career but I do have a funny relationship with horror," Fierberg says, "When I was a kid my mother used to take me to the movies on a Saturday and drop me off so I could go and watch a double bill. One day she dropped me off and they showed *Eyes Without a Face*; I must have been six years old and I remember being so terrified that I would run out into the lobby and then occasionally peek in, but it was one of the scariest things in my life. So I didn't like horror and throughout my whole life I suffered terrible nightmares. And then when I was called to interview for *A Nightmare on Elm Street 4* I told my friend that I don't want to interview for this horror film, but they said, 'look, you always take the interview,' and so I did, I went in and met Renny Harlin. There had been a number of storyboards done by David Lowery, who has gone to work on huge films by Steven Spielberg and on all these major studio movies, but these storyboards were like something for an art film, they were beautiful images and they were not your standard shots, so I thought, 'oh, this is going to be more of an art film,' and so I immediately went and watched Wes Craven's original *A Nightmare on Elm Street* and thought it was great. After that I decided I would go back and embrace this horror thing and pretend I never had all those nightmares, I said to myself, 'I'm old enough now, I'm not six years old.' I went in with the attitude of really trying to convey what a nightmare is and how it looks and feels. I give credit to Bob Shaye for allowing me to do that. New Line were a distributor of foreign films and sometimes they would have access to stuff that wouldn't be widely seen, and one day somebody took us to a screening of a film called *Chinese Ghost Story* and that was doing all kinds of unusual things with the editing; it would cut from a super wide angle shot to a super telephoto shot. This really inspired me, so instead of having all the shots in a scene be done with a 40mm, we were cutting from 18mm to 75mm and continually shifting the perspective. I could shoot a small object with an 18mm and then shoot the actors with a 75mm. It was very dynamic and it was fun to go from slow-motion to regular motion and creating all these elaborate, dramatic shots. I credit that to the style of Asian filmmaking that I saw in *Chinese Ghost Story* and also in the John Woo style of filmmaking. However, nobody in the United States knew who John Woo was at that point and I would say that *Nightmare on Elm Street 4* was the first movie to really utilize that style of filmmaking in a Hollywood context; now everybody does it. That aesthetic came very intuitively to me as it did to Renny, so we were a visual match made in heaven. We almost had a psychic ability when it came to planning shots, we both knew what the next shot had to be. There was a cut of the movie at one point and the pizza sequence was originally edited very Hong Kong–style, like cut-cut-cut-cut-cut moving into this pizza. I thought it was brilliant, but they toned it down because they thought it was too extreme, but I wish they hadn't."[58]

When it came to crafting the intricate special effects sequences, Fierberg would block the scenes to get the best out of special effects man Steve Johnson's gruesome creations, and few were more elaborate or gorily inventive than the famous roach motel sequence. "Steve was pretty hands-on in working with Fierberg on how certain things were going to be shot," Benson recalls, "he was very picky about how things looked and so he would work with Fierberg and check to see how something was going to look through the camera as he would have some ideas on how to frame it. But that cockroach transformation scene was a blast! Having producers allow 'Screaming Mad' George to go wild on that was just like someone handing Salvador Dali a canvas and saying, 'here, go paint!' But not everybody understood what George was trying to say when he was explaining it. I understood what George wanted a hundred percent, I understood his artistic vision—which is why I stayed with him so long—but not everybody did and so I could have been a little more vocal. I was quite young and I didn't want to step on anybody's toes on a big film, but I

Director Renny Harlin (left), producer Rachel Talalay (center), and cinematographer Steven Fierberg (right) (courtesy Steven Fierberg Collection).

should have interjected more because it wasn't easy for guys like Mick who would have to go in and look at what George was doing but couldn't understand what he was saying, so there would be a bit of a translation issue with George's heavy Japanese accent and inevitably something would get lost in translation. But that whole effects sequence came out really well and it is one of the most disturbing things in the film. Brooke Theiss was fantastic and game for anything. I absolutely adore her. She is unlike most people we put in the makeup chair and as effects people we put them through a lot; I've seen the gamut of emotions in that chair, from angry to irritable to everything in-between, but Brooke was really patient and really sweet. She has told me on numerous occasions that she would do it all over again. It takes a certain kind of person to do that kind of stuff."[59]

A Nightmare on Elm Street 4: The Dream Master continues the previous installment's discourse on psychologically disturbed teens of broken homes, those emotionally abandoned by parents who are otherwise busy nourishing their own neuroses with alcohol and other forms of harmful, numbing self-medication. Alice and Rick's father, Dennis Johnson (Nicholas Mele), is a burnt-out white-collar executive type who treats his children with disdain, blaming them for the death of his wife and the misery that plagues his life. While the subtleties of this relevant theme of parental abandonment and the emotional fallout from such occasionally gets lost among the thunder and bluster of the film's action, Brian Helgeland's script does provide rich narrative motivation for Alice's discontent in life. She carries the burden of assuming the roles of wife and mother to her troubled father and overcompensating

A model for the Roach Motel sequence (courtesy Nick Benson Collection).

brother, envisioning for herself a dead-end life working in the local diner schlepping plates of pizza by day and coming home to a drunk father who chides her repeatedly for what he sees as unsatisfactory home keeping. "You call this vegetation a meal after a ten-hour workday? What the hell am I, a rabbit?! Christ, Alice, try to think a little more!" the angry and imbibed Dennis says before his daughter fantasizes about breaking the dinner plate to pieces before him and scolding him for drinking his life away. Further signs of troubling ignorance by the Elm Street elders are displayed when Kristen's mother Elaine (Brooke Bundy, returning from *A Nightmare on Elm Street 3*) barely acknowledges the death of her daughter's two best friends while deceitfully drugging her dinner with sleeping pills. Indeed, it is the tragedy of Kristen's doomed relationship with her indifferent mother that leads to her untimely though spectacularly surreal death at the end of the first act, that which leaves an opening for Alice to assume the role of the heroine and chief Freddy nemesis for this and *A Nightmare on Elm Street 5: The Dream Child*. Indeed, one of the production's most noticeable aspects is the replacement of Patricia Arquette with Tuesday Knight playing the previous lead character, Kristen, whom audiences may have assumed will remain the survival girl of this film after having emerged successfully from the nightmares of Part 3. However, the series continued its revolving door of strong female leads taking the reins in the battle against Freddy, and so Kristen, the last of the Dream Warriors, duly succumbs to her nightmares at the forty-minute mark.

"When I first got the audition for the film I was ecstatic," Tuesday Knight enthuses, "I was totally aware of Freddy and the fact he was a big deal. I loved the first and third one. The second one not as much, I had to grow to like it more than I did when I first saw it. I think it swayed away from the ideas of the first film quite a bit, especially having Freddy exist outside of the dream world, though I do love *A Nightmare on Elm Street 2* now. But I was extremely excited to audition for the fourth film and when I went to read for it they said I was going to be replacing Patricia Arquette. So they told me to go watch *A Nightmare on Elm Street 3* and look at the character and see how Patricia played it, which I did but when I started filming I just let that go and did it my own way. I didn't want to copy her, I wanted it to do it organically and make it my own. The whole production felt like a big thing, you could tell from all the great elements that were going into it and you knew when you were filming these really cool elaborate scenes that you were working on something that was going to be huge and special. And this was the first one where Freddy really came out funny, he has that great charisma and personality, he is so witty and has that distinct swagger. There is something about the way Robert plays Freddy which is actually sexy, it's to do with the way he walks or slithers around. Freddy has the kind of energy of a dangerous, decadent rock star, it's the same kind of dark, seductive energy. It was surreal working with Robert. The first time I met him he had his makeup on and he was so nice. Robert loves to talk, so conversations with him are always fascinating because he is a natural storyteller and he would tell me about everything, whether it was Hollywood stories or about his house or just anything. So the whole time I'm thinking, 'I'm sitting here talking to Freddy Krueger and in a few minutes he is going to be terrorizing me.'"[60]

Actress Tuesday Knight (courtesy Tuesday Knight Collection).

"It's a shame that Tuesday Knight wasn't in the film for longer," Fierberg says, "but they were extremely eager to get to the new girl and because of that they cut the best scene of the film out. They felt it was taking too long to kill Kristen before they switched to Alice so they deleted this sequence that we shot with Tuesday, a scene which is probably the best work I've ever done. It was a scene where Tuesday comes out of her house at night and walks forward as the camera cranes up and looks down at her on her lawn, then she turns and the camera drops to the ground, I mean really fast, and her own house has now become the Nightmare house—Nancy's house from the original—with no cut. She turns, starts running, the camera pulls back and then she's running down this nightmare tunnel; it was scary and really, really surreal. It was achieved with two shots: a wide shot and then a close-up which becomes the crane shot and super wide shot. How we got away with it was you saw a wide shot of the house and then you cut to the close up; they had the façade of Kristen's house cut in half and they pulled it back to reveal Nancy's house which had been built behind it. So we had people on each side of Kristen's house façade who were pulling it apart so that when the camera was in position you saw Nancy's house. And they took that scene out because they thought it was taking too long to focus on the new girl, but everyone who worked on that scene remembers it, it was a tour de force.

Even though it was the best scene in the movie I understood why they were anxious to get to the point that Alice becomes the lead girl. Her side of the story allowed me to play around with some interesting visual ideas that relate to the themes of her character. You know, *A Nightmare on Elm Street 4* is a very catholic movie in some ways, that's the kind of story that Renny wanted to tell, and I was able to really work with that. I like to look for a lot of references in art, especially in paintings and photography, but there was a sculpture by Bernini which was very influential to me on this film and it was *The Ecstasy of St. Theresa*. That sculpture is kind of violent and kind of erotic, it has Cupid about to pierce St Theresa who looks to be in the throes

The façade of the iconic Elm Street house (courtesy Steven Fierberg Collection).

of orgasm, and there's a scene in the film where Alice is in the church and these little boys start singing in a choir and I set up the shot so that the light passes across her face when just as she has this look of ecstasy come across her and we had her pose just like St. Theresa. I only spoke to the actress who played Alice, Lisa Wilcox, about six months ago and she had no idea that what we were trying to do was to get her to pose like this Bernini sculpture, but Renny was one-hundred percent behind me in doing that."[61]

Though Tuesday Knight didn't last the entirety of the film, she did leave a major impression upon fans as well was as her director. A pop star with three albums to her name, including an excellent eponymous 1987 pop release for CBS Records, before landing the crucial role of Kristen in *A Nightmare on Elm Street 4*, Knight was able to parlay her talents beyond the onscreen action when director Harlin realized he had the ideal singer for a *Nightmare* theme song in his midst.

"The soundtrack was such a huge part of it and that is down to Renny because he was so into the musical element of the film," Knight affirms. "How my song "(Running from This) Nightmare" came about is because I found out Renny was looking for music and so I asked him if I could present him with a song. He said yes, so I went into the studio for about three hours and did that song and then went back to Renny and played it for him and he flipped out. It was amazing. I didn't know where it was going to go in the film and when I found out it was going to be the title song I really, really freaked out. When I first saw the film and heard my song come up at the beginning I thought I was going to pass out, it was like, 'oh my god, this is insane!' That feeling is so hard to explain, I was so grateful and it was such a big moment for me. It was my love song to Freddy, I made it all about him. I worked on it with Michael Egizi, who has done a lot of music for films and TV shows. Renny gave me such an opportunity in choosing my song for the theme and it is because of that song that I have been able to place over fifty songs in films. I would never have had that chance without my experience on *A Nightmare on Elm Street 4*."[62]

The film was able to tap into the pop culture zeitgeist with its terrific soundtrack which brings together pop, rock, rap, and new wave artists including Billy Idol, Blondie, Divinyls, Dramarama, Go West, The Fat Boys, and most tryingly for producer Rachel Talalay, Sinead O'Connor. When it came to choosing the songs to be placed in the film, Talalay had championed the O'Connor track, "I Want Your (Hands on Me)," after it captured her ear, but doing so led to some contretemps with her co-producer and New Line boss, Robert Shaye, over the expense that would be incurred in acquiring the rights to use it. Music Supervisor, Kevin Benson, who previously worked on the excellent soundtracks of previous New Line films such as *My Demon Lover* (1987) and *The Hidden* (1987), had managed to secure the rights to the other chosen songs for a tidy sum of $5,000, but when it came to the aforementioned Sinead O'Connor track, the price was double. O'Connor's debut album *The Lion and the Cobra* had just broken out and singles from the record began charting as well as receiving airtime on MTV and radio, and so the potential for the film to be tied with an artist whose career was becoming stratospheric was too great to ignore.

"I had this infamous argument with Bob about the Sinead O'Connor song," Talalay recalls, "We put it on the temp, and then Bob found out it was going to cost

$10,000…. Bob went ballistic. We were on a mixing stage, and Bob came in and went fucking nuts. I said, 'This is perfect for the scene and this is gonna be a huge, huge hit.' He said, 'You don't fucking know this!' He's yelling at me in front of everybody. He took me into the ADR soundproof booth and he yelled at me. And everybody's just looking at him ranting, and they can't hear what's going on. I just argued for why I thought he should spend the money. He came out of the booth and said to the mixers, 'What do you guys think?' Everybody said, 'I think it's a really great song. I think it works really well.' He went, 'Oh, okay!'"[63]

Sure enough, "I Want Your (Hands on Me)" became the third hit single from O'Connor's *The Lion and the Cobra* and duly made the rounds on radio and television, Talalay's intuition having proved fortuitous as now the film would be linked to the Irish singer whose star was fast in ascent. Making further use of the commercial and cultural influence of MTV, a music video was filmed for The Fat Boys' track, "Are You Ready for Freddy?" Utilizing full marketing crossover potential, the amusing pop promo features tantalizing clips from the film interspersed with the comically inclined rap artists being terrorized by "Uncle Frederick" in the Thompson house. While he's at it, Freddy joins the three MCs in spitting out some dope rhymes. This was 1988, at the height of Freddy-mania, so the idea of everyone's favorite child killer-turned-cult hero rapping on MTV was just another sign of pop-culture's acceptance and warm embrace of *A Nightmare on Elm Street* as a cinematic phenomenon. Production designer Mick Strawn was there to enjoy the Boys' company.

"The Fat Boys were hilarious," Strawn says, "We had these scooters on the set that some promo company sent over for us, and somebody had to watch The Fat Boys all the time because, you know, they're The Fat Boys, and when it came my turn to get on a scooter and go round the parking lot with them we stopped at one point and ended up having a discussion about who was the baddest villain of all: Leatherface, Michael Myers, or Freddy. And the one with the gold teeth, Darren, who later passed away, he wasn't getting into the discussion at all, but the other two were going at it back and forth until Darren just pipes up and out of the blue comes out with, 'you know, Freddy gonna kill ya! It ain't even a contest cause Freddy gonna get ya in yo dreams! In! Yo! Dreams!' And I just started cracking up and literally fell off my scooter. But they were wise words: Freddy can get you in your dreams."[64]

As was now typical, a new composer was brought in for the latest installment, this time being the eminent Craig Safan, who was noted for his work on high-profile television shows including *Cheers*, *Amazing Stories*, and the 1980s revival of *The Twilight Zone*, as well as the films *Fade to Black* (Vernon Zimmerman, 1980), *The Last Starfighter* (Nick Castle, 1984), and *Remo Williams: The Adventure Begins* (Guy Hamilton, 1985). It would be the bombastic score of the latter film which drew the attention of New Line Cinema head Robert Shaye, leading to Safan taking the reins from Angelo Badalamenti, who previously scored *A Nightmare on Elm Street 3: Dream Warriors* to magnificent effect.

"I got the job of scoring *A Nightmare on Elm Street 4* because immediately before that I had done a film called *Remo Williams: The Adventure Begins* which was directed by Guy Hamilton. For that I had composed one of those giant scores, the

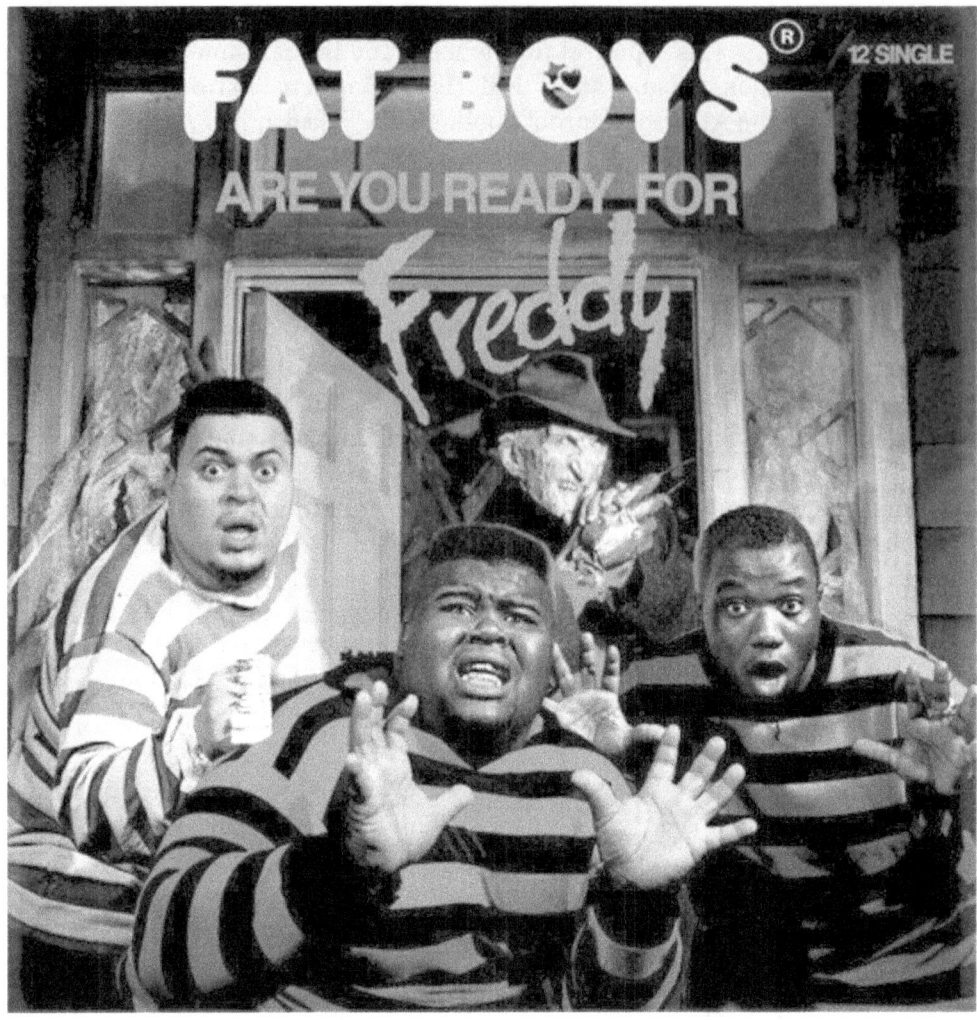

Cover art for The Fat Boys single, "Are You Ready for Freddy?"

most complex score I had ever written. Bob Shaye saw that film and he loved the music, so he called my agent and asked, 'can Craig do the next *Nightmare on Elm Street* film? Because I love what he did on *Remo Williams*!' and that is literally how I got the job. I never interviewed with Renny, it was totally Bob Shaye who brought me in; he was the big cheese over there, he was the studio boss."

This was not the first time Safan found himself working on a Robert Englund picture, as one of the composer's very first film scores was for the Henry Fonda-starring comedy road movie, *The Great Smoky Roadblock* (John Leone, 1977), which also featured an early supporting role from the future Freddy Krueger, Robert Englund. "I was about 24 years old, I was really young," Safan recalls, "and that movie, *The Great Smoky Roadblock*, was a disaster, but it was the first time I worked on a film with Bob Englund. He was in the movie playing this character named Beebo and I wrote a really cool little theme for him. It is ironic that he ended up becoming Freddy because Bob is such a nice, sweet guy. We always say hi when we run across each other because we go back that far. But prior to taking the job on *A Nightmare on Elm Street 4* I had never seen any of the films, so I had no idea what it was all about. I went and watched the original and I listened to the score by Charles Bernstein. Charles is a friend of mine, we have known each other forever, but I took that famous theme of his and incorporated it into my own stuff, though for the most part I ignored it as it was a completely different kind of score. I have never heard the music from *A Nightmare on Elm Street 2*, even though its composer, Christopher Young, is also good friend of mine. I know he took a huge part of the budget to record with an orchestra and I don't think he made any money on it; and I have never heard Angelo Badalamenti's score for *A Nightmare on Elm Street 3* at all, though I'm guessing it's quite electronic. They didn't have a huge music budget on *Nightmare on Elm Street 4* and I don't know if Bob Shaye thought I was going to do a huge orchestral score or what, because the music that he liked from *Remo Williams* was this big, big score, but New Line didn't have the money for that kind of thing. I was getting tired of that kind of score myself, so I thought this would be perfect for me to record in my studio at home with my Synclavier and my electronic gear and I could make a lot of my own samples and come up with some great sounds. I started doing electronic music in college in the late-60s so the whole transition to electronic music in film scoring came natural to me. I was doing the orchestral thing all along too but I always had my finger in the electronic world from the days where there was just plug-ins and no keyboards, when they were just sound machines."[65]

And so the score for the film is entirely electronic, eschewing traditional orchestration in favor of utilizing the sounds of then-prominent synthesizers. For the composer, this meant being able to work alone in devising the musical tone of the film, recording all the elements of the score himself and without the stress of the ticking studio clock and the attendant host, and cost, of session musicians.

"There was no real recording session because there was no orchestra; there was no showing up and seeing a hundred-piece orchestra, it was just me laying it down and mixing it; it's more of a tapestry process when you are working with electronics because I'm the only musician, so it's not like you are paying people to sit there for three hours and dealing with all the financial elements of that. Renny pretty much left me alone. He and Rachel Talalay would occasionally come over to my studio to listen to what I was coming up with and we did spend a day together spotting the picture, which meant going through the film inch-by-inch and talking about where each piece of music should appear. There are a lot of songs in the film so when we spotted the film I would have to be told where a song was going to be placed so I didn't have to worry about coming up with anything for that part. There isn't much of a through-storyline for me to follow in the film, it is fairly incomprehensible, each scene is like a vignette; you have the kid in the water bed, you have karate scene, you have the girl who turns into the cockroach, you have the diner, you have the scene where they keep going in circles on a loop, and so each kill or each set piece and part of the film is like a vignette and I thought that each one should have its own specific sound. For example, in the first scene with the kid in the junkyard I just used to a lot of metal percussion; the scene that plays on a loop is circular and so I used a lot of repetitive eighth notes, you could never put your foot down onto where the downbeat was; and then when the girl becomes the cockroach and she goes into the roach motel I used a sample contrabass clarinet that just made this weird, horrible sound like what you would hear if you close-miked a cockroach; that's where my head was. My music for the karate scene was pretty on the nose and that's the one I'm least happy with because it's the most clichéd, but I am proud of the whole final reel where Alice is fighting Freddy in the church, you have the image of the bodies coming out of him and there's all the stained glass. For that I got to use these big Bach organ sounds, so I liked that whole segment. But my concept of the music was to give each segment its own individual style and looking back on it, I do think the music is good if not something I listen to anymore. I did work hard on it trying to get what I wanted from using the synthesizers. We didn't have computers back then, except with the Synclavier on which you wrote in these commands, but working like that was very limiting and you really had to work hard to find your own sounds, and then to sustain a whole film, I mean it's one thing if you are writing a three-minute pop song and you are looking for one really cool sound but on a film you have two hours of material which has to have some variety."[66]

With style, pop culture savvy, and fun in abundance, *A Nightmare on Elm Street 4* remains one of the most popular films of the franchise as well as a commercial behemoth for the fledgling New Line Cinema, who were by now branching out into more commercial filmmaking with the likes of *My Demon Lover* (Charlie Loventhal, 1987), *Hairspray* (John Waters, 1988), and *Torch Song Trilogy* (Harvey Fierstein, 1988). In taking a chance on the persistent Harlin, Robert Shaye ended up with his studio's biggest hit to date, one which solidified the popularity and commercial value of his Elm Street brand name. Tuesday Knight considers the marriage of aesthetics of Harlin and Fierberg to be crucial to the success of the film:

"Renny and Steven are the ones who brought all that flashy MTV style to it and made it such an appealing film to people who might not necessarily be Freddy Krueger fans or horror enthusiasts. Steven's visuals really made it exciting and together they brought everything to a higher level, it was just so different for horror at that time, it was exciting. It was a crazy shoot, we did so much in those six weeks, but Renny was great and his vision for the film influenced everything on the set, right down to us actors and how we performed. I loved Renny, he and I had a great connection from the very beginning. In fact, it was so good that everyone thought we were having an affair. We weren't, but everybody thought we were, even though I was going out with someone else at the time, and that was Andras, who is in the movie! But we had such a good connection and I thought he was so creative; he really let us express ourselves and do what we do and bring some of our own stuff to the roles, certain improvisational stuff and things like that. I thought he was wonderful, I had a great experience with him and I would love to work with him again."[67]

"I had just worked with Chuck Russell on *The Blob* and Renny was an entirely different kind of filmmaker," Nick Benson says, "he would just come in and be like, 'okay, what are we doing?' and we would tell him what we're doing and he'd go 'great!' and he would just disappear with the two blondes he had with him. So it was relatively easy. More so than not it was a crew-run film; in my opinion Renny was just there to guide everything, but the crew really ran it all, we knew what worked and what didn't. That's the great thing about working on a film that far into its franchise: you know how things are run and you know what works."68

"We were out somewhere in East Bumfuck, San Fernando Valley for the junkyard scene," Englund recalls. "I had just done a television series, I had been working non-stop for a year, I was exhausted, I had a cold, and you have to kind of psyche yourself up to put that makeup on, and we were shooting nights, which really does something to your body clock. So we had been there for a week or so and I remember I was sat in my chair, wrapped in a blanket, it was three or four in the morning and I was tired. But I remember getting up out of my chair and walking fifty yards down this canyon of old cars and they were testing out all the lights and all of a sudden these broken vehicles came to life, the lights were like eyes coming alive; it was so incredible that it informed me of the sense of surrealism and imagination that was going into this film, and it was all practical effects. And then Renny showed me a rough cut of the junkyard sequence on the video assist and I could see that he was really going for that MTV style of editing, it was very energetic, and it made me excited about the project. By showing me the little rough cut of what he had shot, even though it was in black and white on this little monitor, in the middle of the night, on location, all of a sudden I had all of these ideas and I just wanted to get to work. Renny knew his star was a little under the weather and he offered me some stimulation."69

Meanwhile, horror filmmaker and historian, Mick Garris, considers the elevated humor of Freddy's fourth outing to be a key to its mainstream acceptance: "I think one of the reasons that *A Nightmare on Elm Street 4* did as well as it did was that *Dream Warriors* injected a lot more humor into the character of Freddy and then they really amplified that in Part 4. And so having a monster who can crack wise really appealed to kids because there's that forbidden quality to it; you're not supposed to watch scary movies when you're a kid, but with Freddy, even though he was the most vicious of child murderers, he was also funny. So that combination of horror and humor, and the idea of whistling in the face of death, is what allowed it to be embraced as well as it was, because the whole concept of mortality is not something that children are really aware of. And so they like that walk through the graveyard where they do so safely, because they don't think about what the results could be, they don't think of the danger, they think of the spooky fun of it all. Freddy became more of a comedian than a scare show by this film and that didn't do any harm at the box office."70

"I love the film and I love the *Nightmare on Elm Street* franchise," Fierberg affirms, "the first is still the most beloved by everyone and always has been, and we knew that when we were making Part 4 but we were hoping we could be the next best film. The one thing I regret is that they already had a release date of August 1988, and we started late for some reason, we were pushed back two weeks, which in a way was better because it gave us more prep time, but then they only gave us two weeks from the day that we finished shooting to the day they had to have 2,000 prints in the theatres. It had gotten to the point where we had a release date in two weeks' time and I'm still color correcting it! This is not like today where color correcting is done digitally, this is printing the film and screening it in a theatre every day for a week. All the visual effects still had to go into it, all the green screen stuff. So on the first day of screening it there is this notice on the screen for the first fifteen minutes, 'visual effects shot to be added' and every day as I proceeded there would be less of those. They were working twenty-four hours a day, and my impression of it is that even though the film had a main editor, there were several people cutting it at night, perhaps three editors altogether working on it. At one point they sent a negative to a lab in Canada because they had to make a thousand prints in a day because the lab we were at couldn't do it. It was insane, but it was a great team effort; everybody was pushing themselves to the limit to make it the best it could be. It was inspirational that way."[71]

"The film was so big, it just went crazy," Knight recalls. "The trailer was on TV like every five minutes, the box office was swarming, it was incredible to watch this thing erupt before our eyes. It was a big deal, I will never forget the commercial that ran announcing it was the number one movie in America. New Line were very happy with it and I don't think they even expected it to become as big as it did. I saw it again recently at a reunion screening for a lot of us who worked on the film and it was the first time we had seen it in a theatre since it was released and it was incredible. I couldn't believe how good it still is, it has held up incredibly well. It's so much more than just a horror film, it has everything: action, comedy, and horror. And of course it has a great theme at its core about female empowerment. I loved it."[72]

"Working on *A Nightmare on Elm Street 4* definitely opened a lot of doors for me," Benson admits, "and a lot of the people who were on that film have gone on have major careers in the industry working on massive productions. But this was a

Renny Harlin (left) and Steven Fierberg in front of the Freddy soul chest (courtesy Steven Fierberg Collection).

huge movie for me going into it, having been a fan and knowing the franchise had become so big; I was still quite young and fresh in the business, so for me it was like, 'holy shit, I'm working on *A Nightmare on Elm Street* and I'm here working on Freddy Krueger's death!' That was a little bit intimidating, and then when I saw it for the first time I was blown away. It's a real rock n' roll movie, I just absolutely loved it and I was really, really proud to have been a part of it. I still get work today because I was part of that film, I never thought it would still be opening doors for me at this point in my life, three decades later. Those of us who worked on it still treat each other like family, we're still friends. There's a lot of other films I've worked on that I don't speak to any of the cast or crew from, but the people from *A Nightmare on Elm Street 4* have remained in my life. The 1980s was a great time for horror filmmaking, it really was a second Golden Age for horror."[73]

"I have never paid much attention to the success of the film," Safan says, "nor did I ever see Bob Shaye again after working on it, and so it wasn't until later on that I found out that *A Nightmare on Elm Street 4* was particularly successful and is fondly remembered, because it is a film I get asked about quite a lot. I just thought the whole series was a great success and we were just another one, but I have discovered that this is particularly well-regarded. When we were making it I thought it was pretty campy; I mean the meatball head on the pizza and some of the catchphrases, it was so cheesy that I had to restrain myself from making musical jokes, but I just played it straight. I thought there was a lot of style but very little substance, I didn't find it scary at all. It's more about grossing you out than it is about making you feel unsettled. It's not *Night of the Living Dead* scary, it's not even *A Nightmare on Elm Street* scary! There was no sense of reality to it and I think a good horror film should have some sense of reality to ground you and make you think that the threat is real, but in our film all these kids are dying and everybody cries for like one second and then they are back to their normal life going about their business, and of course that's not the way it would happen. Had the film used some sense of reality then these deaths would have a deeper impact on the characters. I just couldn't imagine who was going to buy into it. But then it turned out to be a good movie, I think that Renny did a great job visually and his style was perfect for the kind of story we were working with. It was the fourth film in the series and so it wasn't perceived as something new or fresh, but Renny was new and it was he who brought that pop sensibility of the MTV era to the film. The visuals are very strong, it's very slick, and while a lot of that style of shooting is probably clichéd now, at the time it was fresh and innovative. The only thing that bugged me is the way he mixed the movie, which was frustrating to me, but in retrospect he made the right decision because that's the way movies were going, which is that rather than having the music being up front it was just another element with the sound effects. So compared to *The Last Starfighter* where the music was very much up front, the mix on *A Nightmare on Elm Street 4* was frustrating. If it was up to me I would have put the music way more to the foreground—I wonder why!—but as it is, the music is more of a texture and that is where film music has gone in the last twenty years; if you look at a Christopher Nolan *Batman* film and compare it to a Tim Burton *Batman* film you will hear the difference; these days you don't even know what the music is, or whether what you are hearing is music or sound effects. Is it a musician or a machine that you hear underneath? But that's the way most films have been done since *A Nightmare on Elm Street 4*."[74]

"The film had a huge opening," Fierberg recalls, "There was a lot riding on it. The script tied into something very primal and whatever our screenwriter, Brian Helgeland—who is now a big deal in Hollywood—tapped into with the script it has struck a chord with so many people. I have met a lot of people who tell me how important this particular film was to them growing up, that it expressed something about childhood and how they saw the world and they connected with it. So there is an emotional core there and I think the kinetic energy of the way Renny directed it and the way I filmed it made for an exciting, fun watch. And they let the character of Freddy change a little bit so as to add humor to him, and the fact that you could see his face perhaps helped him be embraced by a lot more people. And of course the set pieces were pretty impressive, especially for that time; it had some big scenes. Overall, I think it stands up so well because it is a huge, fun, exciting movie with an emotional depth, and all of that combined with Renny's vision, which was so well-executed, really made for a great film. It was made by a great team, we all enjoyed the thrill of it."[75]

"*A Nightmare on Elm Street 4* is beloved by a lot of people," Englund says, "and it certainly has a place in my heart because it has one of my favorite sequences in the entire franchise and it's the scene where Alice leaves the diner where she works and gets in the truck with her boyfriend and then the scene just keeps looping, and looping, and looping. As elaborate as some of those other set pieces are, that scene is very surreal and genuinely unsettling, and yet it was done so simply. I love that it feels exactly like a nightmare, it's what dreams do. Another thing I love about this film is that Renny Harlin really did leave me alone to develop my character and bring another dimension to it. It's my favorite performance as Freddy."[76]

3

Welcome to Primetime, Freddy!

"That was then, this is now. Springwood's nightmares are just beginning."
—Freddy Krueger

In the midst of the *Nightmare on Elm Street* franchise's pop cultural approbation and in the throes of massive financial success, New Line Cinema chairman Robert Shaye devised the cunning plan to turn his prized property into a syndicated television series. By this time Freddy Krueger had become young America's favorite film villain, with his image adorning everything from toy dolls, water pistols, clothing, lunchboxes, and costumes. And of course, he wouldn't be a teen idol of the 1980s without having his own pop videos rotating on MTV, as Freddy did when he joined The Fat Boys and Dokken for singles promoting the previous two hit films. And so while another theatrical sequel was duly set in motion as the public embrace of the property was at its peak, Freddy attempted to conquer television. New Line joined forces with Stone Television and Lorimar to bring Springwood to the small screen with *Freddy's Nightmares*, an anthology show that would span forty-four episodes across two seasons. Upon the series premiere in October 1988 fans might have been surprised and concerned to learn that their titular anti-hero was to rarely feature as a diegetic character within the narratives of the episodes, rather his presence is largely that of an infamous name uttered in terror and whose memory haunts the subconscious of Springwood's population. While he does appear in some stories, Freddy's role is predominantly that of host and curator of the dreams to come. However, despite his lack of presence, *Freddy's Nightmares* is a rewarding experience for the Elm Street devotee for numerous reasons, including the fact that the town of Springwood is expanded to take the viewer on a deep dive into the Middle-American milieu that Krueger has corrupted.

The pilot episode "No More Mr. Nice Guy," directed by *Texas Chainsaw Massacre* legend Tobe Hooper, functions as a prequel to the events of *A Nightmare on Elm Street*, depicting the backstory that Marge Thompson relates to Nancy in the first film and subsequently takes us on the guilt-ridden journey of Lieutenant Tom Blocker (Ian Patrick Williams), the man who lights the torch that makes Freddy immortal. The episode begins with the prosecution of Freddy over the slaughter of twenty children, a horrendous tally which may be only the tip of the iceberg as the FBI are confident that they can link Freddy to serial killings all over the state of Ohio. Devastating details are relayed for the jury, including the names and fate of several Freddy victims, such as the horrific deaths of Virginia Cross, aged eight, and her four-year-old brother, Mike Cross, found in a dumpster a block from their home; Bobby Doyle, six years old, only identifiable through dental records. After Freddy is acquitted on a legal technicality, he returns to his dungeon of horrors in a disused industrial space and immediately reunites with what is likely to have been his method of luring his young victims, an ice cream truck; he excitedly tears a tarp off the vehicle and rhetorically asks of it, and the audience, "ah, together again! Are you ready for Freddy?" Tobe Hooper utilizes some interesting visual techniques in this scene, at one point offering us a tour of Freddy's lair of torture subjectively through the villain's own eyes, just before the angry parents and local dignitaries, including a dentist, a lawyer, chief of police, all upstanding professional people who gather together as the Springwood vigilante mob, arrive to serve Freddy the justice he deserves after the legal system has failed them. But as Freddy says, "Springwood's nightmares are only beginning," and from here the show takes us through forty-four episodes of the town's denizens being haunted by various social and psychological malaises, some directly in battle with Freddy, others just having the misfortune of living in a less-than-idyllic Springwood and thus experiencing the phantom's malignant presence that has permeated the community.

Perhaps the biggest coup for *Freddy's Nightmares* was luring Robert Englund back as the bon vivant villain, lending the series immediate credibility as a genuine product of the *Nightmare on Elm Street* universe, whereas other television versions of big screen horror franchises such as *Friday the 13th: The Series* didn't feature its famous monster at all. The show also retained much of the crew from the films,

Robert Englund as Freddy Krueger in the television series, *Freddy's Nightmares*.

meaning those behind the scenes were already frequent visitors to Elm Street. Englund recalls the allure of the enterprise:

"How they got me was on board was, first of all, they let me direct some of them; I got my DGA card and I directed several episodes. Secondly, they paid me handsomely. And also it allowed me to help my friends, my crew, to make some good money because what happened was I brought all of the crew from *A Nightmare on Elm Street 4* onto the series because I figured if we did that movie and the TV show back-to-back then by the end of it we'd all have a lot of money and be better off. All of these kids had been working real hard on the first four films and I thought that by doing this they would finally have enough money to buy a house, or to get married, have a new car, or whatever they needed to do. When you added the two salaries from *A Nightmare on Elm Street 4* and *Freddy's Nightmares* it was good money."[1]

"You cannot do a show with Freddy and not have Robert Englund," says series writer-director-executive producer, Bill Froehlich. "That character is so important to him and he was very helpful in assisting me with maintaining the *Nightmare on Elm Street* tone and feel. He was in all the intros and outros and interludes and we had a lot of fun creating those with him. There were times when we were filming those and he would suggest trying different things and adjusting other stuff to be truer to the character. He took it very seriously and clearly understood the character from the feature films, so we were clearly welcoming of any and all suggestions he had in wanting to maintain the truth of the character. There were of course moments when he wanted to do something but we just didn't have the budget or the time, but we would continue to creatively spit ball and come up with something else that we could do within the restrictions of our timetable and budget that he felt good about. He wanted to protect and honor the creation of that character. He came to the set as Robert but there was a point where you saw him fully invested as Freddy, he made the shift and that is his artwork."[2]

The show's potential to exploit television's regulations and restrictions due to its mooted late-night slot meant the possibility for some thematic darkness and a creative playground for any filmmakers willing to join the production. And when it came time to hiring, New Line's Robert Shaye took a relaxed approach; "Anybody who wanted to direct one could direct one and anybody who wanted to be in one could be in one and anybody who wanted to write one could write one,"[3] Shaye says.

Meanwhile, Bill Froehlich took a more discriminating approach to sourcing talent, given his more hands-on engagement in the day-to-day running of the show. "I brought in a number of directors that I had known prior to this," Froehlich affirms, "but I also brought in some directors that I had the fortune to meet for the first time while working on the show. I was able to give some talented people chances that they weren't getting elsewhere, and these were talented people, and in some cases it was because they had a reputation for doing a certain type of show; executives like to pigeonhole you, which meant it would be very difficult to get opportunities in something which would allow you an opportunity to grow. So I knew some of these directors were stuck in that situation and I wanted to give an opportunity to prove they could handle the job and that they could do something different; for the most part, I was right! There were a couple of times where we had to help someone because the schedule was just crazy. Ultimately, my choosing directors came down to a number of factors and it usually depended on practical elements, I had to feel that they could work fast enough within our schedule and budget; another thing was that even though they had to be capable of working fast I did not want them to be what we in this business call a 'traffic cop.' By that I meant that I wanted more than someone who would just turn up and say, 'okay, let's shoot a master, two over-the-shoulders, and two close-ups' and then move on. A lot of television directors can make great money coming in and doing just that, but I wanted people with an aesthetic. I looked at as much of their work as I could in advance and if I saw a distinctive creative quality and a sense of risk-taking then I hired them, because you really had to have some grit to do something this cheaply and this fast while wanting to deliver quality. Being that the series had an anthology format I thought it was a great opportunity for directors to put more of a creative stamp on their episodes. A lot of television work in the 1980s and 1990s, including some very successful ones, followed a strict formula and there was a lot of repetition because people loved seeing the same kind of thing every week, and a lot of us who were creating those felt very creatively hemmed in and we wanted to break out a little more."[4]

"There was a lot of creative freedom afforded our directors," Englund confirms, "some of the episodes are incredibly stylized and because the show is formatted into these short segments we felt that they should have a distinctively stylish look to them. But by the time it got around to my turn directing the budget had already been slashed, so on 'Cabin Fever' I did the first segment in a more traditional classic style and then the second half I did all handheld, very cinéma vérité, so there are two very different approaches to the filmmaking there in one really good episode. The first segment is my homage to *The Twilight Zone* and it stars Brett Cullen and Lezlie Deane, who went on to star in *Freddy's Dead: The Final Nightmare*. I had discovered her on *21 Jump Street* with Johnny Depp, and she was really talented, kind of like a voluptuous Jodie Foster, and I cast her in my movie *976-EVIL*. Lezlie had her own punk band and I remember one time when my wife and I were in Paris, at a hotel we could never afford but being put up by the publicity department of some movie I was doing, and we were having room service late one night, some lovely French food with a glass of champagne, and we turned on the TV and there was Lezlie Deane with long blonde hair and really shiny lipstick, a real goth kind of look, and she was being interviewed with her lover—she was in a lesbian punk rock band—and I was just like, 'Oh my god, that's Lezlie!'"[5]

Following Tobe Hooper's memorable pilot episode the directorial reins would be handed over to Tom McLoughlin, whose horror pedigree includes the low budget 1982 independent horror film *One Dark Night* and his heavily ironic but entirely brilliant *Friday the 13th Part VI: Jason Lives* (1986), which revitalized the increasingly moribund *Friday the 13th* franchise and marked him as a major filmmaking talent. The fun sense of self-awareness and lively aesthetic construction of the sequel led to it being not only a box office hit and fan favorite, but further propelled Jason Voorhees towards pop-culture horror icon status, thus providing Freddy a financial and cultural rivalry which would be played for laughs (and money) years later with the 2003 monster mashup, *Freddy vs. Jason*. It was following his successful sojourn to

Camp Crystal Lake that McLoughlin was approached to bring his edgy and profitable sensibilities to Elm Street, as he recalls:

"I came to *Freddy's Nightmares* due to a combination of two things. After I finished directing *Jason Lives* I was asked to direct *A Nightmare on Elm Street 4*. I went in to New Line Cinema and had some meetings with them and I said I was happy to read the script and hear what it was all about. I didn't want to do another *Friday the 13th* right then because I didn't have any cool ideas, so I thought I might try the *Nightmare on Elm Street* series and see if I could bring something interesting to that table. But when I went in there I found out they were already shooting second unit material; it's standard practice for a major movie to have four units all filming at the same time but being where I was in my career in those days I didn't want to jump in on a project which is already under way, I want to be there from the very beginning. So I turned it down. But I was still on New Line's radar as somebody that they wanted to be involved with and then Mick Garris got involved with *Freddy's Nightmares* and he recommended people he knew and I was on that list. So I met with the executive producer of the series and landed one of the episodes, which was 'It's a Miserable Life,' the second episode of the series right after Tobe Hooper's pilot."[6]

Mick Garris is a filmmaker whose name would become synonymous with the horror genre in the years following *Freddy's Nightmares*, having gone on to direct several Stephen King adaptations for film and television, including *Sleepwalkers* (1992), *The Stand* (1994), and *The Shining* (1997). Prior to that his work included producing and directing documentaries for major cinema releases such as *The Thing*, *Videodrome*, and *The Goonies* as well as working on Steven Spielberg's *Amazing Stories* as a director, writer, and story editor. Garris and Spielberg would develop one of their amazing stories into a feature film for the latter's production company, Amblin Entertainment, and the project would become the 1987 science fiction comedy, **batteries not included*.[7] That same year New Line Cinema would offer Garris the opportunity to direct his theatrical debut, *Critters 2*.

"I was very grateful to New Line because they allowed me to make my first feature film, so when Bob Shaye asked me if I would do an episode of *Freddy's Nightmares* I said, 'Anything for you, Bob!' He had given me such an amazing opportunity with *Critters 2* so I was happy to do it. *Freddy's Nightmares* was really a director-for-hire situation because the show was done so quickly, but because it was an anthology show it had more flexibility in regard to the aesthetics you could bring to it. You are not consigned to the same style, the same characters, and the same locations, so that sets you free, though you are limited in terms of bringing ideas or themes to the table. On series television you don't agree to a script, you agree to a timeslot, but I was happy to work on it because it was shot in town and friends of mine were making it."[8]

The bizarre, surrealist aesthetic of *Freddy's Nightmares* also proved to be the métier of filmmaker William Malone, who had directed the low-budget science fiction horror films, *Scared to Death* (1980) and *Creature* (1985). Malone was brought on to the series by former UCLA friend and producer, Bill Froehlich, allowing the director to bring his distinct visual aesthetic and pitch-black sense of humor to the episodes "Heartbreak Hotel," "Lucky Stiff," and "Easy Come, Easy Go."

"Bill Froehlich is a great person," Malone says, "I became friends with him at

Director William Malone calls the shots (courtesy William Malone Collection).

UCLA and so I knew him for a long time. Then when he was in the position to be hiring directors he remembered that I was a good horror guy. For some reason whenever I get hired on these television shows they are already a few seasons in, which is good because it means you are coming in to something which is already a well-oiled machine where everybody knows what they're doing and you don't have to reinvent the wheel. Plus, by that time the producers are usually fed up with the show and don't care, which is great because you can go and do whatever you want to do. But Bill wanted guys who really knew and loved the genre and so a lot of the directors and writers who worked on *Freddy's Nightmares* were really big horror fans and they enjoyed doing it, and that was rare because back then because if you worked in that genre it was considered slumming it, but now it's mainstream, it's a big deal. A lot of directors working on horror films and TV shows back then hated doing it and they would tell you that they hated it, but that was not the case on *Freddy's Nightmares*, we had the likes of Tom DiSimone, Ken Wiederhorn, Mick Garris and some other guys who are all big horror fans, they love the genre. I had seen and loved *A Nightmare on Elm Street* when it first came out and it was a great film and part of the reason I loved it so much is that it has a surreal quality. I'm kind of a closet surrealist, or maybe not-so-closet, so it really suited me to work on this show which was so bizarre and which allowed its directors to be creative."[9]

"Bill Malone had been a friend of mine and I knew that he was really talented, Froehlich affirms. "I tried to get him work on previous shows that I did and it never quite worked out; for the life of me, I just couldn't understand how Bill wasn't getting more work, because I knew exactly how good he was. So when it came to *Freddy's Nightmares* I called him up and said 'you've got to come in,' and he said 'I'm there!' and he was fabulous, he rocked. He brought great ideas and an amazing visual sense, he did one of the things that I wanted a lot of the directors to do, which was to bring a real cinematic sensibility to the episodes as opposed to just slamming through it."[10]

The series didn't just rely upon directors of high horror credentials either, as producers brought in up-and-coming filmmakers who had been making their mark in Hollywood in recent years in a variety of genres. One of those was Lisa Gottlieb, hot off her Columbia Pictures teen comedy, *Just One of the Guys* (1985), and who would direct the sixth episode of the first season, the excellent "Saturday Night Special."

"When I was starting out in the industry, if you were going to go into feature films you couldn't direct television," Gottlieb recalls, "but as soon as I made *Just One of the Guys* that line started to get a little shaky, so I was very pleased to get the call from one of the producers, Jill Donner. I went in and met with Jonathan Betuel and

1st assistant director Richard Schor (left) on set with producer Gil Adler (center) (courtesy William Malone Collection).

Gil Adler to work on the script. Don Bohlinger came in later. Jill Donner isn't credited with writing the episode but she is the writer I met with mostly; this was before she went off to do *Baywatch* and make the big bucks! I've heard that the reason I was initially called is that the guys were all moaning, 'oh, the studio and Robert Englund is bugging us to hire female directors, but there's no good female directors around,' but Jill said, '*Just One of the Guys* is hilarious and so well-directed! Lisa works really fast and I just spoke to her agent, she wants to do it!' She told them that I had made a studio film with an eight-week schedule and I delivered it in six-and-a-half weeks. Columbia had begged me to have the film wrapped and everybody home before the Christmas holidays, which I did, and that sounded good to these guys because the *Freddy's Nightmares* schedule was so tight. It was a very low budget enterprise but we had some amazing talent working on it and I managed to give all my friends jobs: Bobby Lesser, Scott Burkholder, and Joyce Hyser. Kevin Yagher was there doing Freddy's makeup and he was awesome; I knew some of the other people going into it, including the UPM [unit production manager] Scott White, from a previous film that we worked on together; I was friends with the DP, David Calloway, and I had previously worked with the camera operator, Henry Lebo. When he left to go work on another show they moved the First A.D., who was female, up to camera operator, so *Freddy's Nightmares* was very open to women. Robert worked with female directors in a lot of his theatre work and he had the instinct to be very inclusive, he always wanted a very diverse group of people working with him. Everybody loves Robert, he is one of the best people in Hollywood. So going into it I knew there would be a great crew of people working on the show and I actually took over from my friend Ken Wiederhorn; he had cast this young woman who he was over the moon about and that was Mariska Hargitay. She was there one day when I was shooting and when we were introduced she said, 'I'm so nervous, this is such a big thing and it's my first break!' She was very tall, had legs forever, really slim and beautiful and I told Ken about her background, that her late mother was Jayne Mansfield, who was killed in a car accident and the kids were in the backseat; he didn't even know! Mick Garris was so great to me. When I was there for the week leading up to shooting I was asking him a lot of questions and he was just a complete gentleman. One day I said to him, 'you know, you're on this set in this funky-ass North Hollywood warehouse and you are wearing a really nice pair of slacks and shoes, not Nike's, with a shirt and tie!' And he said, 'Well, I looked at the shooting schedule and I thought that if I'm attending my own funeral I will dress up in formal attire.' And I just cracked up because it was so true, it felt like they were pulling the rug from under us before we even walked out on to the set. Mick said he was only shooting what he needed, no more, and I said, 'I'm doing the same thing!' Mick was fantastic, he would help you with anything you needed, he gave me his phone number and said 'if you need anything just call me.'"[11]

Garris' presence also proved particularly helpful to the series showrunners, Gil Adler and Alan Katz, as his familiarity with the horror fraternity meant he knew the right people who could bring some skill, vision, and efficiency to the production. "Gil had been a friend of mine for years," Garris says, "so when they were looking for directors I helped them out and recommended all the of people that I knew and made some introductions. It became a little bit of an incestuous family and then when Gil made

Tales from the Crypt a couple of years later he brought in me and some of those same guys on to that show as well. One of the crucial people I introduced Gil to was the composer, Nicholas Pike. I had worked with Nick on *Critters 2* and he is a brilliant guy."[12]

Nicholas Pike is a distinguished, Emmy Award–winning composer whose career has taken him from low-budget horror films such as *C.H.U.D. II: Bud the Chud* (David Irving, 1989) and collaborating with the world's biggest pop stars, including Michael Jackson, to being the musical director of NBC's *The Bonnie Hunt Show*. "I never saw any of the *Nightmare on Elm Street* films prior to working on *Freddy's Nightmares*, in fact I still haven't. None of them." Pike admits. "But some of my friends like Charles Bernstein and Pat McMahon worked on them and I knew it was this big horror thing at the time. I was familiar with the image of Freddy: the striped shirt, fedora hat, and burnt face, and that pretty much told me everything I needed to know about it. A flute student of mine had introduced me to Junior Hornrich when he came to New York to orchestrate and conduct a movie and it was through that project I met the guy who produced *Alfred Hitchcock Presents*, so I hit up him up for a job scoring an episode of that show and that's how I got started out here in Hollywood. After that I was hired by New Line to do the music for *Critters 2* and then I was pulled into *Freddy's Nightmares* from various connections to that film, mainly Mick Garris and Bob Shaye."[13]

Upon joining the series Pike set about creating a haunting, memorable theme tune which is both unsettling and dreamlike in its tone and composition, recording the score in a house in Laurel Canyon which was owned by his engineer, Michael Jay, who had a home studio set up in his living room where the composer would lay down the music with some of the best musicians in the business, including renowned session guitarist Dann Huff (Whitney Houston, Michael Jackson, Barbra Streisand), who contributed the unnerving heavy metal guitar line which mimics the childlike synthesizer melody.

"Dann Huff was the pre-eminent session

Composer Nicholas Pike takes a break from recording the *Freddy's Nightmares* score (courtesy Nicholas Pike Collection).

Michael Jay's Laurel Canyon home studio, in which the score for *Freddy's Nightmares* was recorded (courtesy Nicholas Pike Collection).

guitarist in LA back then," Pike says, "he played on a lot of major albums and I worked with him many times until he left town for Nashville, where he's been having great success as a producer for about thirty years now. The budget for the music on *Freddy's Nightmares* was reasonable and we could have gone to an outside studio but when you go to a recording facility like that you don't have the luxury of time, your mind is always on the clock and you are aware of how many hundreds of dollars are going out the window by the hour. It was kind of wild and unruly back then. I had this company bring over all my racks of equipment to plug into Michael's gear, and he had this Sony F1 digital two-track recorder that was like a shoebox that attached to a VHS recorder which digitized the signal and put it onto a videocassette tape. It was the pinnacle of recording technology back then, but Michael was very much into the most up-to-date gear and had all of these kinds of gadgets. For the sound and tone that I had in mind for the music, I decided to go for these screeching bowed cymbals which I coupled with Dann's guitar so as to give it all a very metallic edge, very threatening and evil. I remember sitting in an office in New Line and listening to the main title theme that I composed and it was on a cassette tape that you shoved into this machine in the wall. I remember there were a lot of cooks in the kitchen on that show but there was nobody dictating to us what the musical style should be, they left me alone once I came up with that main title sequence because they loved it. There are some traditional elements to it such as the heavy metal guitar, but otherwise it is pretty out there. I also did the first three episodes, but after that I brought in two friends to take over, Junior Hornrich and Randy Tico. They did the bulk of it after I left, although there were other people brought on at a later stage. Junior is a Brazilian composer and percussionist who did the score for John Boorman's *The Emerald Forest* and it is he who really launched my career as a film and television composer, so when it came time for me to leave *Freddy's Nightmares* I gave it to Junior and Randy, but unfortunately when they took over the budget decreased."[14]

Indeed, as the series progressed the production hit upon some serious issues, including the logistical nightmare of producing the series according to Lorimar Executive Vice President Les Moonves' plans for selling it in various formats to accommodate multiple time slots. Moonves designated the second season of the series to be the final one and therefore wanted to maximize profits by distributing the show in an innovative though complicated manner that meant writers were required to spin an intricate narrative web across the season with each one-hour episode containing two tenuously linked plots which were also designed to tie into other episodes across the series on occasion. This allowed the series to be aired as either an edited half-hour single story or full one-hour two-story episode, and, somewhat ambitiously, as a two-hour feature-length piece comprised of four thirty-minute interconnected stories; the latter strategy also meant the series could be sold to the home video market as feature films. Lorimar stood to make a lot more money through these multiple avenues of airing the series, but with production due to resume imminently and the slew of second season scripts having yet to be written, Moonves had to call upon producer Bill Froehlich to pull the series back from brink of disaster and, with little time to prepare, deliver the required twenty-two hour-long stories which could be split into forty-four half-hour stories out of which eleven two-hour features could be gleaned. Froehlich's previous television credits include *Scarecrow and Mrs. King* and *MacGyver*, while he had just finished being the showrunner of the sophisticated romantic comedy series *A Fine Romance* when it came to an end after failing to replicate the success of the show it was designed to replace, *Moonlighting*. Froehlich recalls the situation that led him to *Freddy's Nightmares*:

"They put *A Fine Romance* on at eight o'clock on a Thursday night opposite Bill Cosby when he was killing everybody in that timeslot, so we ended up being cannon fodder. Soon enough I was looking for my next project when I was approached by Les Moonves, whom I had known for quite a long time. He called me and said 'I'd like you to take over this series we're doing called *Freddy's Nightmares*. We're only doing two seasons, it's being done in a special way, and I'd like you to run the second season.' But then he revealed that there was a bit of a problem; they were due to start production in seven days and they only had one script which was not in good shape and they had no other stories or scripts that were ready to go. That is a terrible position to be in prior to the start of production. Normally you would have to shut everything down and take time to build up a number of scripts, because once you begin production the beast of time begins to chew you up as everything moves so quickly and your attention is split between all the elements you have to deal with. This came about at a time when there were several projects that I wanted to focus on more than this, but I looked at the situation and realized they were in real trouble. If I can use a combat war term, it would be like parachuting into a Hot Landing Zone, and I thought for the sake of my sanity I shouldn't really do it. So, I politely turned Les down. But he kept coming back at me, saying 'I know you know how to do this, we know we're in trouble, so would you take this over for us?' My agent said, 'they're giving you great money, they're giving you all these perks, and they're going to give you a development deal after it, so you should really consider doing this.' But there was another reason why I was holding out, which is that I didn't think I could do justice to the *Nightmare on Elm Street* movie franchise, I wasn't sure we could replicate what made the films so successful, because in 1989 you couldn't go that far with Standards and Practices and so I thought we would be too restricted. So, I went in to see Les one last time with a proposal that I assumed would get me kicked out of his office, but I leveled with him and I was honest. I said, 'Les, I know you are in a lot of trouble here with the pressure to get going, and I only see one way of helping you with this and that is for me to have complete creative control. Nobody, including you and everyone at the studio, can tell me what to do creatively, because I will need to be able to make decisions very quickly. I can't get caught up in the bottleneck of having to deal with different levels of executives; if your executives can keep up with me, I'd be glad to look at their suggestions and comments because we'll need all the help we can get, but I cannot go through the normal process with this.'

There was another person in that meeting and it was Scott Stone, whose production company was working on the series under the aegis of Lorimar, and I said that my criteria would include him. I literally just met Scott and I'm already telling him he can't have any input! But I offered him a stipulation, because he was responsible for the deficit financing, meaning that Lorimar gave us a budget and if we had to go over that budget to complete an episode then Scott was responsible for that. So my stipulation was: 'If I stay on budget then I can do what I want when I want in order to get this done, but if it looks like I am going to go over budget or if I do go over budget then you can step in and we can work it out together because it is your money on the line.' I wanted to be fair about that. Scott turned out to be a fabulous guy, we worked very well together, and ninety percent of the time I did stay on budget. But I turned to

Les and said, 'I know you won't accept this because you guys always have your finger in the pie, but this is the only way I can see it working.' And I also told him that I want to add some tonal feel and some psychological elements, the kind that you might find in *The Twilight Zone*, and to insert some black humor in the style of *Alfred Hitchcock Presents*. I thought that if we combine those ideas with the elements of horror that comes from the *Nightmare on Elm Street* films then we could deliver what the heart and soul of the franchise was all about. After I finished saying this to Les I just got up and started to leave because I thought he was going to boot my ass out of there, but then he said, 'Bill, where are you going?' and I replied, 'Les, you're not going to let me do this.' 'Yeah, I am. You start Monday!' And this was on a Friday!"[15]

"It was like playing three-dimensional chess," Froehlich elaborates, "because the logistics were outrageous as you had the storytelling logistics and the production logistics to deal with. Here is an idea of how we decided to work it out: in the first half-hour of an episode we might have certain sets which might come into play in the second-half of the episode, and you might also need those sets in a later episode which would connect with this episode to make a two-hour feature. So we had to figure out if we required the same sets at a later stage, if we could afford to keep them, and whether could we go back to the same location again if we needed to. This is the kind of logistical planning that was going on as we were trying to write good characters and stories. And we were doing this for one-third the normal budget of a network television series. It was nuts! But when we did accomplish this and the episodes

1st assistant director Richard Schor (right) and executive producer Bill Froehlich enjoy filming *Freddy's Nightmares* **(courtesy William Malone Collection).**

started airing and beating the competition, every studio in town sent production and development executives over to my office to meet me and find out how the hell we were doing this, how we were able to make a one-hour episode on one-third of the budget and in fewer days than that of any other show whilst delivering something at the level of quality that we were able to put into it. I told them exactly how we were doing it and then they kind of slinked out of the office and went back to their bosses to tell them that we were achieving all of this successfully because we had eliminated all the executives."[16]

Freddy's Nightmares proved to be a springboard for many of its talented crew to go on to illustrious careers on major film and television projects in the ensuing decades. Production designer Greg Melton has gone on to work on *The Walking Dead*, *Agents of S.H.I.E.L.D.*, and *The Mist*, while writer Jonathan Glassner went on to be executive producer of the 1990s revival of *The Outer Limits* before co-developing *Stargate SG-1*. Michael De Luca was one of New Line Cinema's brightest and most ambitious young employees, a writer with designs on becoming an executive (with a wardrobe to match) and he wouldn't be long climbing the ladder to become one of the studio's major players. As president of production, he spearheaded such New Line success stories as *Seven* (David Fincher, 1995), *Boogie Nights* (Paul Thomas Anderson, 1997), *Austin Powers: International Man of Mystery* (Jay Roach, 1997), *Rush Hour* (Brett Ratner, 1998) and *Blade* (Stephen Norrington, 1998).

Mick Strawn recalls that "when Mike De Luca used to write on *Freddy's Nightmares* he would come in dressed in these suits with the narrow black tie. We used to hang out all the time in my office out the back and one day he said to me, 'nobody talks to me, they completely ignore me!' and I said 'well you're dressed like a friggin' accountant, Mike! Get yourself some Levi's and a couple of horror t-shirts, then come back and people will notice you. As it is you're wearing 'The Man' camouflage. Get rid of that crap!' He came in the next week with a new wardrobe and from then on he became the Mike De Luca we know."[17]

"Mike was young and ambitious," Tom McLoughlin says, "he was involved with New Line from early days. To Bob Shaye, Mike was the kid with his finger on the pulse of what was happening in horror and pop-culture, he knew what audiences wanted. And he often got it right; it was Mike who convinced Bob to do *Teenage Mutant Ninja Turtles* and some other things which became huge hits for New Line, and now he has gone on to become one of the heavy hitters in the business."[18]

"There really was some amazing people coming through the show," says Strawn, "so many cool directors coming and going, but when it comes to a TV series like this the director is really the guest. They should really call them 'Guest Directors' because that would give more of a clue how directors work on a TV show, they step in and they step out. You give each one what he needs for his particular episode but even before they're brought in you are pretty much locked in as to what you're going to do anyway. I got to work with Tobe Hooper on the pilot of *Freddy's Nightmares*, which was interesting. I remember having a meeting with him to discuss about the look of his pilot and it essentially went like this: '[mumbles] well yeah, I was thinking [mumbles] that we could, eh, that we could [sighs and mumbles] if the expansion of the overall [mumbles], eh, hmmm, you know, Freddy and the colors…' and it just went on and on and on like that, and at the end of the meeting I'm thinking, 'okay, so I'm on my own!' And that's how it went. I worked away on the design of the show and he never argued with me or said anything, I just kind of stayed away from the guy because I thought he was so fucking weird! But you also had the likes of Mick Garris, who I had worked with before on *Critters 2*. I built the town of Grover's Bend in the film and my name is there on the list of the town's occupants."[19]

Special Effect Coordinator Andre Ellingson also recalls working alongside the many talented filmmakers who stepped behind the camera on *Freddy's Nightmares*. "I was still so young when I started on *Freddy's Nightmares* that my brain was just absorbing everything that I should be doing. My goal was always to be a director; I had directed all my own movies in film school and that's what I wanted to do, and so throughout my career, no matter what I do, I'm always close to the director watching them work and asking questions. I love finding out how they made that leap into directing, who gave them their first job, and all of that kind of thing; everybody has a different story, and working on *Freddy's Nightmares* exposed me to a lot of different directors who had a lot of different experiences. Some of these guys were already established and then you had a lot of younger directors with less experience and this was a step up for them; this show was a really good opportunity for those guys because they were getting to work on one of the most popular franchises of the day and New Line was a great studio to work with, when they recognized talent they put you to work. One of the *Freddy's Nightmares* directors, Michael Lange, who shot *Mother's Day* and *Deadline*, also worked on the show that I do, *Criminal Minds*, and we recognized each other straight away; the last time I saw him I was twenty-six and then I meet him when I'm fifty-six and he remembers me. He's this big, friendly guy who has been directing for thirty-five years and I always remember working with him on *Freddy's Nightmares* because I loved his personality; so as this young kid who wanted to direct, I really latched on to him because he was so passionate and brought amazing enthusiasm to his job. There was so much talent coming through that show, people who went on to become huge, and one thing I will never forget is the day Brad Pitt came in to appear in the episode, 'Black Tickets.' I happened to go into the front offices and all the girls are acting giddy so I said 'what's going on?' and they're like, 'oh my god, you should see this actor that just came through!' And at this stage nobody knew who Brad Pitt was, he was an unknown, but even then he had all the girls going crazy over him. Then I saw this dude and he had charisma coming out of his eyes and I'll never forget just thinking, 'look at this young guy coming in here and just ripping it up!' I remember working with him on the effects for one scene where somebody put piranhas in his Jacuzzi, and so when my buddy Chris was working with him on some big movie a couple of years ago I told him to ask Brad if he remembers the scene from *Freddy's Nightmares* in the Jacuzzi and he did! Brad turned around to Chris and said, 'yeah, of course I do! That was one of my first gigs! Sitting in a blood pool with piranhas on *Freddy's Nightmares*.'"[20]

Like the *Nightmare on Elm Street* films, the television series touches upon various themes that Wes Craven set out in his original film, themes of child abuse, familial discord, bullying, peer pressure, grief, loneliness, sexual identity, and divorce, all par for the course in the Springwood milieu. For Bill Froehlich the influence of Rod

Andre Ellingson on set with Freddy Krueger (courtesy Andre Ellingson Collection).

Serling and his seminal masterwork *The Twilight Zone* was crucial to informing the series with a depth of such ideas, with the producer having been tutored by the legendary writer in the early days of his career after the two met at Ithaca College, where Froehlich was a student and Serling a visiting professor.

"I got to take seminars with Rod for four years and he talked me into being a writer after he read some scenes and short stories that I wrote. I really wanted to be a director or a producer, but Rod pulled me aside one day and asked what I planned on doing and I replied that I wanted to go out to California and make movies and television, and he said, 'well, you can write your way into directing' to which I responded with, 'Rod, I'm not a writer,' and he looked at me and said, 'yes, you are! Bill, you have been writing scenes and stories for me for four years and I'm telling you, you're a writer.' That floored me. I never considered that someone on his level would think that something I was doing was any good. Both mentally and emotionally it opened doors for me. In my head and in my heart, he was a mensch to me. Rod always said that a writer must always have a point of view, you must take a stand and you should write about the elements of your time. Rod was a deep and heavy proponent of using writing to achieve social justice and we know one of the great lasting effects of *The Twilight Zone* was that a lot of them were morality tales with themes that addressed human nature and our behavior. So the challenge that I found when I was doing *Freddy's Nightmares* was to find ways to bring as much of that as possible into the show, and that was very challenging because I didn't think the *Freddy's Nightmares* genre allowed us as much flexibility as they had in *The Twilight Zone*. There were certain storytelling rules and regulations that we had to follow to ensure that it stayed within the feel of *Freddy's Nightmares*, but for the most part we tried to bring some important themes to the episodes. Though there were times where I feel we weren't able to go as deep as I wanted to but we felt that if we can at least touch upon it then a person watching might find an emotional connection, it could be something that says to somebody, 'hey, you're not alone.'"[21]

In Mick Garris' *Killer Instinct*, Lori Petty's track star Chris Ketchum is haunted by memories of her recently deceased mother incessantly pushing her to win as she is failing to meet the sporting standards expected of her. Despite being in mourning over her mother's death, Chris is insensitively scolded by Coach Wilson (Lee Kessler) by saying that "she may have been your mother but she was my friend," and further mentioning that they were friends through school, sports, marriage, and divorce. This alludes to yet further broken homes in the supposedly idyllic American Dream town of Springwood, and another source of confliction for Chris, being the child of a broken home. Chris' fiercest rival is Nickie (Yvette Niper), a beautiful and naturally athletic bourgeois kid whose wealthy parents are also pushy, to the point that Nickie says to them that her medals might as well be theirs.

While such themes are relevant and apropos to those ideas introduced in Craven's original film, they weren't necessarily the most important element for the directors working under the intense schedule of *Freddy's Nightmares*, as Mick Garris says, "Wes certainly brought these ideas to his films and there is something in the Elm Street world which is intellectual and deep and worthy of analysis, but unfortunately when it came to *Freddy's Nightmares* the directors didn't get to explore them in any great detail. The main characters are young, so their dilemmas are identifiable to other young people watching, but beyond that I don't think the themes played as big a role in the TV series as they did in the films, here it was more of a 'boo!' and a 'ha-ha!' So we just had some fun creating memorable special effects moments, such as decapitating Lori Petty, which was a lot of fun to do! I don't think anybody saw it coming."[22]

In one of the best episodes of the entire series, Tom McLoughlin's "It's a Miserable Life," ambitious teenager Brian Ross (John Cameron Mitchell) has aspirations to leave Springwood to become a liberal arts student—as noted in his yearbook—but his desire for a more metropolitan lifestyle is constantly rebuked by his hard-working, blue collar father who has supported the Ross family with his Beefy Boy fast food restaurant, repeatedly making snide remarks to Brian about wishing to attend college in favor of working the grease pits of Beefy Boy in perpetuity. "This place clothed you and fed you, I can't believe you're turning your back on it," Brian's father says when his son reminds him that he is leaving to pursue his education in September. But despite needing to clock out and return home to fill out his applications, Brian is made to pull yet another graveyard shift in the burger joint. As Brian whiles away the boredom of manning the counter by throwing hoops with onion rings, an ominous biker can be heard pulling up to the drive thru speaker and begins taunting the youngster with "you can't run, you can't hide, you're ours, Beefy Boy!" in a voice that sounds suspiciously like that of Freddy Krueger. Moments later the biker returns to the service window and pulls a gun on the despondent youth, shooting him in cold blood. But then Brian's girlfriend Karyn (Lar Park Lincoln) arrives to pick him up only to find him asleep on his shift. From there Brian begins to experience further nightmares and visions as his anxiety about being grounded in Springwood for his entire life begins to take its toll on his mental health. The episode deftly moves in and out of the elastic dream world with elliptical surrealism and provides a dense discourse on the predicament facing small town kids with opportunities and ambitions bigger than those of their parents. Brian is intellectually capable of being accepted to his chosen liberal arts college, but he is stultified in the menial routine of his father's business, that which he is expected to assume responsibility for some day.

"Teen angst and teen mental health are both important themes in the context of this episode," McLoughlin says, "I love working with teen characters because this is the time in your life where you experience so many things for the first time: first time you get your heart broken, first time you fall in love, first time that you take drugs, first time that you realize that your parents don't know what they're talking about. It's the first time we get to make choices on our own and some of those choices can be really bad and some are ones you learn and grow from. In 'It's a Miserable Life' you have this character who is caught between these two worlds, dream and reality. When you see the motorcyclist arrive at the window you're not quite sure if he is there for real of if the character is imagining it. Those are themes I love to work with but when it came to creating the next picture or the next episode in each of these franchises it was always a case of 'we've got to give the audience this, this, and this,' because that's what they expect: some humor, a really incredible kill, something that ups the game and that we haven't seen before, which is why you see these increasingly elaborate set pieces as the films go on and become something bigger. On the series we were working with such low budgets we couldn't afford to do big set pieces, we really had to find something creepy, and of course we didn't have Freddy as part of the storytelling but we still wanted to create that nightmare realm and have these moments that are surreal and unsettling, things you see in a bad dream. But the making of that episode was pretty much what they call a 'clusterfuck.' I only had a half a script, which was written by Mike De Luca, and it was the first half of the episode; for the second half we kind of improvised a lot. All of that stuff in the hospital hadn't really been worked out. They just trusted the directors and allowed us to make the episode we wanted to make out of the basic material given to us. It was crazy on one hand because I was shooting and shooting and shooting so much material which hadn't been planned but there was nothing in the script which dictated anything in particular for the hospital section. I had the benefit of both John Cameron Mitchell and Lar Park Lincoln, they are great actors and we really tried to make the scenes believable and character-related, so when we got to the hospital we put in every crazy thing imaginable; the only thing that was scripted was her mouth being sewed up, or certain other effects gags. But a lot of the other stuff, like when she looks out the door and sees the old man, and the wind coming through the hospital, that was just stuff that I created on the day and I was lucky to have a really good assistant director who protected me to get the stuff that I wanted. He would prioritize the day so that I could work on the things that were really important to me. So I had a lot of creative freedom on that episode and I know that I had Bob Shaye upset at how crazy the schedule seemed to be and because of all the footage we were shooting, but at the premiere party for it Bob came over to me and said 'I really love what you did,' so it felt like all the excesses that occurred were justified."[23]

For her episode, "Saturday Night Special," Lisa Gottlieb managed to insert some deep satire into her cautionary tale of the dating game in the 1980s, taking on several key institutions of the decade. The episode is based around the exploits of a couple of lonely people who feel the need to exaggerate their qualities and attributes as potential lovers. Gordy (Scott Burkholder) is one such lonely guy who has been rejected by his dream woman, the athletic beauty, Lana (Shari Shattuck), and decides to embrace the fashionable world of video dating where he is coached into creating an absurd profile reel—"now you're going to tell us all about your life, very naturally, just as if you were sitting in your own home," Gordy is told while being instructed in how to sit, how to smile, and how exaggerate what limited qualities he may possess. All of this works wonders for Gordy as he receives a call from Lana looking for a date. The second segment of the episode deals with Lana's friend and housemate, Mary (Molly Cleator), a dowdy and unlucky-in-love woman who is convinced by Lana to undergo expensive cosmetic surgery—"what price beauty?" Lana says. When Mary emerges from her surgery she is no longer the plain old frumpy recluse of before, but a glamorous and vibrant young woman (now played by Joyce Hyser)—"I can't believe it's really me," she says, "It's just the way I dreamed it." And of course, Freddy Krueger will play a part in this dream, meaning her new image will come at a greater cost than a mere financial one. It seems that the answer to Lana's question of "what price beauty?" is: Mary's life. A vision of Lana, via Freddy, appears in the mirror to Mary upon her ultimate mental breakdown and regales the moral of the story: "I told you, once you were different then everything would be different. But you wanted to be perfect and now you are, so enjoy yourself. You deserve it!"

Gottlieb provides further satirical jabs at the seedy working environment of Springwood Realty, where Lana and Mary are employed. There is certainly no equality in the workplace when it comes to beauty, as their smarmy boss, Mr. Fadiman (Vinny Argiro) disrespects the hard-working Mary while he flatters Lana into using her natural beauty to close a deal with wealthy out-of-town real estate client, Mr. Rawley (Robert Lesser), suggesting that Lana gives him that "special personal attention that Springwood Realty is famous for." Of course Lana is simpatico with this working arrangement, viewing it as an opportunity to climb the corporate and financial ladder, "I know, I know, a woman should be valued for who she is and not for what she looks like, right?" she says to Mary sarcastically before admitting that "the way I see it is Life's just one big beauty pageant and like it or not we're all contestants from the minute they slap your butt and tell your daddy it's a girl." Mr. Fadiman also alludes to Mr. Rawley's "Springwood Beautification" project, meaning that even Springwood isn't safe from a cosmetic makeover, as he tells Mary that the town's property market went soft "after that Krueger business" and disparagingly remarks that "Springwood is just like any other town, only with affordable housing." Mr. Rawley's plans are to discard of the ugly people and places of Springwood by building a new upscale shopping center on a historic site, a move that Mr. Fadiman says "won't hurt the town's new upwardly mobile image." Wittily, he also remakes that "beauty is in the eye of the deed holder!" The shallow allure of beauty is the focus of much of the episode's horror and comedy, as Gottlieb takes aim at the obsession with plastic surgery and the false impression of everlasting cosmetic perfection. This leads to some particularly hilarious moments in the episode, though the director had her share of battles with some complacent editors.

"Robert Englund comes from theatre and so do I," Gottlieb states, "so we would have long talks about the subtext of what is going on in the episode. In each of these stories in the show, and in the films, are little morality tales, whether it's someone who is too ambitious, or you slept with the wrong person, or you lied about something, or whatever it is, Freddy is there to teach you a lesson, he is like the arbiter of morality in a completely amoral universe. In my episode, for the second segment with Joyce Hyser and Bobby Lesser, the script was very much flirting with the idea of the beauty myth and what it would feel like on both sides of it. I went in and said you've got to really play up this myth, I want the man to tear her shirt off in a moment of passion and find that she's a mannequin under the clothes; that to be the beautiful thing that she is meant she was artificial. And they loved that, although when I shot it and took it into the editing room they all fought with me, they said, 'This won't cut in! What are you doing? We have no idea what you are doing here!' So I told the editor to go take a break and I will put it together, so when he came back I ran it for him and he said, 'Oh that really works! But I still don't understand what you did.' And I said, 'I shot it in order to cut it exactly the way it's cut. That's why you didn't get it when you looked at it.' When he saw it he realized there were very few choices and that shut him down, because I had shot it with the editing in mind and I shot the exact choices I wanted him to have. I only needed that one choice to make that moment work. He was a little snotty about it because it looked as though I cut the line ahead of him. I'm sure the other directors had moments where something went well after somebody had said, 'That's not going to work! You better cover yourself and have an exit plan!' And I normally do too, but on this scene everybody said 'it's not going to work, you're wasting our time!' but after seeing it cut together and seeing it when it aired they all said 'you were right, we were wrong, and we hardly ever say that, Lisa' and I said, 'Good! You should say it more often, especially when you absolutely know you're absolutely wrong. That would be really refreshing if you admitted it more than just once!'

We cast Shari Shattuck who was this typical, blonde TV actress who came in to read and was very good and very funny but of course on her résumé it said she was a championship ice skater, so that was the winning combination. And Scott Burkholder is a terrific actor who I cast as Gordon, the guy who couldn't get a date; Scott even asked if we wanted him to go learn ice skating, but we said no, though I did bring them in for rehearsals. Mick Strawn and I found a nice skating rink and we went back there with a bunch of art department people the day before we were going to start filming and when we arrived there was Shari! She lived near it and booked the place out to practice ice skating! She admitted that she hadn't been on the skates in a little while and wanted to be prepared for her shots. Molly Cleator played the woman who turns into the Joyce Hyser—Plain Mary versus Pretty Mary—and I had seen her in a number of theatre productions and I knew she would give a lot of emotional life to this girl who wishes she was pretty."[24]

Also cast in the episode is Robert Lesser, a skilled and versatile theatrical actor who has appeared in his fair share of classic and cult films, including *David Holzman's Diary*, *Die Hard*, *The Monster Squad*, *Running Scared*, and *2010: The Year We Make Contact*, and is cast in the "Saturday Night Special" episode as romantic interest, Mr. Rawley.

"I knew Bobby Lesser from mutual friends," Gottlieb says, "we all went to each other's parties, so I got to know him and whenever I would hold these script readings in the big dining room of my little arts and crafts bungalow in the middle of Hollywood I would always ask Bobby in to read. So we would work together whenever we could and I actually wanted him to be in *Just One of the Guys* but it didn't work out because it was out of state and it would have involved travel, but generally I would cast Bobby in anything I do."[25]

"Looking back on it now, I'm realizing what an enormous franchise *A Nightmare on Elm Street* has become," Robert Lesser says, "When I was cast in *Freddy's Nightmares* I hadn't seen any of the films. There was a terrific bunch of people cast in that series and it had some first-class writers and directors. I watched 'Saturday Night Special' again recently and it reminded of the good time I had making that episode. It was certainly the only time I got to kiss a beautiful actress, on screen at least. When we were making it there certainly wasn't a feeling of it being some kind of prestigious production, it felt more like a B-movie kind of set. But it was a good job, a fun part, and I enjoyed being around my wonderful cast mates who gave terrific performances, and of course Robert Englund is great, he is an extremely talented actor and a very charming person when he is not in that makeup. It has some interesting themes going on about plastic surgery and knowing who you are, it's all about identity. It was a classy little piece of storytelling and the great thing about having all of these wonderful writers and filmmakers on the show was that they could bring their different sensibilities and themes to it. Lisa was in sync with this story and it was very nicely done."[26]

"Bobby's a really cultured, artful, creative guy; he's a total sweetheart and funny as hell," Gottlieb enthuses, "I have always told him 'you're a terrific hipster but you can play any businessman or any right-wing conservative, you have this universal look and you can turn your New York accent on or off, so you should be working all the time!' But the truth is he does work all the time, he does a lot of theatre; it is hard to keep that kind of nomadic career going doing great work in small roles and appearing in maybe only one or two scenes. You hope that it would move you up to something like second-lead in a movie, but a lot of the best actors that I know in Hollywood have that kind of career and that's the life that they lead: small roles in films and a lot of work in theatre. I'm always going to love this episode and I am most proud of the moment where Bob Lesser is making out with this woman and when he opens her dress he sees it's this silver mannequin underneath and then we cut to a shot of him and he says, 'wow, I've seen some bad boob jobs but this takes the cake!' That line made the whole show worth it."[27]

"Lisa was a good friend of mine," Lesser affirms, "and she was totally absorbed in this opportunity of getting to work on the show and she enabled me to take on what was an unusual part for me. When I see these lists of 'Ten Best Episodes of Freddy's

Nightmares' I don't see anyone including our episode, which is a shame, but it must be Number 11, just missing out on making the list because it was damn good! You can mention it in the book, '"Saturday Night Special": the overlooked gem of the series.'"[28] Robert isn't wrong, "Saturday Night Special" is indeed the overlooked gem of the series.

Further episodes throughout the series delve into the dark heart of Springwood and continue the core thematic discourse of dysfunctional families. Director Michael Lange's episode "Mother's Day" is a classic example of the show's juxtaposition of the dramatic and the absurd. Teenager Billy (Byron Thames) moves into Elm Street with his mother, Jane (Judith Baldwin), and his overbearing stepfather, Al (Arell Blanton). Once again, the subtext of child-parent distrust is present but is played to extremes in both halves of the episode. The link between the two segments is Billy's pretty neighbor and love interest, Barbara Gamble (Jill Whitlow) and in the second half we are given an insight into her own disturbing relationship with her emotionally distant mother, Sherry Gamble (Elizabeth Savage). Sherry is the host of a trashy radio talk show, is on her third marriage, is ignorant to her daughter's life, and yet enjoys a position as a mouthy moral authority on-air under the guise of her dispensing straight talk. When Barbara anonymously calls her mother's show under a pseudonym to discuss her issues, she is told "your mother doesn't care." Sherry's unsympathetic negligence leads to one deranged caller killing his landlord after the host refuses to take the severity of the call seriously and makes a dangerous throwaway comment. Lange amplifies the comic absurdity in this half of the episode, as seen when Sherry tries to ring her lawyer from her jail cell and the cartoonish mousy gibberish on the other end is made deliberately audible. It is episodes such as this which herald the fact that the *Nightmare on Elm Street* property had by now entered a whole different realm of humorous horror far removed from the austere milieu of Wes Craven's original film.

Child's Play writer John Lafia contributed another socially conscious episode to *Freddy's Nightmares* with his entry, "Rebel Without a Car," in which lead girl Connie (Katie Barberi) is delighted to receive a full scholarship to attend Springwood College. This nicely sets up a class conflict between Connie and her boyfriend, Alex (Craig Hurley), as two working class kids with differing social ideals: him learning to be a mechanic and her with aspirations to an upwardly mobile middle-class life beyond the confines of their small town. A ghostly apparition even reminds Alex of his social limitations when it warns him, "I've never been out of Springwood, and neither will you!" The second segment of "Rebel Without a Car" might as well have been titled *Scenes from a Class Struggle in Springwood*, as it details Connie's life in college and her conflict with the snobbery and haughtiness of the elitist sorority sisters that she aspires to be part of. This is depicted in several scenes, such as when Connie endures a humiliating interview it is mentioned that she "went to Springwood High … a public school!" in a most politely derogatory manner; worse, the interviewer refers to Connie as "a financial aid case" and suggests she would feel more at home with the "racial and ethnic diversity" of the college dormitory where other kids receiving financial assistance dwell. She is also sneered at for having worked in Springwood's fast food restaurant, Beefy Boy (in a nice nod to Tom McLoughlin's episode, "It's a Miserable Life"). The prestige of being a sister in the Omega Kappa Pi sorority house is something the girl aspires to as a social and cultural ideal, but she is demeaned by those she wished to call her peers; "Omega Kappa Pi isn't about change, it's about tradition" says one of the sorority sisters when they are told they have to cut back on certain luxuries such as cooks and cleaners, before tricking Connie into servitude under the guise of initiation. These are the kind of interesting themes that are explored throughout the two seasons of the show and which relate to those in the parallel film series, though not all episodes, if any, are primarily concerned with such intellectual ideas; the mandate was chills and spills, first and foremost. But for those willing to explore all forty-four episodes to mine for such, the series provides many great opportunities to study the fractured society of Springwood.

When it came to putting *Freddy's Nightmares* together, the production benefited from the kind of young and enthusiastic crew who were well aware they were working on something that was on its way to being part of the horror lexicon. One of those was Andre Ellingson, who had also worked on the previous two *A Nightmare on Elm Street* films. He notes the intense labor involved in bringing Freddy to the small screen, but also the career opportunities that awaited the ambitious:

"I was just having a great time, I was young and excited to be working on an Elm Street show. When Mick Strawn got the call to do *Freddy's Nightmares* at some point in 1988 he hired me as the Construction Coordinator, so my job was to work directly under Mick and be in charge of building all the sets, and then one day I walked by his office to ask him a question but he's on the phone, so I stand leaning in his doorway waiting for him to finish his call and then he pauses, he puts the receiver to his chest and says to me, 'Do you know any Special Effects Coordinators?' and then I replied, 'I'll do it!' so Mick picks up the receiver and says into it, 'Okay, I got the Special Effects Coordinator, what else do you need?' I've never looked back in my whole career. In that moment I went from a carpenter to an effects coordinator, with just the flip of the phone. And I didn't even know what smoke machines were, what balsa wood was, what pyrotechnics were, I hadn't a clue! Me and Mick would read the script together and talk about how to do each gag and I just picked it up as I went along and it worked! But *Freddy's Nightmares* was an extremely busy show! There were a lot of effects and blood gags that kept everyone constantly working, not to mention all the sets."[29]

"Oh god, I figure there were about 320 sets over the first season, and 22 or 24 sets per episode," Strawn recalls, "we had one main living room set which we would dress as everything you could possibly imagine and then we had three other sets and every night we would change those three over to something else. I'm drawing as fast as I can and picking out furniture and colors; it was absolutely lunatic. I don't think I slept for about eight months. One night I was driving home and at this stage I hadn't brought the car to get washed for a long time and the windshield is starting to smear with half an inch of dust, so when I got off the freeway and got to my house I walked in and just started crying, because I'm just so tired and exhausted. My wife is like, 'oh my god, what's wrong?' and I'm just blubbering, 'my car, my car!' I was just totally fucking losing it. After I did the first season I said 'no, that's enough!'"[30]

"Mick Strawn never slept," Gottlieb confirms, "I loved Mick and I remember him saying to me 'even though your episode is only the sixth one I'm already burnt out, I don't even know what color to paint the walls!' But we had so much fun designing the episode, deciding on the background colors and the wardrobe that the characters would wear; we really tried to art direct it to where things would have a specific color scheme and have moments where certain colors would punch in. So I really enjoyed working with Mick on that. We had a very short schedule and we shot both chapters in five days, it was unreal. They would schedule half a day for the effects but of course we would be there for the whole day. It was exactly like making an indie film where you have very little money, but I would come in early just to get some extra work done and there was Mick Strawn working with the painters trying to get everything ready and being a complete burnout wearing the same clothes as he did yesterday. I would tell him to go home but he would just say 'if I go home and go to sleep I won't come back in the afternoon, I'll be gone for the day!' I would see people being worn out all the time, there were no days off between episodes; if people had Sundays off they would still come in and work and that would be after wrapping at 4 a.m. on Saturday and they would have to be back on Monday at 7 a.m. It's a difficult way to work and you really want great production values and high quality, but it's challenging to achieve that while working that fast because it means you are constantly making compromises."[31]

Production designer Mick Strawn (courtesy Mick Strawn Collection).

"There was a lot of craziness," Bill Froehlich admits, "it was a very intense schedule but there was an immense creative spirit and freedom that allowed us to get what we really wanted onscreen; it was the kind of lunacy that you could only get away with on *Freddy's Nightmares* and a great example of that was the episode that I directed called 'Dust to Dust.' We had a great cast including Sandahl Bergman, Tony Dow, Amy Lyndon, Martha Smith, and Richard Brestoff. But I was trying to figure out what to do with these characters who in the beginning of the story crash-land in the wilderness and end up becoming cannibals, and the idea just hit me one day. I walked into one of our writers' meetings and I said to Jonathan Glassner and David Braff, 'I got it! I'm going to write one half of the story and I want you guys to write half,' and they asked me, 'well, what are we going to do with it?' and I said, 'they are going to be recovering cannibals and they are going to fall off the wagon and the person they fall off the wagon with is an astronaut who has ingested an organism that he brought back from space.' Jonathan and David just looked at me and said, 'have you been drinking?' Another episode that I directed, 'Do You Know Where Your Kids Are?,' was at the end of the season and one of the things you do as an executive producer is plot out the nature of the season both in the way the stories unfold and the way production unfolds. So I said, 'okay, we're starting behind the eight ball but I want to spend money on the first half of the first three-quarters of the season in order to put more production value into it in order to grab the audience and pull them into the series,' so we did that. But that meant in order to bring the entire season in on budget we had to start spending less money on some of the later episodes. So when we got to episode seventeen we had to start paring the budget back and had to develop those stories so that they could be shot on either fewer locations or fewer sets, something where we could control the money. We shot these episodes in five days, which was insane because normally a television episode would be shot in eight days, and we had only one-third the budget of a regular network series episode. So, by the time we got to 'Do You Know Where Your Kids Are?' I decided I would direct it because I didn't want to hire another director and put him through what I knew we would have to go through, and it meant I had more control over things. This episode had to be shot in four days on an even smaller budget than usual, so I did the same thing on that episode that I did on the whole season: I spent the first three days putting more visual shots in, moving the camera and trying to make it as interesting as possible. But by the fourth day we still had seventeen pages to shoot. Now, production crews like the work they're doing but because many of them have been doing this job for years they can get a little jaded at times and they know exactly what a call sheet looks like. So when everybody showed up that morning they looked down at the call sheet and they realized there were seventeen pages to be shot they thought, 'holy shit! We're going to be here all night!' Everybody had a sour face upon reading that but I pulled them all together before we started shooting and I said, 'look, we all know how to read a call sheet, we all know what this means, but you are going to go home on time tonight!' and I could hear a couple of guys in the background grumbling 'Bullshit!' But I said, 'we have done all of the intricate camerawork on these sets in the first three days, so here's how we're going to get this done: we're going to shoot with three cameras, we'll put them in three positions, lock them down, and all movement is going to be with the actors; they will come in and out of the close-ups and coverage according to how I'm placing the cameras and we will knock these scenes off like that.' I told them we will be done with half of this by noon lunchbreak and we were. And the crew realized, 'oh my god, we are going to go home on time!' It was another example of this show being creative and fun, but also of knowing how to plan and know what you're going to do and how to accomplish it."[32]

"Typically we had very short schedules," William Malone says, "and I remember one time they asked me to direct the interstitials, which are the intros and parts in-between the two stories with Robert Englund, and I was shooting my episode at the same time. This became problematic because the sets were in two different places, so I was literally running between the two. I would set up a shot on one set and then run to the other one, so it would be like, 'Action! Okay, cut!' and then run back and call 'Action!' on a different scene. We were trying to get a lot done on a very tight schedule and not a lot of money."[33]

"Oh my god, the hours!" Ellingson exclaims, "I couldn't even imagine what it must have been like for the older guys in their forties and fifties, it must have killed them. We got through that first season because it was non-union and we would work fourteen, sixteen, maybe eighteen hours a day. There were some days where I would just sleep in my office on the set instead of going home. The exterior locations were

William Malone (center), surrounded by various crew members, directs (courtesy William Malone).

all around North Hollywood, but we didn't go out very much or very far, sometimes when we wanted exterior shots we would just shoot outside in front of the stage. We built all the sets in a warehouse on Webb Street, North Hollywood, and I'll never forget it because I spent two years of my life there around the clock. It was crazy. We would finish a fourteen-hour day filming and the construction crew would be out in the parking lot waiting for us to leave so they could come in and work ten hours building and painting sets, then we would come back in the morning and shoot it for fourteen hours. Then they would come back, tear that down and build another set. And so on. It was just a machine. The crew was young and we cared about it. At its most intense we had some twenty-hour days on that show, and I mean if I work more than ten hours a day now it's like, 'put me to bed!' It was abusive, but it was the best place I could be, it's where I wanted to be, surrounded by these people and working."[34]

"I didn't have any money on that show, all I had was paint! And I used it!" says Strawn, "I painted these really deep, intense colors but the DP would come along and do this horrible blanket lighting. David Calloway was the DP and he came from *Falcon Crest*, he came from the soap opera world and you see it, it feels like you are watching a soap opera at times. To get that kind of lighting he used this thing which was like a ceiling made out of nothing but light bulbs, meaning there was no directionality to the lighting, and we tried everything we could to sabotage it. We would take the old panels that they had, which were these electrical connections, and ran clear tape all the way along the copper edge so that when they'd put them together they wouldn't work. The grips would be going around with flashlights in their mouth trying to find out what's going on, they couldn't see the clear tape, so they'd have to get rid of it. Then all of a sudden the lighting got better. We did the best we could! The more light he'd put on things the darker we'd make the set."[35]

"My whole episode is set and filmed out in the sunlight," recalls Mick Garris, speaking of his episode, *Killer Instinct*, "it was a dash for the finish line, literally and figuratively, and it's filmed out there in sunny Southern California. Not very scary. Though there were some wonderfully dark episodes, particularly Bill Malone's ones, 'Lucky Stiff,' 'Heartbreak Hotel,' 'Easy Come, Easy Go,' those are very stylish and brooding and dark and I love that. The show could have benefited from more of that kind of approach."[36]

"David Calloway was a great DP," William Malone says, "He is a very talented guy who really knew photography, and composition and lighting has always been very important to me. I've always felt that a lot of horror films lack any real sense of atmosphere, so I was very keen to have a lot of atmosphere in my work. I've always thought that there is no reason why low budget movies shouldn't look great because it doesn't take you any more time to light something well on a low-budget movie than it does on a big-budget film. David was very keen on having *Freddy's Nightmares* look really good and so he and I were a good pairing. Everyone on that show treated me really well, I think they were always bemused by me because I was always coming up to them and saying, 'hey, is it okay if I do this kind of shot?' and they would be like, 'I don't know what you're talking about, but yeah, go ahead!' I was forever trying to do these shots that, at the time, I didn't know how they were achieved, so I was trying to do stuff that you would normally use a Technocrane for and here I was trying to do it on a dolly; the camera department was just going 'what is he trying to do here?!' I was really left alone to do what I wanted on *Freddy's Nightmares*, there really wasn't any restrictions other than having to come in on time and on budget, so I saw the show as a chance to go to film school, because I didn't go to film school per se, so here I had a chance to try any wacky idea that I came up with. So I pulled out all the stops, anything I could think of."[37]

"I haven't seen all of the episodes of *Freddy's Nightmares*," Tom McLoughlin admits, "and I'm not sure how much restrictions were placed on later directors coming in, but I certainly had a lot of creative freedom on my episode, particularly with the visuals. I really wanted to make my episode have the feel and tone of a *Nightmare on Elm Street* film. I'm a huge fan of surrealism, in particular the work of Luis Bunuel and other filmmakers who push the edge of reality, and there are many moments in my episode with elements of surrealism. I was able to talk to the director of photography about how to achieve that feel, something visually stimulating which tells the story in a very interesting photographic way, such as the use of diffusion and wide angle lenses, or things like the POV shot during the operation or the perspective of the bullet being shot at John. Anything that can heighten the weird and creepy elements, because that is what people want from this kind of show. The use of diffusion on the lens and heavy fog was stuff I brought in to help it achieve a more dreamlike or surrealist tone because I was all for bringing in any details that enhanced the weirdness of the episode. So I was able to define the look of *Freddy's Nightmares* pretty easily because of the amount of control we could bring to it and because I was working

Actress Janet Keijser with cinematographer David Calloway on set (courtesy William Malone Collection).

with the most amazing talent who helped me a lot. The Beefy Boy burger joint was a whole set that we built so we didn't have to go in to an operational establishment; our production designer Mick Strawn was able to create one so that we could do whatever we wanted in there and get all kinds of great shots. Mick can take a little and make it a lot, he is such an extraordinary talent."[38]

Strawn recalls a recent reunion with his former director, whereupon they reflected on the hard labor involved in working on *Freddy's Nightmares*: "I was up in Seattle working on a film as the First A.D. and the production designer and some people there are telling me 'we have Tom McLoughlin coming on Friday!' I have my production head on and the name doesn't register with me, it never occurred to me who it is. So I get to the set on a Friday morning there's this guy Tom sitting by the set in a chair and when I go over I realize who it is and the first thing he says to me is, 'the last time I saw you was thirty-two years ago when you built a fast food restaurant in a parking lot for me!' And all of a sudden it hits me: it's Tom McLoughlin! I built the Beefy Boy burger joint for him and we did some really weird things on that episode, every gag you could possibly imagine."[39]

Freddy's Nightmares has maintained a less-than-stellar reputation in the three decades since its initial airing and has proved elusive to own on any home video format. Fans have been limited to collecting the original 1980s VHS tapes as digital issues of the series have been curtailed due to poor sales. Warner Home Video canceled their planned DVD release of the series after the tepid commercial response to their initial Volume 1 taster which consisted of the first three episodes of season one. Mercifully, two of those, including "It's a Miserable Life" and "Killer Instinct," have been ported onto further DVD and Blu-ray releases of the film franchise as supplemental features, meaning fans cans savor a tantalizing glimpse of the series while waiting and hoping for a complete set.

"It's so hard to get a good copy of *Freddy's Nightmares*," Strawn says, "all that's out there are multiple-generation bootlegs from back when generations made a difference in the quality. Every time it's duped it loses something. Some of them are so bad you can't even see anything! I'm not even certain I would want to see them though, because I'm pretty sure if I watched an episode I would fall asleep because I would immediately be brought back to being on the set and be reminded of how exhausting it was. *Freddy's Nightmares* was just a blizzard of hard labor."[40]

"It's not necessarily a bad thing that the show is kind of forgotten," Garris says. "Both Tobe Hooper and Tom McLoughlin's episodes are great, but my episode, 'Killer Instinct,' is probably my least-favorite thing that I have directed. It's not something I really put on my resume. I was a new filmmaker at the time and I was learning the ropes. It was so fast, in fact it was a sprint; there was so little time to put thought and construction into building sequences. It was a case of 'let's put the camera here, have this much movement, then move on and see how it works.' I wish I could have had another day so that there could be more style and atmosphere put into it. But, you can't whine about what you didn't have, you make the most with what you have, and all of us did that albeit some more successfully than others, and my hat goes to off to Tobe, Tommy, and Bill, who in my opinion directed the standout episodes on the show."[41]

"*Freddy's Nightmares* had a great premise," McLoughlin states, "and I think it was Bob Shaye's idea, of having this one-hour show be split up into two half-hour segments and you could watch one segment and it would work as a complete story in and of itself, or you could watch both and see the story be expanded upon in the second half. Bob thought that the structure of the episodes meant it would work if channels wanted to broadcast the show like that. Bob trusted us to make the show the way we wanted to make it, and I don't recall him ever visiting on the set of my episode but I did get the notes that would come down from dailies and notes regarding the schedule, which in my case was going all over the place, as were our working hours each day. We were under the imperative to provide what the audience demanded, whether it was more gore or sex or humor, and we certainly provided the horror and comedy. But those genres work best when viewed in a communal setting where people are reacting together to what is unfolding. That's why the *Nightmare on Elm Street* films worked brilliantly on the big screen."[42]

"Freddy was so popular in the wake of the fourth film," Garris says, "and so *Freddy's Nightmares* was just an opportunity to capitalize on the brand in syndicated television. The producers of syndicated television see the money directly, rather than with a network where you make your deal for the season. This was done very cheaply and shot on 16mm and not on 35mm which was the norm at the time. Most one-hour shows were at least seven-day shoots, and on network television shows it would be eight or nine days for a one hour episode, but *Freddy's Nightmares* was being shot in five or six days and made in such a way that you have two different stories that share the same characters in the hopes that they could be split up for syndication later on if they weren't able to make enough episodes. As far as I know they were broadcast in their full-length hour-long versions whenever they aired, but it did not do particularly well because it was resigned to late-night television. In Los Angeles it played on Channel 9 at 11 p.m. and there just isn't a whole lot of money to be made from a syndicated show that goes on at eleven o'clock at night."[43]

The show's gleeful mixture of gory violence and absurdist humor did not sit well with lobby groups and critics, with the negative reaction being so fierce that some television stations gave in to public pressure and canceled the series outright. One such was the Canadian channel CHCH. Despite being aired in a Friday midnight slot, when children are safely unaware of the show while being tucked up in bed, the call to withdraw *Freddy's Nightmares* from the channel's programming was the result of a campaign organized by an Ontario teacher named Ernest Robinson, who took exception to the show's horror elements, saying, "I would hope this would be the first step in a no vote of responsible parents against the people who are exploiting our kids." In his campaign, Robinson gained the support of various teachers' organizations, city councils, and catholic groups, ultimately succeeding in his objective of having *Freddy's Nightmares* pulled from rotation. Upon being bombarded with letters and phone calls of disapproval of the show, CHCH bowed to the pressure, prompting their spokesperson to remark that "it's the responsible thing to do if we're offending people."[44]

"Well, that's what we were trying to do!" Mick Strawn confirms, "We wanted it to be funny and shocking. But the lasting result is that we have a horrible reputation among 'true' horror fans because they think we ruined Freddy. But what we did do was make the character a hundred times more accessible, it allowed Robert to really play with the character's personality and that is the key to Freddy's success with audiences. When I was a kid the horror icon we looked up to was Vincent Price, he represented the horror genre at that time, he gave horror character, and I think Robert Englund did that in the eighties with Freddy Krueger and influenced a whole other group of filmmakers that didn't have anybody at that point who was a standard bearer for the genre and who had such an immense personality. No one has more personality than Vincent Price and Robert Englund."[45]

"What happened on *Freddy's Nightmares* is really kind of sad," Robert Englund says, "We started out with this great budget and this excellent idea that we were going to change American Television; we were going to be on very late, ideally at 11.00 or 11.30 at night, but certainly after prime time—'Welcome to Primetime, Bitch!' And we were going to be syndicated and this meant we could get away with more, or so this is what I was told: we were going to be on late and we would be dark and we could do whatever we wanted. We could have more violence, people could smoke cigarettes, they could drink, and we could be a little sexier and infer stuff that you wouldn't be able to do in an earlier time slot. Tobe Hooper's pilot is wonderful and very dark and it gives everybody the back story and lets them in on where the show is going to go. We were going to have some fun; that was the plan, not campy fun but more carnivalesque, and we would have that countered with some dark, macabre imagery. But we were really only able to get away with that on the first couple of episodes, which is where we were able to do all of that without the fear of the controversy that was to come."[46]

"*Freddy's Nightmares* really took a lot of glee in breaking the rules and taboos that were set by network and syndication television and commercial television." Garris confirms. "Our mandate was all about being scary and breaking taboos and being that we didn't have a network, because with syndication you go directly to individual stations, that was a huge relief because you don't have Standards and Practices nor do you have specific advertisers coming in with their input. The issue of too much violence never came up on my episode or on Tobe's because there was no network overseeing everything, but when my episode was first shown on the local station they edited it and they're not allowed do that, it's a DGA [Director's Guild of America] thing; so when they re-ran it they had to put it on in its full uncut version. You constantly have to raise your stakes if you're a horror show that has already been on for a year and you are going on for another year because if you stay the same then people are going to tune out, they're going to say 'been there, done that.' It's the same with the horror genre in general, and so many filmmakers think they have to amplify the gore rather than amplify the storytelling."[47]

"We never got an edict down saying you have to cut this or that," Malone recalls, "and I didn't know what you couldn't do, so I pulled out all the stops. The only time we were censored was when we censored ourselves, because we knew how far you can go on regular television."[48]

When the second season ran its course, *Freddy's Nightmares* was no more. The show was the victim of bad scheduling, multiple controversies, and a somewhat apathetic if not downright negative response by the end of its run. In retrospect, it might seem baffling that the television edition of such a hugely successful parallel film series could falter as much as it did, but given that the next big screen entry, *A Nightmare on Elm Street 5: The Dream Child*, was released the same year *Freddy's Nightmares* shuttered and marked the beginning of the film franchise's commercial decline, perhaps it was a sign that Freddy had overstayed his welcome and was heralding cultural fatigue with the property.

"It's a shame," Robert Englund says, "what transpired and what happened was that they kept taking our budget down and the reason for that was they didn't keep the promise of having us on late at night. They had us on in the Bible Belt and in Texas and other conservative territories at 4.30 in the afternoon or 6.00 in the evening, opposite the news, and so we couldn't have a dark show, we couldn't have a sequence in a church or have something sexy or violent at that time of broadcast on syndicated television. That meant we were losing markets and so they lowered the budget and then they lowered the budget again. I believe we originally had ten days to shoot an episode and then it went to seven days for a while, but then pretty quickly it went to five days in the end, and it was just impossible; nobody was sleeping, the scripts weren't as good because they couldn't be as dark and nasty. I kept thinking, 'just get us on late at night!' The *Friday the 13th* TV series was on late at night everywhere and it was opposite the big talk shows, so the hip young people who didn't want to watch the old movie stars on the talk shows—and talk shows back then were pretty unhip—could switch the channel and watch *Friday the 13th*. That's the audience that we were promised, but they got crazy with the syndication and torpedoed the whole project."[49]

Fangoria editor Tony Timpone recalls being distinctly unimpressed with the television version of *A Nightmare on Elm Street*, the franchise which had helped build his magazine's reputation and increase its circulation. "I was never a fan of *Freddy's Nightmares*. I think it was flawed from the get-go. They filmed it on a real shoestring, the production values are really poor and then they made the mistake of doing an hour show with two interconnected stories instead of keeping it a half-hour show with a single story, the whole thing was very sloppy and hard to follow. It was nice to see Robert on a weekly basis but the production values and the writing really weren't up to snuff, they just banged it out; it was at the point where Freddy was really getting overexposed and the last thing he needed was a TV show. The *Friday the 13th: The Series* was a far more successful transition to the small screen than *Freddy's Nightmares*, it was a pretty well-written show and it brought in some great directors too, including David Cronenberg, George Mihalka, and a lot of Canadian horror veterans. It was a well-constructed show and the production values really weren't that bad, unlike *Freddy's Nightmares* where they were pretty atrocious."[50]

Tom McLoughlin, who lent his talents to both *Freddy's Nightmares* and *Friday the 13th: The Series* was well aware of the perils of changing or diluting the big screen formula for the small screen: "I was in early talks with executive producer Frank Mancuso before *Friday the 13th: The Series* was even written and his feelings were that he wanted to do a show with which they could cash-in on the title 'Friday the 13th' but have it be in reference to the superstition around the date and not be associated with Jason. I told him that he was running a risk by calling it *Friday the 13th* because the expectation will be that it is a show with Jason and when people find out he's not in it there could be a backlash. At least *Freddy's Nightmares* had the central character present, even if he was just introducing the episodes. The problem with the whole thing was that the success of the movies taught producers and studios that audiences were buying into all of these elements such as the more extreme gore and the more humorous side of Freddy, so it got to the point where they thought they could milk that, so they make Freddy this facetious entity, his one-liners became like James Bond quips and it just got bigger and bigger until it lessened his ability to scare us. If you have Freddy enjoying it too much and talking to us directly, it undermines the horror factor of it all."[51]

Indeed, if *Freddy's Nightmares* can claim legitimacy to the Elm Street universe, it is largely due to Freddy Krueger's appearance in every single episode, albeit limited to the role of host, with the exception of some episodes in which he is a diegetic character within the narrative. Amplifying his playfulness, Robert Englund brought a great sense of irony to his self-referential master of ceremonies; as the engineer of the nightmares to unfold, the actor draws upon his witty and wicked sense of humor as he directly addresses his audience in the extremely entertaining wraparound segments.

"They shot Robert Englund's section on a separate stage," McLoughlin recalls, "and I would go over there and talk to him about the lines and what I wanted from the wraparounds. They were just one or two shots, such as the one of him coming up out of the boiling grease or speaking to the camera saying a snappy line or issuing one of his wise-ass retorts; they were just these tiny little parts to make it feel like his presence could be felt throughout the show."[52]

"I actually did three of the wraparound segments with Freddy," Garris says, "I did them for my episode and for two other episodes to follow. Robert and I are friends and we had some conversations about it, but he didn't need any direction, he knew best how to make Freddy work, certainly much better than I did. So the direction was more technical, working with the special effects and figuring out the movements and how best to portray Freddy within the frame. The show was really a celebration of Freddy, he was the star of that show. Freddy was basically the Crypt Keeper, so there was no surprise that Gil and Alan became producers on *Tales from the Crypt* later on, it was the same sort of format … but with more money! That show was run by Richard Donner, Walter Hill, Bob Zemeckis, and Joel Silver."[53]

"It was a lot of fun shooting the special effects shots for the interstitial sequences with Freddy," Gottlieb states, "because Robert Englund is a genius. They have done everything you could possibly do to a character over the course of the Elm Street film series, so Robert has been though every kind of effects gag and he's game for anything. I would have a meeting with him to go over the special effects scenes in front of the green screen and I would say, 'okay, we're going to have you chop your own arm off,' and he would say, 'oh, this is how we did it in *A Nightmare on Elm Street 2!*' or whatever one it was. And then one time I had him stick one of his long razor fingers into his own eye, which sounds gruesome but when you are shooting these pieces it is so hilarious and so silly because Robert knows exactly what he's doing and has such a good time doing it; everything he did to improve an effect gag made it better."[54]

"I believe they called that set where Freddy did his introductions the 'Hall of Dreams,'" Andre Ellingson recalls, "I ended up getting my SAG card because of the prop skeleton that is in the background on that set. How I became a member of the actors' union is because one day they wanted to do a TV promo for the show and they wanted to use the skeleton to deliver a line. That meant the jaw needed to move, so I put some monofilament on it and some smoke behind it and I moved its mouth to mime the words 'jump my bones, baby!' and I said the words out loud as I was doing it so I could get the rhythm of the jaw movement right. Well, I spoke the words like Freddy would say it and unbeknownst to me the sound guy was recording it, so one night I'm at home watching TV when the commercial comes on and I hear my voice speaking for the skeleton! They used me for the commercial and so I ended up getting my SAG card because I went into the producer's office the next morning and said, 'Hey, I just saw the commercial and noticed they used my voice.' So they had what's called a Taft Hartley, which means if you do more than one thing on camera you are eligible for the union, so I went and performed a stunt in a shot and that then meant I was able to make it into the union. If the sound guy had not been rolling they would have gotten Robert to record it, but they used me instead. Maybe the lab they thought it was Robert's voice! And from there I ended up acting in one of

Andre Ellingson playing a priest in a scene with Freddy Kruger (courtesy Andre Ellingson Collection).

the episodes, 'Do Dreams Bleed,' where I played the priest; I don't know what they were thinking because I was only twenty-seven years old, a little young to be playing a priest, though I was kind of obscured so it worked. I'm not an actor, but it is fun to spew out a couple of lines and get paid for it."[55]

"It wasn't a critic's show," Lisa Gottlieb says, "but I never had any worries about it being a critical success. It was for fans of Freddy Krueger and for the kids who stay up late at the weekends watching horror movies. I had mixed feelings about the script but the writers were very open to listening to my comments and they did make a few changes; I certainly took some big risks with casting but they went for it, so all-in-all I had a very good experience on *Freddy's Nightmares*. I met some producers and writers on that show whom I stayed friends with, such as Gil Adler. I would come and pitch him story ideas when he was running a horror company after *Freddy's Nightmares*. He never looked at me as a 'horror' person but he liked how I handled the comedy in my episode. Gil was great to work with and I remember I tried convincing him to use this local LA band who I happened to know because one of them was dating one of my friends, and I wanted them to do the music for my episode. They were called The Fibonaccis and they were this art rock band, kind of like LA's version of Talking Heads, who used to perform their own versions of horror movie music. I showed them my cut of the episode and they composed this really fun score but Gil had been looking for a permanent person to do the music for the show, an in-house composer who could commit to every week and every episode. Gil did allow me to ask The Fibonaccis to do it but he was straight with us, he made the deal with the band though he told me he was trying to cook up a contract with these other guys to be a more permanent presence. That's Gil, he's an honest person and that's probably why I stayed friends with him. And sure enough when it came to mixing he said, 'you should skip the mix,' and I asked why and he said, 'well, you will be upset when you hear the score because it's not your friend John's score.' And I said, 'Oh, is it the guy with the synthesizer in his basement? I told you I'm not crazy about synthesizers unless they really make it sound like it's not a synthesizer.' So Gil said, 'listen, let's have a party the night it airs, invite all your friends and we'll have a good time, you'll like it and we'll celebrate. Really! We love the episode!' So we had the party, which Gil didn't have to do for us but it was fun, though I certainly wish my original score by The Fibonaccis was left in it. However, I watched it again a few years later when I was teaching at USC when one of my colleagues screened it in one of his classes and I thought, 'you know, the score works!' I just wasn't able to hear it at the time we made the episode. *Freddy's Nightmares* was very fast work and long days but I am very proud of it and I am particularly proud of the look that we got and the way we set up the subtext of the beauty myth. It upped my game working with all of those special effects. It was just fun, a good experience all around and I felt that I was welcome there for the most part; it's always touchy in that world, it's always a little nutty, but I had a great time making it."[56]

"Because of *Freddy's Nightmares* I went on to work on some other great shows like *Tales from the Crypt*," Nicholas Pike enthuses, "Gil Adler was the man who produced both of those shows and because of him I got to have some enjoyable experiences scoring them. You can do anything when you are working in the horror genre because there always has a sense of tension and weirdness attached which feeds your creativity. On a romantic comedy there's not a whole lot you can do sonically, you can't really bring unusual sounds or be very experimental, but you can when you are working in horror. When I was growing up in England I was a choirboy in Canterbury and there were evenings where we would rehearse and when we would leave the choir practice in the cathedral we would have to walk a couple hundred yards back to the choir school through these catacombs that have been there since the 900s; people are buried there and the wind would be howling and the rain would be pouring down, so we would run through there at a hundred miles per hour to get through as fast as possible, it was the creepiest place you possibly imagine. So that fueled my imagination and was perhaps an influence when composing darker material. Looking back on it, I'm still very happy with the music, I think the instrumentation stands up today; perhaps the underscoring a little less so, it sounds really cheesy but it is of its time. Though I do think that the main title theme is really cool."[57]

"Some of the episodes were pretty awful," William Malone admits, "they really were, but it was great fun to work on them and it was an opportunity to try out things, so I have nothing bad to say about them. I got to work with a lot of really talented people in *Freddy's Nightmares*, people such as Wings Hauser who is a great actor, I was very pleased to get him on the show. On my episode 'Lucky Stiff' I worked with Mary Crosby and she was just a joy, a wonderful person to work with. I also had David Lander in there and we had some very funny conversations because we thought of that episode as a comedy. When I look back on it now I just chuckle because I see certain things which were funny when we were shooting them and one of those was filming the coffin scenes with David; he was claustrophobic, so when we put him in the coffin he had difficulty with that. There is a scene where he is in the coffin and his mouth lights up as he is speaking, and this being a cheapo production I literally had to get a little tiny bulb and wire the side of his mouth and put the bulb inside his mouth, but he was a good sport about it. That was a great thing about *Freddy's Nightmares*, it was fun and it was a great learning experience. We could really get away with a lot as long as we brought it in on time and on schedule. It was a great place to try out ideas and many of the things I would do later in my career I was able to do on *Freddy's Nightmares* first. By season two it was just a cash cow, they didn't care what we did as long as they were making money."[58]

"I think that every episode of *Freddy's Nightmares* has something in it that you remember," Tom McLoughlin says, "and it's because the directors were really pushing the envelope of what they could do on television. It was such a surreal show that we didn't have to do too much to make it much more creepier; we didn't have to come up with anything too elaborate, we could work with smaller, more inventive kinds of effects and give it this subtle but strange tone. It ended up being funny and twisted, and it really made us laugh on the set as we were doing it. We were all young and we loved that we were out all night making these crazy, bizarre and hilarious things."[59]

"I laughingly look back at this and think it was a great adventure," Bill Froehlich admits, "I got to work with amazing people and a terrific crew who just loved what they were doing. It was the only time in my career where I had complete creative control, aside from my feature film, *Return to Horror High*, so I remember it with deep fondness. I also remember the exhaustion because I didn't sleep much for that year, because you are in the midst of something that is demanding of all your time you are swept up in the rushing storm of it; we had great fun but we also felt constantly rushed and always under the gun. Something that I have taken with me from the whole experience is realizing that if you can face the challenges that arose with *Freddy's Nightmares* then you can face anything. And the other thing I took from it is to make sure you have got a lot of great people working with you at all times. In the United States it ran as a first-run syndication show, which meant that it aired at different times all over the country and so it wasn't like appointment television where everybody saw it at the same time on the same night each week. But we were very surprised and pleased to discover that it beat all the competition in the late-night timeslots, which felt pretty good. It is fascinating to me that it continues to have a lasting resonance and that it has continued to mean something to people from different generations. Just recently some teenagers told me that they discovered it and loved it, and that is really cool to hear thirty-one years later. So, I'm delighted and surprised that *Freddy's Nightmares* has had a lasting impact on viewers and on the people that worked on it."[60]

4

The Birth, the Death, and the Resurrection

"It's a boy!" —Freddy Krueger

Following directly on from the storyline of *A Nightmare on Elm Street 4: The Dream Master*, Alice Johnson is now dating the man of her dreams, Dan Jordan, but she is soon revisited by the man of her nightmares, Freddy Krueger. Heralding the horror to come, Alice begins to suffer from horrific flashbacks to the inception and conception of her terrorizer and it is here she witnesses the fate of Freddy's mother, Amanda Krueger (Beatrice Boepple), a nun with the religious order who runs an insane asylum. One night, Amanda is locked inside the overcrowded hall with the violent inmates by careless orderlies and is brutally defiled; as a result, she falls pregnant. With increasing regularity, Alice is put in Amanda's shoes and even experiences the shocking birth of the son of a hundred maniacs. "Sister, this is one of God's creatures," the midwife says to Amanda, "take solace in that." But such consolation won't keep Amanda from rightfully disowning her demon spawn; she later confronts her evil offspring in a holy showdown and declares "Your birth was a curse on the whole of humanity. I will not let it happen again!" But Freddy will experience a re-birth via Alice's son, Jacob, as entering the mind of the unborn child allows him to regain his power by manipulating the fears of Alice's friends, including pretty girl Greta Gibson (Erika Anderson), comic book enthusiast Mark Gray (Joe Seely), and budding athlete, Yvonne Miller (Kelly Jo Minter).

Alice and her pals have just graduated from Springwood High, and it is at their ceremony that we meet their parents and get an insight into the kind of pressure put on these kids to achieve the social standards of the Springwood upwardly mobile. In doing so we meet a roll call of dysfunction and domination, the true sources of the anxiety that plagues the teens. The most egregious of these ghastly Elm Street elders is Greta's narcissistic, hoity-toity mother, Racine (Pat Sturges), whose obsession with cosmetic perfection is absurd to the point that she chides her aspiring model daughter for licking a lollipop: "Greta, that's not what a cover girl puts in her body!" The reality of Greta's situation is that she is suffering from an eating disorder because of her mother's insistence on her becoming a glamour magazine cover star. Greta cannot even partake in poolside graduation festivities with her friends because Racine has a photographer coming over for dinner and insists that she not mess up her hair.

Further unfortunate parental units are present, including Dan's father (Burr DeBenning), who sleazily remarks "Alice, you look sweet today!" Mr. Jordan is incessantly pushy about securing his son's future on the gridiron, as we see when he tries to influence and convince Coach Ostrow of Dan's athletic prowess. Alice's father, Dennis, stays out of sight, not wanting to embarrass his daughter as the disgraced former drunk among the well-preened and well-heeled parents of his daughter's peers. Though sober, Dennis remains a tragic symbol of the dysfunctional broken family, that which is all too familiar in Springwood since the Freddy Krueger vigilante killing; his appearance is a raw reminder of the shameful legacy of lies and the emotional toll it has taken on the town's families, and he only reluctantly joins his daughter for a group photograph upon gentle persuasion.

When it comes time for these teens to meet their demise, Freddy will evoke all of the negative traits of their parents to taunt them in their final moments. Dan is tormented by the words of his mother and father when their voices are respectively channeled through Freddy just before the young man is dispatched in a most gruesome automotive manner. Freddy mimics Mrs. Jordan when he adopts her voice of disapproval and admonishes him via a radio call-in show with "I'm calling about my wayward ex-son, Daniel, who's been acting like an ungrateful, unmanageable dickweed ever since he was seduced by that bimbo slut whore Alice." And in quoting Mr. Jordan, Freddy quips: "this boy has a need for speed," a reference to the father's insistence on a football scholarship. So while Freddy drives Dan to his death on a hellish high-speed motorcycle, the line that Mr. Jordan used to sell his son's abilities to the football coach takes on a deadly irony.

While in mourning upon Dan's passing, Greta is made to sit through one of her mother's bourgeois dinner parties where much older men comment lecherously upon her looks while her mother demands that she fawn over the commentators with gratitude. "He was just a friend of Greta's, not someone special" Racine callously informs her guests as Greta grieves. From here Greta is tortured and taunted with an overabundance of food, force-fed by Freddy as her mother and the guests laugh along at her peril until she is ironically stuffed to death.

"If Freddy wants to get even with you he finds out your tragic flaw," Robert Englund says, "When he finds out that Greta is bulimic he helps her binge and purge, he stuffs her to death ... it becomes wonderfully Kafkaesque. There's an awful lot of that kind of formula to these films where the audience are anticipating and are looking forward to how Freddy is going to deal with one of his victims and we've done that a lot with humor and if there's been any progression it's that they have allowed me to explore the sort of relish and humor that this demon has."[1]

Aspiring comic book artist Mark is doomed to the gloomy prospect of a life spent running his father's warehouse business and once again Freddy echoes the parents' disapproval of their children's interests in his method of murder, in this case he uses Mark's skill and interest in pop art against him. And so in a battle between Mark and the frankly embarrassing creation of "Super Freddy," the teen succumbs to his nightmare when he is turned into the very thing he loves: a 2D comic book paper drawing, whereupon Freddy literally cuts him to shreds after evoking Mark's father, quipping: "I told ya, comic books was bad for ya!" And to bludgeon the point

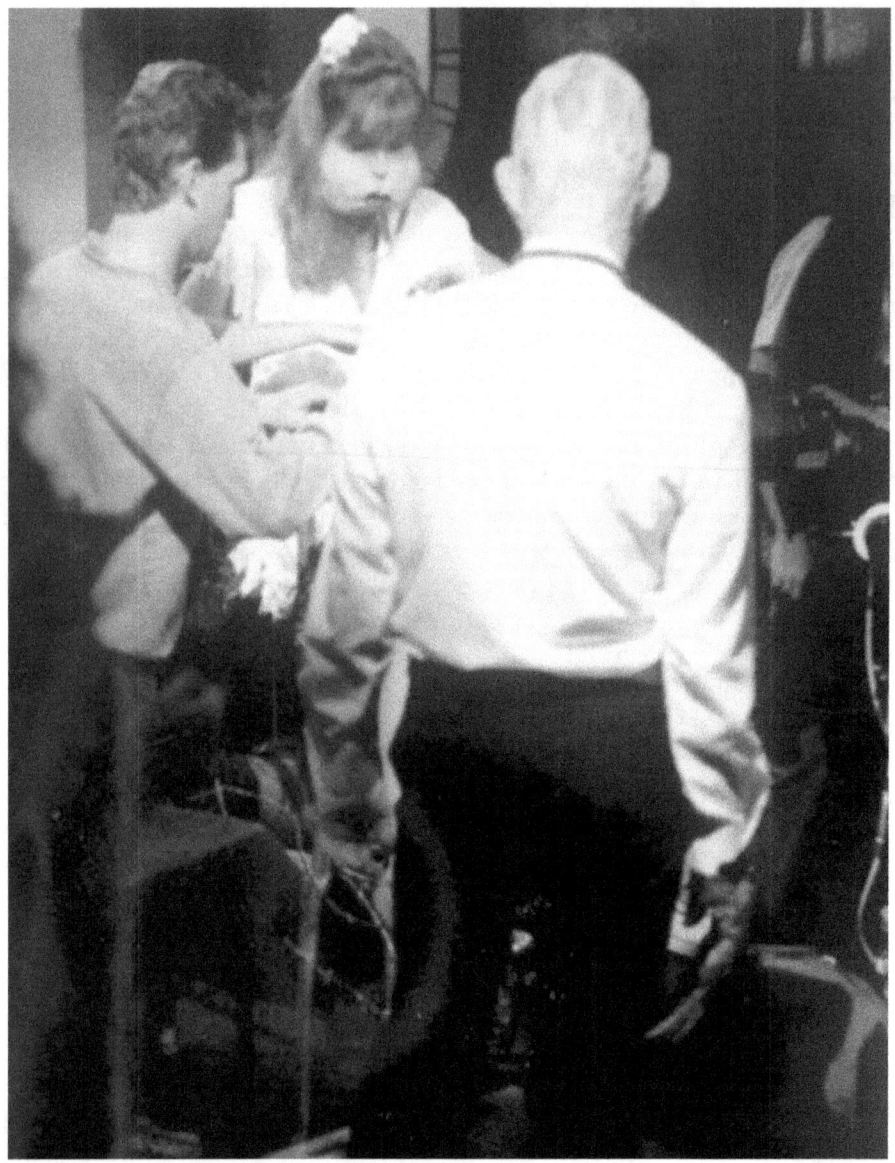

Special effects coordinator Andre Ellingson sets up a scene with actors Erika Anderson and Robert Englund (courtesy Andre Ellingson Collection).

of parental oppression home, it is made to look like the storage units of his father's warehouse have collapsed on top of him. On the nose, yes, but a witty thematic gag regardless. Once again, the aspirations of the children and their refusal of their parents' roadmap for their lives is the catalyst for their demise.

Before his death, Mark seems to sum up the theme of the entire series when he references the Greek myth of Melicertes, whom he says, "kills his kids because he didn't like the way they were running the kingdom." Whether broaching Greek mythology is a worthy highbrow endeavor or perhaps too obscure a reference for this film depends on how deeply one reads into such themes while enjoying the thrills and

4. The Birth, the Death, and the Resurrection   155

Mark (Joe Seely) enters a nightmare through the panels of his comic book.

spills on screen, but for those of us to whom the *Nightmare on Elm Street* series has always been about the ignorance of parents who push their rebellious children into danger due to their own fractured worldview, then Mark's mentioning of Melicertes is most indicative that the filmmakers behind this sequel are at least honoring the more intellectual ideas that emerged in Wes Craven's original *A Nightmare on Elm Street*. While the parents depicted in Craven's first film were at least well-meaning if misguided in their attempts to shield their children from the truth, as the series proceeds with each successive entry the parents become far more malevolent in their manipulation of their offspring, snuffing out their dreams well before Freddy begins snuffing out their lives.

As New Line Cinema scrambled to get a fifth film in motion to capitalize on the success of *A Nightmare on Elm Street 4: The Dream Master*, the search began for story concepts that would take the series back to its darker origins. New Line development executive Michael De Luca was a fan of the burgeoning literary horror movement of the 1980s known as Splatterpunk, and he duly put out the call to some of the major names associated with it, bringing in writers such as John Skipp, Craig Spector, David J. Schow and other authors to pitch ideas for the sequel. In the end, the final film would utilize some elements from a joint script submitted by Skipp and Spector along with those of screenwriter Leslie Bohem. The latter had unsuccessfully pitched the notion of introducing Freddy's spawn in the third film of the franchise, only to be belatedly called back to bring those ideas to fruition now that the fifth film had an ideal character in Alice to be fertile carrier of the demon seed. Next on the agenda was to find a director, and none seemed more suitable than British-Australian filmmaker and comic book enthusiast, Stephen Hopkins, whose sole prior directing credit was the 1987 slasher film, *Dangerous Game*. Like Renny Harlin before him, Hopkins knew his way around a low-budget independent production and was primed to step into the intense schedule of an *Elm Street* film. The director's dark comic book sensibilities married well with New Line Cinema's vision for the film to tie in with the Splatterpunk aesthetic.

"It was the same as with *A Nightmare on Elm Street 4*, when I saw Steve Hopkins' film I thought, 'god, there's a real vision here,'" Rachel Talalay says, "and he came in with a real strong Art Director's point of view to sell himself for the film. He came in with these incredible gothic drawings of where the dream world should go. He wanted to direct the film and they were incredibly impressive. I think he probably got the shortest shrift in terms of the series because there was the least amount of time and probably the worst concept to go with Freddy's baby."[2]

Indeed, introducing Alice's baby and the attendant questions of shame and stigma surrounding teen pregnancy, single parenthood and abortion are loaded issues too consequential for the blithely fantastical and darkly humorous material at hand. In the aftermath of Dan's death, Alice finds out she is pregnant, and she begins to have ominous visions of the ghostly Elm Street girls in white skipping rope and singing the "*One, two, Freddy's coming for you*" lullaby that usually heralds the imminent presence of the tune's titular demon. Soon, Alice realizes that Freddy is gaining power through her unborn child, and while discussing such deadly implications of her pregnancy with Mark, he asks her if she would consider aborting the child, but Alice replies, "No, I can't do that, I saw him inside of me growing. He's part of me and Dan, I want to keep him." "Okay, then we'll find another way," says Mark just as flippantly as he asked if she would terminate the fetus. Somewhat more thematic gravitas is given to the child elsewhere, when a vision of the youngster, Jacob, appears roaming in Alice's nightmares, where she finds the dream child forlorn in the abandoned ruins of the old Thompson house. Unaware she is speaking to her future son, Alice queries the boy as to the whereabouts of his mother, to which he replies that it is she. "Who said I don't like you?" she asks her son. "My friend with the funny hand," replies Jacob dejectedly.

Dream child Jacob (Whit Hertford) and mother Alice (Lisa Wilcox) share a moment.

Whit Hertford's portrayal of young Jacob brings rare pathos to the film and offers the only genuine emotional cue for the pro-choice versus pro-life motif which recurs throughout. Notions of unwanted pregnancy, unfit parents, and the difficult decisions faced by the pregnant women of the film is a major theme of the narrative, from Amanda Krueger's ill-conceived child through rape, to the rejection of Alice as a suitable parent by the Jordans. "Frankly, we wondered what you intend to do with your baby," says Dan's mother before his father condescendingly questions whether a grieving single woman becoming a mother is too burdensome; they then offer to adopt the child after revealing that the doctor has informed them that Alice is having psychological issues. "You're not taking my baby!" states Alice emphatically. "Well the courts might not agree with you," says Mrs. Jordan sinisterly.

Perhaps the more obvious and immediately impressive component of *A Nightmare on Elm Street 5: The Dream Child* is the expansive and expressionistic visual world that Hopkins and cinematographer Peter Levy bring to life so well. The increased budget allowed for some of the most spectacular and stylish visual elements of the franchise to date, including the dizzying Esher-esque set built for the climax, immersive matte paintings, and a sumptuous gothic production design. Special Effects Coordinator Andre Ellingson recalls the particularly arduous effort involved in rendering such a technically accomplished film: "I don't know how, but I got through *A Nightmare on Elm Street 5* alive, just barely. It was my first feature film as a Special Effects Coordinator and I had only been in town two-and-a-half years and I had just come off the second season of *Freddy's Nightmares* which was just as long and just as abusive as the first season. I remember it being these really long days and it was back when it was non-union, so they weren't paying any overtime and the producers were making a fortune. We were working for nothing but I was still young enough and hungry enough to think it was the best job in the world. I was working with the most famous horror villain on earth, so to me it was all great. At the time it was one of the biggest non-union movies and biggest special effects productions in town, and it was just before digital effects really started to take over, so everything was handmade, done in-camera, and it was very creative. It was old school horror genre filmmaking and everybody who worked on it was artistic and was determined to show what they could do.

All you have to do is look at the sets to see the many challenges that we faced. I mean you had sets which were upside down, inside out, back to front, it was supposed to be a nightmare on screen but it was also a nightmare to build! Mick and his sister C.J. created all of that stuff and we built it, so every day you went to work you were dealing with this hugely creative team of people and we were all working together with the goal of making these great movies. That kind of passion got you through the punishing, endless hours. And especially so when you are part of a special effects crew working with live action, it is the most creative and artistic you can get. But Part 5 was a particularly huge movie, it almost killed me but we got through it and I'm proud of that. But there I was, in my mid-twenties, I had no business being the head of that department at all. I had about fifteen guys on that and these were experienced Hollywood effects professionals and they're wondering how I got the job; *I knew* how I got the job: because of Mick Strawn! Mick had a lot of power

Freddy Krueger takes a shine to special effects coordinator and actor Andre Ellingson (courtesy Andre Ellingson Collection).

at New Line Cinema, they loved him and C.J. because they were brilliant production designers and everything they did, especially their work in horror, is superb, all you have to do is look at *The Hidden* or *Critters*, or any of those movies."³

"New Line took chances," Mick Strawn affirms, "and they had a tendency to hire people who were very talented and stood out but who hadn't gotten a chance yet, and now the vast majority of those people who worked for them have gone on to become the new guard. Some of those people who started in New Line at the bottom are now major players in the industry, some of the top executives at the studios in Hollywood. Evidently, Bob Shaye knew how to nurture talent; he would be behind you 100%, and here's the thing: Bob would be behind you 100% even if he didn't understand a thing you were doing, and that takes big, iron balls! He really tapped into that group of artists that were going to replace the Old Hollywood guard. At that time you still had your big studio union films, the kind of films which were being made by what was left of the old studio system, but then you had the ultra-ultra-low budget work, most of which was horror and which was represented by Roger Corman with New World Pictures and Charles Band with Full Moon Productions. That was just a case of putting out schlock films that were proud to be schlock. But Bob Shaye had more of an eclectic taste and some of the films he produced at New Line were really high quality, it represented the middle ground between the indie underground and the major studios. Cannon Films was another company that rides into that same middle field at right about the same time. Cannon were making a bundle of cash from Chuck Norris and Charles Bronson films, but the Chuck Norris and the Charles Bronson films were paying for the John Cassevetes films and the Jean-Luc Godard films. And that's what happened at New Line; *A Nightmare on Elm Street 5* was being made so they could fund other films. Horror movies were funding all the other genres, because they made the money to allow studios to thrive."[4]

While working tirelessly behind the camera, Ellingson immersed himself in any department that would take him, allowing him to gain valuable experience for his prolific work in Hollywood to come. Such industrious ethic paid off, as after having worked his way from Construction to Special Effects in a single leap from *A Nightmare on Elm Street 3: Dream Warriors* to *Freddy's Nightmares*, Ellingson then managed to gain some screen time in *A Nightmare on Elm Street 5: The Dream Child*, performing as a Second Unit stunt double as well as playing a temporally minor though critical onscreen role which places him as the man who may be ultimately responsible for the creation of Freddy Krueger.

"I play an important person to the whole backstory of Freddy, he is the orderly in the insane asylum who locks Amanda Krueger in with the inmates. My character is up on a balcony with another orderly and this is the crucial moment in terms of how Freddy as a character is created, this is the event that kicked off the entire mythology of his character. It is the rape of Amanda Krueger, and the reason that happens is because my character decides to callously lock her in there. While they're doing a headcount my orderly sees Amanda down there amongst the hundred maniacs and when my colleague gets to a hundred I hit him with a baton and I say, 'that's enough, let's get out of here!' even though I know she is stuck down there amongst these raving lunatics in this pit of hell. My character just doesn't give a fuck and as I leave I look at her in the eye and then turn away, leaving her for dead basically. So my character, 'Orderly Number One,' is the catalyst for the creation of Freddy Krueger. I don't even remember if it was written like that or if the director said, 'look at her when you leave' nor do I recall any action in the script which said that. It may have said that I just shove the other orderly to move on and get out of there, but at no point did it say to exchange looks with her and willingly leave her there. My character doesn't have much screen time but that moment makes him a very evil one. That's where it all began. None of it would ever have happened if I had said, 'Amanda Krueger is down there!' It's a great trivia question: 'who is the catalyst for creating Freddy Krueger?' and the answer is: 'Orderly Number One!'

But getting that role was typical of the way I would just get myself everywhere on these shows, because they were non-union and I would be able to place myself in every department, whether it be casting, construction, effects, or stunts. I was the stunt double for Danny Hassel when he is on the motorcycle and he starts turning into Freddy. That's me filling in on the second unit footage where we had the motorcycle on a little gimbal; we had all the smoke and sparks with fans against a Blue Screen so it looks like he was going down the street. We had four or five units going at the same time and for me it was great because I would get my hands on everything, I just thought 'this job is incredible!'"⁵

With *A Nightmare on Elm Street 4: The Dream Master*, Freddy Krueger most certainly scaled new heights of pop-cultural approbation as a beloved Hollywood horror hero, while the franchise reached its commercial potential with its biggest box office takings to date. But just as though it seemed that the *Elm Street* property couldn't get any bigger, indeed it couldn't. *A Nightmare on Elm Street 5: The Dream Child* was released in August 1989, just as *Freddy's Nightmares* was halfway through its final season and drawing to a close amidst dwindling budgets and controversy. The film was produced on a budget of $8 million, the largest financing afforded any series entry to date, and even though the final box office tally of $22 million brought a return on investment, it was only half of the earnings of its predecessor, a nightmare too real for New Line Cinema and all concerned.

Andre Ellingson playing the orderly who leaves Amanda Krueger behind to be raped by a hundred maniacs (courtesy Andre Ellingson Collection).

"The film was a gigantic disappointment," director Hopkins told *Fangoria* back in 1990. "It was a rushed schedule without a reasonable budget and after I finished it, New Line and the MPAA came in and cut the guts out of it completely. What started out as an OK film with a few good bits turned into a total embarrassment."⁶ Years later the director ruminated that "they can never be as scary as they used to be.

4. The Birth, the Death, and the Resurrection   161

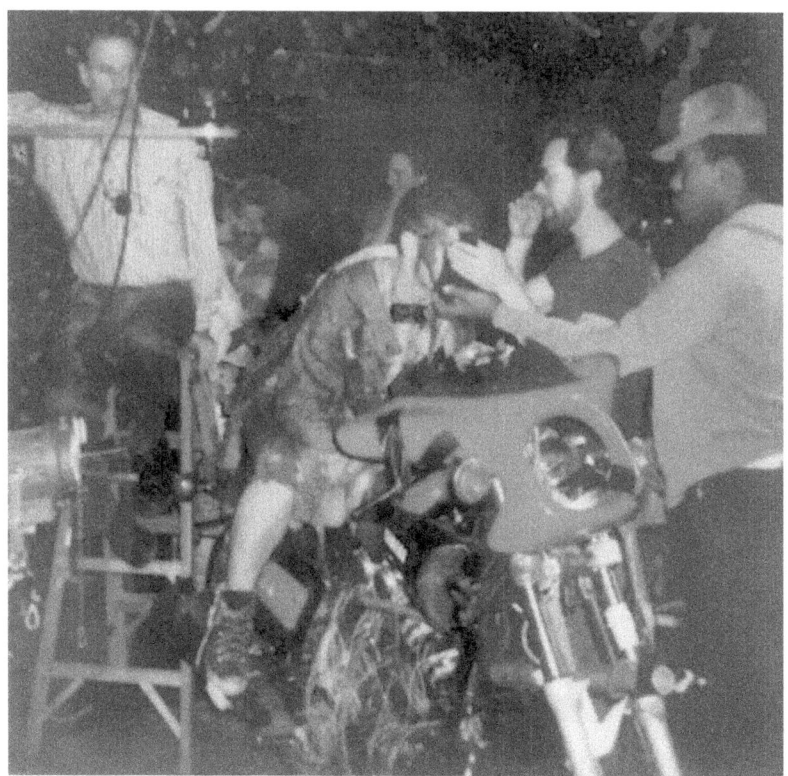

Top and bottom: Andre Ellingson is feeling the "need for speed" as he doubles for Danny Hassel (courtesy Andre Ellingson Collection).

Even by the time I did him, Freddy was so exposed. You can never do a true shocking horror, like a revelation, because he had been so revealed that there was not much left to reveal."[7]

A Nightmare on Elm Street 5: The Dream Child does deliver some decent backstory expansion, but the film suffers from its major aesthetic shift to the joyless, heavy-handedly somber tone. The film's predecessor was marked by thrilling aesthetics, but gone is the rapid editing, the pastel colors, the green-red lighting schemes, the hip new wave soundtrack, and general fun fantasy spirit that permeated the fourth film. Rather Hopkins bathes the film in black and blue hues to create a dark, oppressive atmosphere, heavily stylized to impart its gothic sensibilities. And while this is the least entertaining film of the formal franchise, there are some interesting elements inherent to make it an intellectually stimulating entry. It dares to tackle mature issues such as abortion, bulimia, career, grief, and single parenthood, even if some of it is handled in a rather maladroit manner, but it does attempt to honor the themes that have been a part of the Springwood social subtext ever since Wes Craven considered the dark side of the Middle American milieu in his original film. These sociological ideas have rarely been utilized as prominently within the narrative of an *Elm Street* sequel as they are here. Now the teens of Elm Street are growing up and facing the life-changing decisions which are heaped upon maturing youngsters as they depart high school and enter adulthood to face the real world, but Freddy is here to herald that the real world is actually a hellish quagmire of financial, domestic, social, and moral responsibility. "Those themes are certainly important to *A Nightmare on Elm Street 5*," Robert Englund confirms, "but they are present throughout the entire *Elm Street* series, and that is because they have grown out of what Wes originally planted in there early on. They are wholly intentional but the great thing is that those themes can work on you subliminally. The young kids who just want to enjoy a good Freddy movie with some popcorn while sitting in the dark don't intellectualize those themes, but they are still responding to it on an intuitive level, they are feeling it."[8]

Andre Ellingson in wardrobe to play Dan Jordan in his motorcycle death scene (courtesy Andre Ellingson Collection).

Another quality of the production is in its continuing the franchise with Alice as the protagonist, giving the film a strong and likeable heroine who battles not only dream demons of the subconscious but, across this film and the fourth, battles her own personal demons, those which can be found in any suburban living room, bedroom, or kitchen. Throughout the two films, Alice has to endure the grief of her mother's, brother's, and boyfriend's deaths while taking on the load of being the matriarchal care figure to her angry alcoholic father, not to mention the psychological negotiations she has to make with her own impending motherhood. She does all of this as she dutifully carries on in a dead-end job as a diner waitress, an onerous life to which she has become resigned. With the exception of *A Nightmare on Elm Street 2: Freddy's Revenge*, the franchise has offered an almost exclusively female perspective on the Springwood experience; although the male protagonist in that first sequel is very much a substitute for a traditional heroine, as antagonist Freddy seductively toys with and intimately violates protagonist Jesse's emotional vulnerabilities and burgeoning sexual identity. Alice Johnson is yet another powerful heroine to lead us through this overarching saga of strong, resilient, and resourceful women battling the transgressive fiend Freddy, that which began with the iconic Nancy Thompson, continued with Kristen Parker, and which culminated closest to home with his daughter, Maggie Burroughs, the former Katherine Krueger, in the following film. Lisa Wilcox is resplendent in the role of Alice, bringing the right balance of innocence and world-weariness to draw out our sympathies for the overburdened character, but also believably bringing the necessary toughness that she must harness is going toe-to-toe with Freddy.

"That's one of the things that has really captured people's attention and imaginations," Englund says, "we have a truly great survivor girl in every one of our films and we had wonderful actresses playing those roles. In each one we have a powerful woman who matches wits with Freddy and defeats him or at least holds him off. Those girls are strong and smart and clever and relatable. Our girls survive to fight another day and I think that even more so than *Alien* we were the franchise that really got the first fangirls. I have so many female fans all over the world, and they're not just goth girls, they come in all shapes and sizes and all ages, and that is because they had that incredible identification with the films and the characters, they can identify even more than a male viewer because they are taking the journey with the lead girls. I take great pleasure in knowing that our franchise began the phenomenon of the horror fangirl."[9]

"Sticks and stones may break my bones, but nothing will ever kill me."
—Freddy Krueger

Indeed it won't, as Freddy's purported death which is heralded so definitively in the title of the sixth film only really marks a symbolic demise; the real death on display in *Freddy's Dead: The Final Nightmare* is that of the formal franchise. The film opens with a stark infographic map noting the temporal setting to be ten years from now and revealing that the entire population of Springwood's children has been decimated by a mysterious slate of murders and suicides. All that remains is a despondent adult population who are now experiencing a form of mass psychosis in the absence of the next generation. However, there is a sole surviving teenager left wandering Elm Street, a lost kid simply referred to as John Doe (Shon Greenblatt) who has been struggling to stay awake to avoid confrontation with Freddy Krueger. In a cunning move, Freddy manages to maneuver John outside of the Springwood city limits and into a neighboring industrial town, hoping that the kid will return home with some fresh, immature meat for Freddy to feast on—"now be a good little doggy, and go fetch!" Having hit his head after being thrust from a speeding bus and onto the cold hard pavement of the new town, John is suffering from amnesia and is unaware of who or where he is, nor does he realize that he will be the unwitting catalyst in keeping Freddy's myth alive long enough to claim a few more innocent souls. Taken for a transient, the cops escort him to a shelter for troubled kids and into the care of Dr. Maggie Burroughs (Lisa Zane). When Maggie finds a news clipping that John has been carrying around, she immediately feels a connection to the image of a Springwood water tower photographed in the paper. Maggie begins experiencing mysterious flashbacks to childhood days in a backyard near the water tower, the meaning of which she will uncover while accompanying John back to Springwood in the hopes of curing his amnesia. However, Maggie is unaware that three other youths from the shelter have surreptitiously hitched a ride in her van, meaning that John, being an inadvertently good doggie, has fetched for Freddy. The three kids are Carlos Rodriguez (Ricky Dean Logan), who suffers from a hearing impairment due to the physical assaults administered by an overbearing disciplinarian mother; Tracy Swan (Lezlie Dean), a tough but volatile young woman who bears the psychological scars of being sexually abused by her father; and Spencer Lewis (Breckin Meyer), a rich kid caught up in fraught relationship issues with his father, who treats him more like a material possession than a son. "Nice job on my kid. I expected to see some improvement!" Spencer's father says sarcastically to Maggie. "He isn't a Toyota!" she retorts.

With the kids stowing away in Maggie's van and into Springwood they are fed right into Freddy's glove, his plan to bring new blood back to Elm Street realized. But Freddy gets more than he bargained for in Maggie, who begins to uncover the killer's past and discovers that he had a child. All clues point to John being the offspring sired by Freddy, but it turns out that it isn't an elusive son they seek, but a daughter: Maggie; real name: Katherine Krueger. Thus explaining the recently resurfaced repressed memories of the back yard and the water tower, as it was the location where young Katherine saw her father strangle her mother after the innocent woman had the misfortune to stumble across her husband's sickening basement collection of his criminal misdeeds. Katherine was taken into care after her father's dastardly acts were exposed, upon which her name changed to protect her identity. With the help of shelter colleague, Doc (Yaphet Kotto), Maggie learns that Freddy's invincibility is controlled by supernatural dream demons and that if he is to be defeated for good then he must be brought into the real world to be made flesh and vulnerable.

On the surface, *Freddy's Dead: The Final Nightmare* appears to settle for a series of cheap gags and increasingly absurdist set pieces while in ignorance of the sociological concerns of earlier films, seeming particularly facetious in the context of it

4. The Birth, the Death, and the Resurrection 165

Freddy confronts his daughter Maggie aka Katherine Krueger (Lisa Zane) with memories of her childhood.

coming after its heavy-handed predecessor. But the film isn't as blithe as it may seem, as it features an interesting reversal of the economic milieu of the victims. Freddy has long been a thorn in the side of the Springwood bourgeoisie, and he is in fact somewhat representative of a rarely seen working class element of the town, given the industrial backdrop that we associate with him. But here we see in flashback the mortal Freddy enjoying a comfortable and idyllic suburban life with a wife and daughter, and then later in this film the immortal Freddy haunts children of poverty. Spencer is the sole representative of the typical middle class Elm Street kid with rich but inattentive parents, while Spencer and Tracy are depicted as slum kids with exaggeratedly hideous, overweight, physically abusive parents obviously of lower-class origins. In the lead up to Carlos' death, we are brought to his home, an impoverished tenement building bustling with noise and activity in its graffiti-strewn hallways. Carlos' mother is a disciplinarian matriarch who metes out fierce punishment upon her son for not being "a good boy." Despite his pleading for mercy, she, via Freddy, brandishes the Q-tip from Hell and rams it through his skull from one ear to the other. Tracy's father is stereotypically clothed in the kind of attire that is culturally associated with an uncouth proletarian: grossly overweight and sporting the slovenly dress code of scruffy wife beater vest with suspenders holding up his ill-fitting trousers. Like Carlos, Tracy resides in an impecunious area, illustrated by her shabby abode in which flashing neon lights emanate from a busy downtown street and a cacophony of human traffic and screaming babies resounds from the unpleasant environs. We are given an insight into Tracy's trauma as Freddy adopts the guise of her sleazy, incestuous father, who is introduced framed between her hanging brassieres. Tracy cringes in fear and revulsion as he shuffles his considerable weight towards her and duly commands that she "give Daddy some honey!" before suggestively stroking her arm.

While it may seem particularly cruel of Krueger to stalk these already terrorized kids, a flashback scene to Freddy's youth reveals that he too had experienced the same ordeal of poverty and abuse as his victims. With the aid of novelty 3D glasses, Maggie is able to enter Freddy's mind and take a tour through his memories; it is here we are witness to the life of young Freddy, from a disturbed, bullied child who is taunted in the classroom with chants of "son of a hundred maniacs!" to seeing him endure a physically abusive foster father as a teen.

"The themes of *Freddy's Dead*," Robert Englund says, "as they are of the franchise as a whole, is the sins of the father passed on to the youth, and what is the youth but the future. Freddy is killing our future. Freddy is pollution and poverty, he is AIDS, he is war and famine, and he is suburban complacency."[10]

"We have Freddy dealing with his past as well as all our kids dealing with their past," director Rachel Talalay states. "We've taken our main kids and moved them into the city and out of Springwood, and so we have much more gritty, urban, interesting kids. In *Nightmare 6* the kids' fears are probably the most sensitive and emotional fears that we've ever handled because all the kids are runaways and they all have to do with a certain amount of direct child abuse. These are kids who have overcome their deepest fears and that means a lot to our teenage audience."[11]

Unlike Carlos and Tracy, Spencer meets his demise more comically in a scene where he is subsumed into a platform videogame being played by Freddy. Spencer becomes the game's protagonist and his objective is to avoid a gang of 16-bit variants of his father, who are all sporting leisurewear and wielding tennis rackets. Upon being manipulated by Freddy and his joystick, Spencer succumbs to a chanted chorus of "be like me!" from the angry animated patriarchs. It is clear that Spencer's home milieu was very different to that of Carlos and Tracy's. His is one which may have been more of an existential anxiety to meet the social expectations of a privileged bourgeois family, rather than the debilitating environments of physical and sexual assault, those which were the driving force behind the anguish of Carlos and Tracy, the kind of unfortunate conditions in which young Freddy Krueger was brought up and which he perversely enjoyed. Given such depth of narrative subtext beneath these three young characters, it is no wonder that John Doe turns out to be a red herring; he has no past, no parents, no context, he is essentially an empty character, but a neat narrative device to lead us to the twist in which he is killed off midway through the picture to allow Maggie to take over as lead heroine.

Freddy's Dead: The Final Nightmare is the product of first-time director (and erstwhile *Elm Street* accountant, production manager, producer), Rachel Talalay, who ascended the New Line ladder after years of toil for the studio that began with her position as production assistant on John Waters' *Polyester* (1981). After developing a friendship with Robert Shaye, Talalay began working on further features for the company and fortuitously one of those was to be *A Nightmare on Elm Street*. From there she has been on the inside of the franchise, seeing it grow from a modest independent horror film to pop-culture phenomenon, and by the time the sixth installment was due, it was time for her to take the reins.

"In terms of my directing the film, I had decided that this is something I wanted to do," Talalay says, "I had worked with enough directors and been producing long enough and I had such a passion for the project; and I had just come off producing the film *Book of Love* which Bob Shaye had directed and I thought, 'well, now's the time!' It's hard for him to say, 'I can be a first-time director, Rach, but you can't,' and so I thought I have to do everything I can to get the ammunition together to say 'you've got to let me do this,' because I had never directed anything. So I went and wrote a story outline for *Nightmare 6*, with keeping in mind that we would kill off Freddy and keeping in mind that I wanted to create more story than had been there originally for *Nightmare 4* and *Nightmare 5*, where I think they had just sort of collapsed into convolution. So I wanted more of a story but still keeping the bible of what I knew worked in the *Nightmare* series."[12]

"Bob Shaye really trusted Rachel a lot and that's why he gave her the job of directing," says *Freddy's Dead* cinematographer Declan Quinn. "Rachel had worked on all of the previous films and she was stepping up to direct to close out the series and they trusted her with what was a bread and butter film for New Line. These *Nightmare on Elm Street* films kept the studio fluid to be able to produce other kinds of cinema, so they needed someone who knew what to give the fans and who had the experience and knowledge of how these productions are coordinated."[13]

Freddy's Dead also marks a decrease in the sense of extravaganza that had increased with *A Nightmare on Elm Street 3: Dream Warriors* and marked the franchise since. While there are many elaborate effects sequences, the film is notably less hyper-stylized than the previous two entries thanks to Quinn and his unique style of photography. Having come from a background in music videos and documentaries, particularly some notable work with Irish superstar band U2, Quinn set upon a career in feature film photography in the independent realm, shooting Maggie Greenwald's 1989 film noir, *The Kill-Off* and Jeffrey Reiner's 1991 comedy, *Blood and Concrete*.

"It was a big deal for me to do *Freddy's Dead* as I hadn't done as big a film as that before," Quinn recalls. "I had done a lot of indie films and I had done a couple of films with women directors that got a little attention on the independent scene. As Rachel was stepping up to direct she wanted someone who had worked with female filmmakers before, and at that time it wasn't such a common thing. But I had worked with female directors before and she wanted someone who had some sensitivity and who wouldn't bulldoze over her and be macho about stuff. And she liked the look of those films too, plus I was outside of the usual Hollywood suspects and had a slightly different visual approach, so that is how I got on the list. I was living in Pennsylvania at the time and I went to LA to meet everybody, including Patty Whitcher, who was the Line Producer and very supportive of me. I also met with Rachel and Aron Warner, who was Rachel's right-hand man producer on that, and I got hired right then and there."[14]

As is strangely typical for the cinematographers of the *Nightmare on Elm Street* series, Quinn had little interest or experience in the horror genre. But New Line Cinema were always on the lookout for interesting emerging talent, and Quinn certainly fit that criteria, as he recalls: "New Line understood that by getting hungry people who had experience in the indie world it meant that the work would get done fast and produce good results, and it meant that there wouldn't be too many prima donnas hanging around saying 'I'm not ready yet!' Bob Shaye was very clearly the boss and a pretty hands-on one at that, because he would look at all of the dailies and be very clear about his feelings on what he was seeing; thankfully when he saw our dailies he was very happy. Bob was actually on the set with us as well because he had a scene in the film where he plays a ticket vendor. But New Line had that energy, they would recognize your work from some small million-dollar film and want you to bring that quality to something with a little more money. Working with them on a Freddy production wasn't exactly working on a 'low-budget' horror film—even though other horror films had three times our budget—but we looked at it as stepping up in our careers. I hadn't done any horror films before, so it was going to be a learning experience for me. I'm not a huge attendee of horror films and I don't have a deep knowledge of the genre, and perhaps that appealed to Rachel on some level too. But I did go back and watch all of the previous *Elm Street* films as homework, and I took note of the styles that the filmmakers brought to it, particularly the differing styles from one to the next, how they worked with Freddy and his personality and how that was unique to each director-cinematographer team. So that's all I knew going in. The thread through it all was C.J. Strawn, the production designer, she was there throughout the franchise and knew the look of the films and the sets, so what the DP is going to do is maybe light them differently and give the film a different feeling, perhaps more gothic or less gothic. C.J. was very good, extremely experienced, and really knew the franchise; she is sadly no longer with us."[15]

For those of us who were cognizant of the attendant marketing hyperbole upon its release, *Freddy's Dead: The Final Nightmare* may be most memorable for one particular gimmick used in selling the film: 3D. The fact that Freddy's demise would be memorialized in three glorious dimensions was cause for much excitement for anyone who grew up enjoying the likes of *House of Wax* (André De Toth, 1953), *It Came from Outer Space* (Jack Arnold, 1953), *Creature from the Black Lagoon* (Jack Arnold, 1954), or the more recent *Friday the 13th Part III* (Steve Miner, 1982); the idea of putting on these cheap cardboard glasses that offer an added thrill was something *Elm Street* fans could potentially get on board with. However, the ultimate effect was not a particularly exciting or well-utilized one. The audience is nudged into adorning the glasses when Maggie puts on her pair as she enters Freddy's subconscious, wherein we are introduced to some questionable floating "dream demons" who guide us through the deep recesses of Freddy's mind and his memories of a tortured childhood and adolescence.

"The use of 3D was a decision made early on in the production," Quinn says, "probably before I even came on board. We had a Panavision specialist who helped us devise the 3D sequences and showed us how to rig the cameras. Four-fifths of the film was shot in standard 2D and it's the last reel, from when Lisa Zane puts on the glasses and cues the audience to put their glasses on, is where we switch to the 3D footage. It wasn't so difficult to get your head around the technology but it was cumbersome and slow to use."[16]

"The end of Freddy is really a problem," Talalay says, "not only the question of how do you kill Freddy but also because they made me shoot it in 3D, because to me what could have been cool in killing Freddy would have been if you could make

4. The Birth, the Death, and the Resurrection 169

Maggie signals the audience to put on their 3D glasses for the climax of the film.

this really fantastic effects sequence, but I was completely limited in shooting it in 3D … suddenly you're in this basement with a baseball bat that you can put toward the camera and it's become all about 'how do I make the 3D work?' not 'how do I make the killing of Freddy interesting?.'…And it wasn't even until a couple of weeks before we finished the film that we even knew that the 3D was even going to work. It was terrifying, it was absolutely terrifying. We looked at stuff where we came out with the worst headaches, where stuff wasn't quite aligned, and now most people are seeing the film on video, not in 3D, and it's like, 'what is this? God, this is so lame! And there's these lame visual effects!' What I'm happy with about the demise of Freddy was the whole telling of Freddy's backstory and going into Freddy's head and things like that, I thought that was really good and a really interesting idea."[17]

"When you get involved in a Freddy movie it's a big 24/7 undertaking and you had to move fast," Quinn says. "One of the things you had to do on special effects films back then was that you had to plan your shots months in advance because it took so long to generate the visual effects. I remember having very early meetings with the visual effects team, one company called The Chandler Group and another company called Dream Quest Images and there would be storyboards of these sequences already done that Rachel would have generated with the storyboard artist. We would have sat down at a special effects meeting and figured out how we were going to achieve them and maybe mended them a little bit if need be, figure out what the interactive lighting would be, if we are going to use Blue Screen or Rear Projection, all of that kind of stuff. We had to jump into that early on because a lot of questions needed to be answered.

Quinn continues, "There's one scene at the beginning of the film on the airplane where the floor opens up and the kid falls out, then as he is falling through the sky he opens a parachute and when he looks up he sees that Freddy is up there in the parachute. So we had to figure out how to shoot that scene of the kid descending through the night's sky with the clouds and all of that and it got to the point where it was quite expensive to do because it was a long sequence. So we said 'well, what about rear projection? Is that still do-able?' Nobody had done that in about twenty years. So it turned out there was a company still doing it and had all the equipment there but they didn't do it on the scale we required very often. So we used them and we had a huge screen built in a big hangar in the San Fernando Valley, at Van Nuys Airport; we had this massive structure built in there, 90 feet across by 75, and we had one of the airplane service trucks with the lift on it and we put the projector with a very long throw way back about 450 feet away so we didn't get a hot spot in the middle of the image. It took us days to rig the whole thing and to kill any ambient lighting that was coming in and hitting the screen, but it worked beautifully and was the biggest rear projection sequence done in Hollywood for years. Back then you really couldn't alter stuff by playing with contrast or anything like that so you had to get everything right in-camera. You had to grind it out and we had three units of photography going at the same time, so whenever I would wrap I would talk to the Second Unit DP and see how they were doing and try to supervise that if I could. I had never worked with Blue Screen or 3D or rear projection before, so there was a lot of new stuff which, theoretically, I got it and I understood it, but to make it happen practically I relied on a lot of professionals to steer me right. And that all happened in the prep stage, because by the time you get to shoot a scene you don't have time for silly mistakes. I saw it as a great opportunity to learn, especially using visual effects and compositing, so by the time I finished *Freddy's Dead* I felt I was ready if someone wanted me to shoot a big film with more money and complicated photography, though I ultimately didn't go in that direction, I was drawn toward the independent world to work on films about people, stories with greater emotion and character, that's where my interest was, so I didn't go back to the horror genre. I didn't want to ever go into exploitative horror films, and it can be hard for horror films not to use titillation, or sexual stuff, or things that I consider to be beyond ethical sometimes, but they managed to avoid all of that stuff on *Freddy's Dead*. I'm not the Moral Police but I am just more interested in telling stories about human nature and feelings. I met some great people on this film, such as our Second A.D. Greg Jacobs, who is a successful producer now and has worked with Steven Soderbergh for years; our really great camera operator Mitch Amundsen has become a great DP on major studio movies, and he really helped me out when I couldn't handle it myself."[18]

At first glance, *Freddy's Dead: The Final Nightmare* may seem out of kilter within the *Elm Street* canon, and its tone is certainly in direct contrast to the somber gothic milieu of *A Nightmare on Elm Street 5: The Dream Child*. What one finds is that the film shares a similar aesthetic with New Line Cinema's work with maverick transgressive filmmaker, John Waters, and that is perhaps no coincidence as several of Waters' regular crew came onboard, including Rachel Talalay, who worked with Waters on films such as *Polyester* (1981), *Hairspray* (1988) and *Cry Baby* (1990). As a result, she brings a similar sensibility to Elm Street, thus we get a Waters-style litany of cameos of the celebrity and cult variety, including Alice Cooper as Freddy's deranged foster father, Edward Underwood; Tom and Roseanne Arnold as a couple of delusional Springwood parents; and a returning Johnny Depp delivers an anti-drug PSA before receiving a frying pan to the face courtesy of Freddy. We were reportedly due an even more obvious homage to the filmmaker as Waters' regular, Divine, was set for a cameo appearance which unfortunately never materialized. Cult film aficionados would remember the counterculture hero from Waters' infamous 1972 feature, *Pink Flamingos*, and he was due to appear here in the opening scene but passed away before filming began.[19] The film also contains a distinct kinship with the surreal comedy that was in vogue on television at the time, in particular with two of the most iconic series in American television history, both of which debuted during the film's production. *The Simpsons* and *Twin Peaks* both made an enormous impact upon American culture since their respective debuts and the influence of both shows are evident throughout, from the absurdist, pop-culture-literate humor of *The Simpsons* to the quirky surrealism of *Twin Peaks*. In fact, the film is loaded with references to pop-culture artefacts, from recreations of *Looney Tunes* gags and references to *The Wizard of Oz*, Iron Butterfly's trippy *In-A-Gadda-Da-Vida*, and Freddy's Nintendo Power Glove rip-off, with which he quotes the gaming giant's famous tagline, "now I'm playing with power!"

Director Talalay noted the influence of such media icons when she says, "We've taken Springwood, Freddy's town, to the future and given it a twisted bent, we've given it a *Twin Peaks* edge and a futuristic *Village of the Damned* edge, and that's made for a lot of opportunities for interesting cameos.... I have personally worked to turn Freddy into a combination of the Freddy we had before with a few elements of Bart Simpson added into it. He's really become an evil child.[20] I was conscious in creating *Nightmare 6* that I wanted to create a slightly more fun piece than *Nightmare 5* had been. I felt *Nightmare 5* had been very serious in its gothic horror elements and Hopkins is very much a production designer and he was very into the gothic elements. It was actually the time when *Twin Peaks* had just come out and when Mike De Luca got involved in writing the script we were both completely in love with *Twin Peaks* and I had just come off of the John Waters films and in particular working very closely with John on *Cry Baby*, which was a film full of cameos, so Mike and I came up with the idea that we could get a lot of cameos in this film. I had just been working with Patty Hearst and Iggy Pop and there was the opportunity here to create some David Lynchian type characters. A lot of the weirder ideas came out of watching *Carnival of Souls* and *Twin Peaks*, so there's a slightly more off-kilterish side to my Nightmare."[21]

Indeed, the whole enterprise of *Freddy's Dead* seemed to play upon such self-reflexivity and self-awareness that is inherent in the film itself. It was as if Freddy and the horror genre needed to adjust to the emerging Generation-X and its attendant sense of cynicism and irony. In fact, the film's terrific soundtrack seems to speak directly to Gen-X audiences with its compilation of artists from the early nineties alternative rock music scene, including The Junk Monkeys, the legendary aforementioned Iggy Pop (who provides a closing credits theme song), and rising stars, The Goo Goo Dolls, who are featured throughout with no less than three songs appearing in the film. The Buffalo band provided an accompanying music video for their soundtrack single "I'm Awake Now," which features the musicians being terrorized by Freddy in a movie theater while scenes from the film are sliced into the clip.

A scene from The Goo Goo Dolls video for "I'm Awake Now," with band members Robby Takac (left), Johnny Rzeznik (center), and George Tutuska being haunted by Freddy (above).

To market the film further, New Line put together a memorial for Freddy at Hollywood Forever Cemetery where cast and crew from previous films could go and pay their respects to their fallen nemesis in front of the world's entertainment media. Part of New Line's media campaign strategy also included having Los Angeles Mayor Tom Bradley to controversially declare September 13, 1991, to be Freddy Krueger Day. The studio had pressed Mayor Bradley on the commemoration, which was received favorably and particularly so in the context of the film series having been shot in Los Angeles and given employment to many in the state; however, some civic leaders were not happy with the celebration of a fictional fantasy creation such as Freddy Krueger being honored in a state which had seen much criminal behavior and social disruption in recent times. "It's absurd and embarrassing," Tammy Bruce of the National Organization for Woman said, "Declaring a day in celebration of a character that exists to slaughter people is absolutely horrendous." Echoing Tammy's sentiments, Jerry Rubin, of the Los Angeles Alliance for Survival anti-violence group said, "It's unbelievable. Does that mean you can celebrate by going out and stabbing and killing someone?" And so the vocal disapproval of the cultural approbation of Freddy Krueger went, though one Hollywood policeman, Capt. John Higgins, put the furor into a more practically minded perspective when he said, "While the homicide rate increased 53% the first half of this year, none of the killings were tied to movie-screen mayhem.... I don't know if we've ever had a Freddy

Krueger–type murder up here.... I don't think we've ever had anybody stabbed to death with long metal fingernails."[22]

Despite the free publicity of controversy and the major marketing campaign making it known that this would be Freddy's last hurrah, *Freddy's Dead: The Final Nightmare* was released to diminishing returns whereupon it looked as though film culture and audiences had finally been exhausted by the exploits of the ultimate Hollywood anti-hero. American Cinema itself was undergoing something of a radical shift, as the emerging auteurs of the independent film movement of the late '80s and early '90s began to gain a foothold in the industry thanks to the commercial success and critical acclaim of Steven Soderbergh's *Sex, Lies, and Videotape* in 1989. The rise of the maverick indie film coincided with the end of the slasher franchise boom, which had been on a steady decline with not only *A Nightmare on Elm Street* calling time but with the *Friday the 13th* and *Halloween* franchises all becoming stale, ineffective, and increasingly less profitable, to the point where each of them reached their critical and commercial nadir roughly around the same time. The end of the 1980s saw *Friday the 13th Part VIII: Jason Takes Manhattan* and *Halloween 5: The Revenge of Michael Myers* accumulate their smallest grosses up to that point, as well as garnering some of the worst reviews of their respective franchises. *Freddy's Dead: The Final Nightmare* would follow the trend.

"I think to some extent we became slightly bereft of ideas," Robert Shaye admits, "and as much as I've always tried to say that we didn't want to make a film that didn't really satisfy the audience, and I didn't purposefully do that, with some of these later films we were stretching a little more than we ought to have to create a sequel, because we really wanted to have a sequel and I don't feel embarrassed or guilty or disloyal to the *Nightmare* fans for any of the films that we made. We always tried as hard as we could to deliver good stuff but I think you could only do so much with the idea; after the initial idea, which even in its crudeness was so effective, it became increasingly difficult to embellish on it with new stuff. For the *Freddy's Dead* one, which was ostensibly the last one in the formal series, the most effective thing we could come up with was the 3D gimmick at the end, and it kind of worked and I'm happy with the film. I thought Rachel did a good job, but that was also one of the least successful of the series and that sort of signaled to us that we should let Freddy go for a while and fortunately we were in a position corporately to move on to other things."[23]

"I didn't go in with too much expectation," says Declan Quinn, "because I was so unfamiliar with the genre and the Elm Street series in general. I wasn't too knowledgeable on the arc of the narrative across the series, so the pressure I felt was more to do with the fact that these films were New Line's bread and butter, they were expected to make a lot of money, and I know Rachel certainly felt that pressure too. Because I came from smaller indie films I wasn't quite aware of just how much pressure is on when you are making one of these kinds of sequels, I went in blissfully unaware. I saw it once in the theatre and felt proud of what we did, I thought that we had done a good job, it was pretty scary and funny. We really went for the humor because Rachel wanted to do that, but I didn't have the knowledge to assess if it made for a good or bad *Nightmare on Elm Street* film; my kids were too young to bring them to see it, so they couldn't tell me either. I know that the purists were not so enamored with it and

I was told that Wes Craven didn't like it and that it was the reason why he felt that he had to make the official last film of the series; he didn't want *Freddy's Dead* to be the 'final' nightmare. I thought I would make another film with Rachel but it didn't work out, and it was a once-off for me with New Line as well but it was a great experience and I liked the film. I'm very grateful for the Freddy experience, it opened my eyes to how the genre works and how the technology works and I am just thankful that Bob Shaye and Rachel Talalay gave me a shot. It certainly gave me some clout to have done a Hollywood franchise film like that; if anybody had any doubts about hiring me they would find out that I did that and know I was a capable cinematographer. So it was very helpful, it gave me the Good Housekeeping Seal of Approval. I once had a VHS copy of it when my kids were very young and my four-year-old and six-year-old had managed to sneak it into the machine one time and watched it. Of course, they ended up with terrible nightmares about Freddy, so he has definitely left a scar in my world."[24]

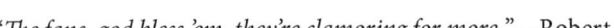

"The fans, god bless 'em, they're clamoring for more."—Robert Shaye

You can't keep a good villain down, and sure enough even though Freddy Krueger was deemed to have met his demise with *Freddy's Dead: The Final Nightmare*, it was inevitable that he would one day haunt Hollywood again. It was just a question of how. This time it would have to be different, with the decrease in box office returns from the last two entries in the franchise it became evident that the traditional Elm Street sequel had run its course by the sixth film; any further adventures of Freddy would have to be an event of sorts. For fans and critics there was only one thing that could mark the announcement of a new Elm Street film as something to celebrate, and that was the return of Wes Craven. Rather than casting a new bunch of fresh young faces and lining them up for the slaughter, Craven would turn the franchise on its head with an intellectual premise that is rarely seen in mainstream filmmaking, let alone horror cinema. Indeed, intertextual films about filmmaking have normally been the preserve of arthouse and avant-garde filmmakers such as Ingmar Bergman (*Persona*, 1966), Dennis Hopper (*The Last Movie*, 1971), Francois Truffaut (*Day for Night*, 1973) and Tom DiCillo (*Living in Oblivion*, 1995), but Wes Craven made the bold aesthetic choice to join them in breaking the fourth wall of illusion and artifice, that which audiences traditionally view Elm Street exploits through. As such, *Wes Craven's New Nightmare* is set in the very real world, its milieu the studio sound stages and Hollywood homes of the cast and crew who actually made the *Nightmare on Elm Street* franchise. And so we meet the men and women behind the Nightmares: Wes Craven, Robert Englund, Heather Langenkamp, Robert Shaye, and John Saxon; further alumni of the series also appear: actors Tuesday Knight and Nick Corri, as well as New Line Cinema executive, Sara Risher.

In its ingenious plot, Freddy begins to haunt the dreams of Heather Langenkamp's son, Dylan (Miko Hughes), around the same time that the actress is asked by Robert Shaye to revive her role as Nancy Thompson in a new *Nightmare on Elm Street* film. The New Line chief admits his desire to satisfy the rabid fan base that is as voracious as ever and who are calling for more product, that which has served his studio very well indeed—Shaye's office is decorated with a plethora of Freddy memorabilia including books, action figures, artwork, and framed articles from trade papers celebrating New Line Cinema's success with the franchise. "The House that Freddy Built" is duly adorned with his likeness in acknowledgment of such.

However, Heather is reluctant to once again visit Elm Street as she has been receiving harassing phone calls from someone reciting lines from the film in a sinister tone. So while the franchise has been a bountiful gift worthy of celebration and continuation by Shaye and his company, for Heather it has only rewarded her with paranoia and anxiety. Such is her fear of the power of the film and its legendary villain, Heather has been cautious of Dylan surreptitiously watching it on videotape, fearing the trauma it may cause the vulnerable child. But despite Heather's best efforts to keep her son shielded from the horror of Freddy, Dylan suggests that it may be too late for such protective measures, as he tells his mother that his stuffed Tyrannosaurus Rex protects him at night from "the mean old man with the claws who wants to come up when we sleep." To makes matters worse, Shaye informs Heather that her special effects artist husband, Chase (David Newsom), has been discreetly working on the new Nightmare already, designing and building the Freddy glove. This news shocks the actress as that morning she had experienced an ominous dream in which Freddy attacks her husband's film set and kills two crew members; all of a sudden, she feels the dream to be an unsettling premonition.

Later that day Heather finds Dylan convulsing and disturbingly quoting lines from *A Nightmare on Elm Street* in an approximation of a Freddy Krueger voice. Heather calls her husband to tell him about Dylan's episode and the distressing dream she had, but Chase's response further unnerves her when he discloses that the two men killed in her dream never showed up for work that day. Chase agrees to leave for

New Line Cinema chief Robert Shaye playing himself in Wes Craven's *New Nightmare*.

home to be there for Dylan, but while in-transit he begins to drift asleep at the wheel and as soon he crosses into the dream realm, he is attacked by the very glove he had been building for the new film. Distraught but suspicious, Heather visits the morgue to see Chase's body and immediately discovers a horrendous gash obviously made by the four parallel razors of a claw. At Chase's funeral and in its aftermath, Heather's visions increase while Dylan's mental health dramatically deteriorates; she is now seeing Freddy Krueger in her dreams at the same time he is increasing efforts to covet her son. Seeking comfort and advice on the strange occurrences, Heather speaks to her former on-screen father John Saxon, calls Robert Englund, and visits Wes Craven in his impossibly palatial hillside LA mansion. Saxon offers some sound paternal advice and dismisses any notion that fictional Freddy could be responsible, putting it down to a mere mortal stalker and the attendant anxiety caused by such. "Hell, Sonny Bono, after a while began seeing his stalker everywhere, even at Mass!" Saxon says. But both Englund and Craven present Heather with the unsettling information that they too have been experiencing troubling visions of Freddy.

As with Heather, the Freddy visiting Englund is not exactly the image of the villain as he once depicted him on screen, rather it is a more frightening demonic embodiment. Englund becomes particularly perturbed as Heather describes the version of Freddy of her nightmares, that which resembles the monster he is presently painting on canvas. He also reveals to Heather that Craven has written Dylan into the script, after which the director himself discloses to her that he began writing the new Nightmare upon experiencing the same vivid dreams. Craven describes the script as a nightmare in progress, a story about what he vaguely refers to as "an entity," an ancient evil which has "existed in different forms in different times" that lives for the murder of innocence. Craven makes a rational philosophical case for the inexplicable events occurring in their lives, ruminating that such evil can be captured or weakened by storytellers, such as himself: "Every so often they imagine a story good enough to sort of catch its essence, and then for a while it's held prisoner in the story. But the problem comes when the story dies and that can happen in a lot of ways. It can get too familiar to people or somebody waters it down to make it an easier sell. Or maybe it's just so upsetting to society that it's banned outright. However it happens, when the story dies, the evil is set free."

While on the surface it seems that Craven is speaking broadly about horror and its place in society, many viewers will be aware that he is also evoking the trajectory of *Elm Street* itself, as it has been both wildly embraced and cautiously suppressed by society. The *Nightmare Elm Street* franchise went through all of those motions that Craven mentions above, having become familiar not only to cineastes and horror buffs but to the greater culture at large, with it being referenced in everything from *The Simpsons* to *Roseanne* and on the national stage, such as in 1988 when then–U.S. President Ronald Reagan made an explicit analogy between the film series and his political rivals. Addressing a Midwestern audience at Southwest Missouri State University, President Reagan unfavorably referred to the economic and foreign policies of the Carter years, claiming that the Democrats' collective memory lane "starts to look like 'Nightmare on Elm Street.'"[25] When the leader of the free world mentions it, something about that particular work of art has indeed struck a nerve within society and culture on a level beyond film appreciation. But the problem with such is that in becoming an entity which has far outgrown its modest origins in becoming a massively commercial enterprise, the truly malevolent primeval horror of Freddy Krueger had indeed become, as Craven would allude to, "watered down." The sinister villain, a vile child killer and molester, was ultimately packaged and sold as a benevolent boogie man no more threatening to late–1980s youth than Frankenstein's Monster or The Wolf Man, as evidenced by the proliferation of merchandise including video games, toys, and other assorted ephemera aimed at children of the day. The important sociological themes inherent became harder to read as the franchise progressed into multi-million-dollar action spectacles with an array of ancillary industries to satisfy.

As implied by Craven, several of the *Nightmare on Elm Street* films ran into bureaucratic problems when they faced censorship in certain regions, including the outright banning of *A Nightmare on Elm Street 3: Dream Warriors* in Queensland, Australia for a three-year period from 1987 to 1990. Other entries in the franchise have endured numerous contretemps with classification boards, with cuts made to several films to appease the MPAA in America and the BBFC in Britain.[26] Horror films often symbolically and metaphorically address various important elements of society that teenagers haven't yet fully comprehended or considered, they can provide the stimulation for an intellectual or emotional awakening and for a rite of passage, and to function effectively they must evoke fear and dread in the young viewer, but by diluting the substance of the material the films run the risk of becoming mere adventure or comedy, an unintentional theater of the absurd and the bizarre. Horror needs to be horrific for it to function appropriately. So when uninformed parents or middle-aged, middle-class appointees to censorship boards consider films such as *A Nightmare on Elm Street* out of any socio-political context and simply treat it as mindless genre filmmaking, the act of burying it or bowdlerizing it to lessen its impact ultimately stymies any important themes or cautionary social awareness that the filmmakers are trying to illustrate and convey, themes which need to be delivered via the conventions of the genre. Banning and suppressing horror invites controversy and curiosity, and in the case of any horror film monster becoming the scapegoat for that society's greater ills they will ultimately become a far more pervasive and malevolent figure than any writer or filmmaker intended. Social suppression allows a monster to outgrow its original text for it to become spoken about in the greater community with fear and suspicion, an omnipresent symbol of evil rather than the character of a fictional narrative.

"I called up Bob Shaye," Craven recalls, "and I said, 'you know, I think I want to make a movie about the phenomenon of the movie and use that as the basis and jump out of the story entirely and also deal with this whole idea of censorship and whether horror films are good or bad and whether they cause people to do things,' because that has been sort of a growing and insistent question continuously asked of me and I think everybody else making horror films: 'aren't you afraid your films cause this or that…?' And my sense was, going all the way back to Greek mythology, that there's a lot of great literature that is about horror, and somehow a story about horror in a sense exorcises it or gives it a form. It's the same as Nancy dragging the hat out of her dream, it's the beginning of being able to come to terms with it, and that if you were to prevent these stories you would in a sense be allowing something that is ineffable to travel unimpeded through our consciousness because it would have a name and it would not have a shape given to it in a sense that we could recognize it. So that became the essence of it, stopping the stories of Freddy has really allowed Freddy to cross over into real life. And it was kind of a subtle warning to the censors on my part, to say, 'back off, unless you want to experience the real thing rather than seeing it in cinema.'"[27]

We saw how an erstwhile facetious horror construction such as Chucky became a mascot of genuine evil when *Child's Play 3* was banned in the UK as moral panic rose in the aftermath of the James Bulger murder in 1993. Society needed to lay blame, and so it chose a fictitious doll that walks, talks, and stalks rather than to question mental health and social milieu that led two ten-year-old boys to commit such a fiendish act upon a toddler. Chucky was no longer confined to the context of the *Child's Play* films, where he could be controlled by the storytellers, rather he became a feared bogeyman whose evil was exaggerated and inflated to a far greater degree than ever intended; he became associated with actual murder. He was "set free" to haunt the culture without context. By not allowing viewers, and teen audiences in particular, to confront the fears that horror serves them, they cannot confront it and overcome it; horror cinema provides a safe, emotional, and intellectual outlet for that to be achieved.

In the panic and fear of moral corruption, calls to suppress art deemed to be wicked or immoral gives credence to it being something to be afraid of, it also denies viewers the cathartic release and engagement with the important themes as well as forbidding the sense of closure that conquering our fears with such stories can provide. When Heather attempts to conceal Dylan from his *Hansel and Gretel* bedtime storybook and from seeing his mother on videotape, she is also denying Dylan a reassuring conclusion, a happy ending, to these scary stories to which he has already begun to engage with. In one scene he pleads with her to finish *Hansel and Gretel*, which she is reluctant to do because of the perceived darkness of the tale; she is so fiercely protective of Dylan experiencing anything to do with horror, no matter how mild, that she even questions why a child would wish to enjoy the Brothers Grimm fairy tale. Craven makes further allusions between the classic German text and his own, having Dylan leave a trail of white pills (in place of breadcrumbs) to follow home after descending to Freddy's hellish boiler room; having Freddy attempting the cannibalistic act of trying to swallow Dylan à la the witch of the Grimm fairy tale in another nod to the text. Dylan, like many children, is beguiled by the fantastical aberrations of dark storytelling, and like many kids he becomes obsessed by the bewitching figure of his mother's film. Through her rejection and repression of horror, Dylan's fascination has increased and resulted in the forbidden texts being rendered even more frightening as a resultant lack of context and clarity. Heather is effectively playing a symbol of a culture that censors without context, like those who sought to suppress *A Nightmare on Elm Street 3: Dream Warriors*, or those petitioners who successfully campaigned to cancel *Freddy's Nightmares*; without being aware of it, she invites real evil and damage into her son's life by quelling his curiosity with the fictional fantasy of art.

"We tried the Ozzie and Harriet thing in the 50's, and that didn't work," Craven says, "We tried the hippie peace-and-love thing, and that didn't work. We tried the yuppie thing and the world got worse. So what's next? There is no clear way for teenagers to go.... No one is telling them the truth they crave so deeply. I make horror movies in which a character comes out of people's dreams and slashes away at anything that's bullshit.... I'm not surprised that Freddy Krueger is a teen hero."[28] And with a story as strong as that of the *Nightmare on Elm Street* saga, the themes at the heart of the franchise and the intelligence of the respective filmmakers was bound to win out in any battle with the moral guardians of the times, particularly with the support of young filmgoers of the 1980s who spoke with their wallets. "It's always gratifying to see how smart the audiences are, because quite often my audiences are the outcasts: the kids with long hair, the blacks and the Hispanics and the people that society discounts, and quite often they are the absolute quickest to grasp what I'm doing; much faster than the civilized critics and people who supposedly have heads on their shoulders. So that's a good sign for civilisation."[29]

"We're more open when we're children," Robert Englund says, "we're not cynical or sophisticated. I remember the first time I saw *Frankenstein* was at a sleepover, I was in the third or fourth grade and it was on at 11.30 at night. And it was unedited! There were commercials but it was uncut, because the scene where Frankenstein throws the little girl into the lake was in there; that was a shocking scene but the scariest thing for me was when the monster hangs Igor on the hook. I remember sitting with my friends, we had popcorn, the lights were turned off, and we were in our sleeping bags. I remember seeing *Horrors of the Black Museum* and it has this great opening where nails come out of opera glasses and poke out a guy's eyes; and then I saw *Quatermass and the Pit*, and what a great, great film. You want those little creases in your brain and that only happens when you're young and you surrender to them more, and they are the kinds of things that stay with you for your whole life. There needs to be a sense of mystery about cinema and that mystery is particularly powerful when we are kids. You try to be cool and you go to the Royal Academy of Dramatic Arts and you do Shakespeare, and Chekhov, and Molière, and Arthur Miller, and avant-garde plays, but it's the experience of seeing horror films as a kid that really sticks, it is those which have certainly stuck with me because those experiences seared themselves into my brain as a child."[30]

In *New Nightmare*, Wes Craven informs Heather that the only way Freddy can be defeated is if she agrees to take on the role of Nancy, the gatekeeper, one more time. In assuming the identity of Freddy's nemesis, Heather must not only face the literal demon, but she must also overcome her psychological demon: the fear and reluctance that she harbors about being the recognizable face of the *Elm Street* franchise. Having been plagued by unsolicited phone calls and mail, she has allowed herself to resent and become fearful of the film that gave her a career as an actress, the film that has financially supported her and was supporting her husband. She has not followed the path of Robert Englund, whom we see as having wholly embraced his place in life as the figurehead of the Elm Street franchise and who has accepted his position as a contemporary horror film icon that he has become because of Freddy Krueger. He is seen here adored by legions of baying fans signaling their love and worship of him as he makes an appearance on a daytime television talk show. Heather is also a guest, but in contrast she is visibly uncomfortable in this intense scenario.

They are on the show to celebrate the tenth anniversary of *A Nightmare on Elm Street*, and while Heather appears somewhat discomposed by the adulation of the audience, Englund hams it up while appearing in full Freddy costume, surprising and delighting the fans of all ages in the audience. We witness the *Elm Street* enthusiasts equally as rabid as they queue breathlessly to get an autograph from the actor outside the studio. The mask and costume of Freddy Krueger affords the actor the cloak of another persona to act out under studio lights and in front of the fans, and he appears at ease with the attention. With Heather there is no mask to assume or to take off, she looks in real life as she does on film, and so there is little to separate Heather from Nancy in the eyes of those who worship the *Elm Street* heroine. Unlike her co-star, she is reticent to embrace life as a public figure. For Englund, being the spokesman for *A Nightmare on Elm Street* has meant taking on TV interviews and convention appearances where he is invariably put under the spotlight to reveal the mechanics and the artistry that goes into making a series of celebrated films. For him it is a precarious balance, being cautious about peeling the curtain back too far in divulging the processes that make the magic of these movies while also embracing the position he is in as a figurehead for the entire *Elm Street* universe. "I think we run a risk," Englund says, "and it's a risk of revealing too much about the process of making films when they parade us around on these TV talk shows and on *Entertainment Tonight* features. But there is such a huge appetite for *A Nightmare on Elm Street* and for Freddy Krueger that there are books about it, there are documentaries, and it is because people really want to find out how these films are made and what kind of minds made them. And it has crossed generations. I have kids and parents coming up to me at conventions, and I can see that this franchise means something very dear to

Robert Englund appears as Freddy Krueger on a daytime talk show and enjoys the wild audience cheers.

them and a lot of this is to do with family. You see, Freddy came home with them, he didn't just exist on the big screen at the theatre; he went home to families via the VHS tape and DVD and I have heard many similar stories from fans down the years that they relate on a very personal level and it usually involves the family."[31]

Wes Craven's New Nightmare was a most welcome treat for fans of the franchise, particularly for any of those who had been underwhelmed by their anti-hero's unceremonious demise in *Freddy's Dead: The Final Nightmare*. Not only did it mark a return of Wes Craven to the director's chair, but the film functions on a variety of levels that entertain and intrigue. Firstly, the film marked the ten-year anniversary of *A Nightmare on Elm Street* and it is partly a celebration of the whole *Elm Street* enterprise. We witness how it has become a personal and professional touchstone in the lives of those who took part in its creation, be it Robert Englund, who became intrinsically linked to Freddy Krueger and thus elevated to status of official horror icon; Robert Shaye, in whose office hangs a silkscreen portrait of Freddy Krueger in the style of Andy Warhol's *Marilyn Monroe*, and which is a nice tribute to Freddy's importance to the fortunes of Shaye and his film studio. And it is a thrill to see Craven playing himself and enjoying a life of luxury looking out over an enviable expanse of California real estate. But perhaps most interesting is the film's discourse on the horror genre and its effects on society and those who make the movies. It uniquely blurs the lines of being an astute "film about filmmaking" while holding fast to the more traditional aspects of the horror movie; certain genre conventions are adhered to as the film plays out its narrative as an actual *Elm Street* entry. But the true invention of the film is in how it deftly plays with the audience's sense of illusion and artifice by allowing us to be privy to the lives of those whose names we recognize from rolling credits and one-sheet posters. For Craven, the ten years in which his creation cultivated a considerable pop cultural cachet, having it emerge as a humble indie horror film to become a studio-making commercial enterprise, was the catalyst for him to acknowledge the monster he had created: "Every one of us in that series has been touched forever by the phenomenon of *A Nightmare on Elm Street*. Robert Englund is always known as Freddy; Heather and Nancy are inextricable, and New Line Cinema has sort of been built on it."[32]

"There is a lot of meta going on in *Wes Craven's New Nightmare*," Englund affirms. "I love that Bunuelian aspect of cinema looking in at itself, when you never quite know that you are crossing the boundaries of illusion, and Wes really brought that to this film. There is a great trick in one scene with Heather, who is playing herself, and she is going to visit her husband who is a makeup effects guy working on a movie, so she goes to the set and there's Wes Craven directing the movie, and there's a glove—so it's a Freddy-esque movie—and if you watch her wardrobe there is a real subtle mutation which is the clue that the dream has started. But by that moment we've already been put on edge by the earthquake, the child being disturbed, the phone call, and it's a very interesting blend of the real and the unreal. Wes did all of that meta stuff again with *Scream* and it was because of the success of the *Scream* films that people returned to *Wes Craven's New Nightmare* via DVD and cable screenings and they were able to see that Wes was doing that meta thing before *Scream*, and so it subsequently became a hit in hindsight. A lot of people really love it."[33]

While *Wes Craven's New Nightmare* didn't set the box office aflame in the way a Freddy feature did in the heyday of the 1980s, it did garner respect from fans and critics who recognized in it the quality of filmmaking and depth of story that usually comes with the best work of Wes Craven. Tony Timpone, former editor of *Fangoria* magazine, considers it of the highest caliber in favorably comparing it with the best of the franchise: "From an artistic, creative angle, *Wes Craven's New Nightmare* is up there with the first and third films. It certainly has the strongest script out of the entire franchise. Of course the first one is the landmark and on the third one Wes Craven came back and worked on the story and you had Chuck Russell and Frank Darabont collaborating on the screenplay; they really made that third film an action-packed *Elm Street* movie and that became the template for all the films after that, they all tried to replicate the *Dream Warriors* formula but then Wes came back with *New Nightmare* and completely reinvented the series and gave us this really great subversive, self-reflexive look at the *Elm Street* movies. It is definitely one of the highlights of the franchise."[34]

5

The Main Event and the Remake

"I've been away from my children for far too long!"
—Freddy Krueger

It was inevitable. There was no way that neither the film industry nor pop culture could leave Freddy Krueger to rest in peace. *Wes Craven's New Nightmare* dusted off Freddy's fedora in the midst of a Hollywood milieu which was taking its cues from Quentin Tarantino and the burgeoning independent movement more than it was from the horror auteurs who ruled throughout the 1970s and 1980s. As such, Craven's brilliant film failed to ignite much interest or excitement outside of those who were already among the Freddy faithful. If one is to consider the formal, canonical series to have ended with 1991's *Freddy's Dead: The Final Nightmare*, then that means it would be more than a decade before the "classic" Freddy would reappear to haunt the dreams of teenagers on Elm Street. It wasn't for a lack of trying, as many screenwriters had attempted to bring Freddy back to the big screen in a novel pairing with his fiercest horror genre rival: Jason Voorhees. While neither *A Nightmare on Elm Street* nor *Friday the 13th* came with a sense of critical prestige, they were indeed cash cows for their respective studios and were beloved by a rabid fan base, and so protecting those legacies was important when it came to finding the right script; but there were also some thorny legal issues which prevented any hastily prepared productions. *Friday the 13th* was owned by Paramount, who held firm to their once-lucrative property until 1989's *Friday the 13th Part VIII: Jason Takes Manhattan* heralded a significant commercial decline for their former money-spinner, encouraging the studio to let go of the property and sell the rights to New Line Cinema. Once in New Line's hands the studio would embark upon producing the next entries in the series, *Jason Goes to Hell: The Final Friday* (Adam Marcus, 1993) and *Jason X* (Jim Isaac, 2001). Both films were essentially placeholders to keep fans satisfied while the complicated logistics of *Freddy vs. Jason* were being worked out. However, both films failed to yield the kind of box office results that a Jason Voorhees-headed picture could once command.

The idea for such a novel pairing has been a pie in Hollywood's sky since Freddy arrived on the horror scene in the mid-eighties and monster movie crossovers are certainly nothing new, nor are they traditionally the canvas for great art; they can be tremendous fun, as is *Frankenstein Meets the Wolf Man* (Roy William Neill, 1943), but they can also be terrible, like *Alien vs. Predator* (Paul W.S. Anderson, 2004), and *Freddy vs. Jason* ultimately made for a passable attempt to appease fans of both franchises. That it took so many years and many more drafts of screenplays to bring this film to fruition is not at all surprising given the many narrative treads, mythologies, and various lines of reality that have been developed or contradicted throughout the two respective franchises; any writer bringing this film to the screen needed to satisfy the massive community of horror fandom that has supported both of these properties over several decades.

Robert Englund recalls meeting an early proponent of the crossover: "*Freddy vs. Jason* has been incubating since the first fourteen-year-old boy came up to me after *A Nightmare on Elm Street* came out in 1984 and said, 'Dude, like, ah, do you think you could kick Jason's ass?' That is one of those male adolescent fantasies which goes back to *Frankenstein Meets the Wolf Man*, this is nothing new; it is an idea from the Golden Age of Hollywood."[1]

Freddy's Nightmares director Tom McLoughlin had made the excellent and financially successful sixth entry in the *Friday the 13th* series, *Jason Lives*, and he was approached to bring together the two horror stars as far back as the mid-eighties, though the director was reluctant: "They asked me about doing a *Freddy vs. Jason* movie around 1986. I said, 'I don't know if that can work; one is set in the dream realm and one is set in reality. That would be tricky but let me think about it.' But it didn't matter anyway because it turned out that Paramount and New Line couldn't come to terms, so that movie didn't happen until years later. In the eighties we had all kinds of different screen monsters, you had Pinhead, Michael Myers, Chucky, and so on, which kind of harkened back to the Universal Monsters such as Frankenstein, Dracula, the Wolf Man, and all of those guys. So when it came to this new breed of screen monsters you had to define them all as individuals. In the *Halloween* series there's this kid who is evil and grows up evil and is like an animal stalking its prey, there's no real heavy agenda there. And he's stalking the same kind of residential tree-lined suburban streets as those of Springwood. It has the same kind of 'evil is coming to town!' idea that the Elm Street films have. *Friday the 13th* was a different

Slash of the titans: Freddy and Jason go toe to toe.

concept in that it's set in an isolated camp and you have these kids being stalked in the darkness and isolation of the woods, and that is what worked so well for that franchise. The novelty of taking Jason to other places, including Elm Street in *Freddy vs. Jason*, wears thin very quickly, it has never really worked at all, whether it was sending him to Outer Space, to Hell, to Manhattan, or Springwood. By doing that they lost what was unique about the series."[2]

After years of tortured gestation, the man hired to finally bring the film to fruition was Hong Kong filmmaker, Ronny Yu. A prolific director in his native land, Yu made the highly regarded 1993 wuxia film *The Bride with White Hair* before bringing pint-sized terror doll Chucky back to life in the comical *Child's Play* sequel, *Bride of Chucky* (1998). New Line Cinema were impressed with Yu's admission that he had never even seen any films from either of the *Nightmare on Elm Street* or *Friday the 13th* franchises, perhaps realizing they had a director who wouldn't be slavishly preoccupied in trying to be faithful to the narrative intricacies and legacies of either property, rather approaching the project with the view to reaching the more casual, nay mainstream, filmgoer. "I think of this as the first film in a series, not the 20th," Yu says. "We're kind of forgetting everything that's happened before and starting from scratch while at the same time showing flash backs ... like a refresher. Everyone knows who Freddy and Jason are so we wanna make a film for the masses, not really the hardcore fans who might remember some details from a sequel 10 years ago."[3]

And so with such a resolve fueling the fires of commerciality, *Freddy vs. Jason* finally reached cinema screens in 2003. It begins tantalizingly with both Charles Bernstein's classic *A Nightmare on Elm Street* theme tune and Harry Manfredini's iconic and instantly recognizable *Friday the 13th* sound effect of "ki-ki-ki-ma-ma-ma." We are then treated to a chilling opening monologue by Freddy over images of him in his boiler room lair, killing a young girl and licking her picture before adding it to a macabre photo album of victims in a moment of homicidal delight. "My reign of terror was legendary," he intones, "dozens of children would fall by my blades. Then the parents of Springwood came for me, taking justice into their own hands. When I was alive, I might have been a bit naughty, but after they killed me I became something much, much worse: the stuff nightmares are made of. The children still feared me and their fear gave me the power to invade their dreams. And that's when the fun really began. Until they figured out a way to forget about me! To erase me completely! Being dead wasn't a problem. But being forgotten, now, that's a bitch!"

And so *Freddy vs. Jason* imagines a world where the former no longer trades on his status as the feared legend of Springwood, having been banished to a fate worse than anything else: obscurity. In order to menace the suburban bedrooms of Elm Street once again he must reanimate the long-dormant Jason Voorhees and manipulate him into stalking Springwood to put the fear back into the fearless teens in town. Once Freddy's name is finally uttered in terror, he begins to regain his power and duly sets about haunting the troubled Lori Campbell (Monica Keener), her boyfriend Will Rollins (Jason Ritter), and friends Kia Waterson (Kelly Rowland) and Mark Davis (Brendan Fletcher). When one teen ends up dead at the house that once belonged to Nancy Thompson and her family, several townsfolk, including local police officers, begin to question whether it could be the work of the notorious Freddy Krueger. Will and Mark both had prior experiences with Freddy and have since been institutionalized in Westin Hills Psychiatric Hospital, where they are being prescribed Hypnocil, the experimental dream suppressant drug that was being tested out on the eponymous Dream Warriors of *A Nightmare on Elm Street 3*. Upon seeing the news report on the recent killings, Will and Mark fear that Freddy is up to his old tricks, and so they escape from Westin Hills to save their friends and any other teens from falling victim to the dream demon. By reviving Jason to do his bidding in bringing terror back to town, Freddy doesn't realize that he has also unleashed a formidable new nemesis who vies for the same victims as he, meaning the two must battle it out on the mean streets of Springwood and on the grounds of Camp Crystal Lake to see who will reign supreme as the ultimate terror titan.

Despite such an auspicious and fan-serving opening with its montage of highlights from the initial franchise and with a suitably ominous monologue from Freddy, the ensuing film is an inconsequentially entertaining if ultimately unsatisfactory monster mashup that fails to honor either of its source franchises in any meaningful manner. It is too frivolous and superficial for the thematic sophistication of the *Nightmare on Elm Street* films, and too aesthetically slick to recall the cheap, grimy thrills of the *Friday the 13th* pictures. Certain themes are present, though arbitrarily bypassed in pursuit of cartoon carnage, though there is one decent strand of continuity in the depiction of the parents actively and surreptitiously medicating their children into a stupor. One of the problems with the film is it was produced in a post–*Scream* Hollywood milieu, meaning that it may indeed have been influenced by Wes Craven but not in the context of *A Nightmare on Elm Street*. Craven's *Scream* is an excellent piece of work in and of itself, but its success led to many imitators and inadvertently instigated a subgenre of its own: the postmodern, ironic, intertextual, self-referential horror. In the wake of *Scream* came *I Know What You Did*

Freddy takes on Jason at Camp Crystal Lake.

Last Summer (1997), *The Faculty* (1998), *Urban Legend* (1998), *Idle Hands* (1999) and of course, Ronny Yu's *Bride of Chucky* (1998). Yu's playful sense of self-awareness stood him in good stead for the lively and cartoonish *Child's Play* film, but the problem faced by such an aesthetic is the propensity to cross the line into parody when the immediate horror narrative of a film becomes undermined by myriad references to extra-diegetic texts which are somehow related to the film—either by director, by star, by genre acknowledgment, or other forms of reference—and which makes the suspension of our disbelief and engagement with the story harder to maintain. Going into *Freddy vs. Jason*, as we do entering any property crossover, we accept that the premise is dictated by outside pop cultural concerns, those being the massive contrivance of pairing the two icons, our awareness of the separate mythologies of both franchises, and the attendant insider sense of humor that is placed to serve fans of both. It is an immediately self-referential endeavor, and we enter into it with a heightened awareness and acceptance that they will be referencing each other with a wink and a nod, but with this kind of film there is always the risk that the diegetic horror of the storyline becomes secondary to our analysis of how successfully the filmmakers have parlayed two separate mythologies into a single crossover storyline. It is harder to immerse oneself in a narrative which constantly reminds us of the novelty that we are consuming.

Director Tom McLoughlin prefigured the 1990s craze for the self-referential horror with his own *Friday the 13th* entry, *Jason Lives*, but like Craven's *Scream*, he skillfully balanced the scares with the laughs, keeping the audience in on the absurdity of the creation they are watching while maintaining their interest in the thrills and spills of the narrative at hand. "There is an issue with reboots, sequels, and crossovers," McLoughlin says, "and that is you can never successfully take Freddy or Jason back to their humble origins and to the creepiness that came with that, because if they are resurrected it will always be a pop culture kind of thing. By the time I became involved with both franchises the characters had been well-established, so I had to consider the mythologies of both characters and how can I develop them without breaking the rules that had been laid down in previous instalments. By the time I got to my *Friday the 13th* movie we'd already had five Jason movies, and by the time I got to *Freddy's Nightmares* there had been three Freddy movies, but nobody had at that point really satirized the genre. So being that mine was the sixth film in the series I felt I had to make some kind of comment about this. Being a James Bond fan my first instinct was to do the classic Bond opening and have Jason walk across the screen and be seen through the barrel of the gun, it let the audience know we're going to have a sense of fun with this. But, I didn't want to sacrifice the fear factor; I wanted to give the kids a sense of humor, and there was some stuff that breaks the fourth wall when the caretaker says 'some folks have a strange idea of entertainment' and stuff like that, but it was crucial that I tried to find a balance so that stuff didn't derail the movie from being a genuinely scary horror film. To maintain that sense of horror I made these really fun kids who you didn't want to see getting killed, but you have to have Jason doing his thing and that is made all the more horrific when these likeable kids are killed, it made for a much more tense horror movie when they are in peril. I think people appreciated that it was more than just another slasher movie, I put more of a story in there, more conflict between the main characters, there's a genuine conflict between Tommy Jarvis and Jason Voorhees, so it's not just Jason moving down random teenagers. And I added other elements which hadn't been brought in before, like car chases and big stunts, an underwater fight and all those crazy kills. So it was a very conscious effort on my part to give it a sense of humor and to make it as scary as possible. But part of the problem with making a *Freddy vs. Jason* film is that Freddy and Jason are two very different types of monsters. With Jason there isn't so much a mind as there is a force. He's got a primal instinct, it's almost animal. This is what he does. With Freddy, there is an agenda, there is a whole backstory of revenge and various themes at play. And because he is witty and has this dark, playful sense of humor, you know there is a mind at play, someone who is very twisted. So with *Freddy vs. Jason* you have two characters which couldn't be further apart and from two franchises which are very different in their approach to horror."[4]

Freddy vs. Jason was a golden opportunity for the publicity machine to go into overdrive and to utilize the iconic imagery of the formidable leading men, especially so when a star as game as Robert Englund is on board. And so the media duly embraced the moment in which two of horror cinema's most lucrative and enduring franchises could trade on their legacies to drum up support for this joint endeavor, with New Line embarking on some promotional activities that were just as amusing as the film. The cunning marketing campaign paid particular attention to the iconic status of the two horror stars coming together for the first time, and so it was billed with due hyperbole as the fight of the century, the Ali vs. Frazier of Hollywood Horror. In July 2003 both Freddy and Jason were lined up to appear at a suitably cheesy faux-pre-match weigh-in at none other than Bally's Las Vegas Hotel and Casino to announce the release of the film "twenty years in the making." The event was MC'd by legendary ringside announcer, Michael Buffer, who informed the rabid audience with his trademark pomp and gusto that in one month's time they will be witness to "the battle of the century." Movie fans and fight fans in attendance were roused by Buffer to welcome the formidable duo onto the podium with a stirring rendition of his trademark clarion call of "let's get ready to rumble!"[5]

For Tony Timpone and his legendary horror publication, *Fangoria*, the idea of a *Freddy vs. Jason* hybrid film was a media match made in monster movie heaven. "We certainly got a lot of mileage out of both the *Nightmare on Elm Street* and *Friday the 13th* franchises," Timpone admits, "those films were major events for *Fangoria* throughout the eighties and I edited the licensed movie magazine of *Freddy vs. Jason*. I think the film is very well made and Ronny Yu did a great job as the director, especially as the fight scenes between Freddy and Jason were really well handled in a comic book kind of way. They are very different villains but both very powerful in their own unique way; if Jason Voorhees is the shark from *Jaws* then Freddy is the Wicked Witch of the West, and it is fun to just see them going at it. But everything in-between the fight sequences isn't quite as effective. At the time I saw it I was disappointed, I thought it could have been so much better, but looking back at it again recently I think it is pretty fun. If what fans wanted was to see these two monsters beating the crap out of each other well then it gave them just that. I don't think it could have been much better for what it is, which is as the title says, *Freddy vs. Jason*.

It's better than some of the critics gave it credit for at the time as it definitely has its fun moments."⁶

Freddy vs. Jason does indeed contain moments that appeal to our core desire to see both of these horror legends stalk the screen once again, and as always Robert Englund brings a tremendous sense of glee and immense joie de vivre to his spirited performance, but in terms of story and themes *Freddy vs. Jason* is perhaps the shallowest of any film bearing the character of Freddy Krueger. It is an unashamedly schematic excuse to match the two horror heroes and have them beat each other into oblivion, and while that leaves audiences wanting for greater plotting and character development, there is no denying the sheer novelty factor inherent and that there are visceral thrills to be derived from the spectacular displays of action that unfolds. Ultimately, it just isn't enough. The ideas and themes behind the *A Nightmare on Elm Street* are far too mature and relevant for it to be reduced to the senseless onslaught of cartoon violence and buffoonery that ensues.

~ ~ ~

"I didn't want you to remember, I wanted you to forget."
—Dr. Gwen Holbrook

Indeed, the 2010 reboot of *A Nightmare on Elm Street* would benefit from viewers forgetting they have seen Wes Craven's 1984 triumph, as the contemporary version positively makes *Freddy vs. Jason* seem like a masterpiece of modern cinema by comparison. This deeply unfortunate reinterpretation of Wes Craven's tale is an almost direct remake, save for some name changes and a further investigation into Freddy's backstory that the original provided. The film is the feature debut of prolific music video director, Samuel Bayer, who is responsible for some of the most iconic music videos to come out of MTV's Generation X era, including Nirvana's "Smells Like Teen Spirit," The Ramones' "Poison Heart," The Offspring's "Gotta Get Away," and The Smashing Pumpkins' "Bullet with Butterfly Wings," and while his heavily stylized imagery is perfectly suitable to the three-minute rock video, it didn't quite translate as well to the big screen. Bayer's *A Nightmare on Elm Street* is a murky, heavily digital product that seems to have been constructed without any affection for what made the original franchise so beloved. In lieu of the brilliant and economical practical effects of Craven's film are expensive CGI animations which have nowhere near the effectiveness of those in the 1984 version. With its dark and obfuscating cinematography, the atmosphere is one of constant bleakness, completely betraying the original series' thematic context of sun-drenched Midwestern America with its bright, sunny, safe, comfortable middle-class environment which is contrasted with its suppressed sordid underbelly. Rather than a subversive reading of such a suburban world tainted by secrets and lies, this film just plants us directly into a gloomy realm with no regard for subtext.

The film opens by having its charmless teens already deep in Freddy's grip. Instead of setting up a scenario of innocence before being corrupted by the malevolent forces of bad parenting, broken homes, and other social ills, Bayer introduces the Elm Street kids as mopey, self-absorbed, overmedicated alternative teenagers. Worst of all, they are drab and identikit, lacking any kind of personality that might make us care about their preservation. There is little depth beyond the immediate generic conventions, but at least there are some allusions to the narratives of earlier films, as with Quentin, the son of the local high school principal. He is revealed to be heavily reliant upon pharmaceuticals, as he explains his need for "speed for kids with ADD," that which he has been prescribed since he was 15. This harkens back to the drugged and despondent kids of *Dream Warriors* and *The Dream Master*, but at least those films set up a familial backstory which explained their psychological malaise. Gone are any allusions to societal issues such as crime, class, divorce, and drinking nor is there any pinning the murders on the bad boy ethnic kid from the wrong side of the tracks like Rod Lane, because it seems that in the Springwood of 2010 everybody is comfortable and wealthy and would be enjoying it more if it wasn't for their miserable kids. Unlike Rod and Tina, who flagrantly display their sexuality with little inhibition, Jesse and Kris (the Rod and Tina stand-ins) are duly attacked but do not succumb to Freddy in the same context of moral abandon by committing carnal sins. Depicting the kids as rather chaste, innocent suburbanites flattens any potential subtext that could arise from the scenario.

The film's unpleasant nature is further enhanced in its most notable deviation from Wes Craven's original film, when it delves further into the seamy details of Freddy Krueger's assaults of children, which are now revealed to be sexual in nature as well as homicidal. The film introduces the unsettling notion that Freddy was the caretaker of a Springwood preschool and reveals that his and Nancy's history goes back to a truly dark time for the children of Elm Street. A sad and unsettling revelation is made when Nancy discovers a horrific stash of photographs depicting her abuse by Freddy, who creepily informs her that "you were my little Nancy," tearing open the wound of her long-suppressed memory of being sexually exploited as a little girl. "Your memories are what fuels me," he says to teenage Nancy as she is dressed in her childhood clothes.

Perhaps most egregious to many fans of the Elm Street franchise, the crucial role of Freddy Krueger is not played by Robert Englund, but by the brilliant Jackie

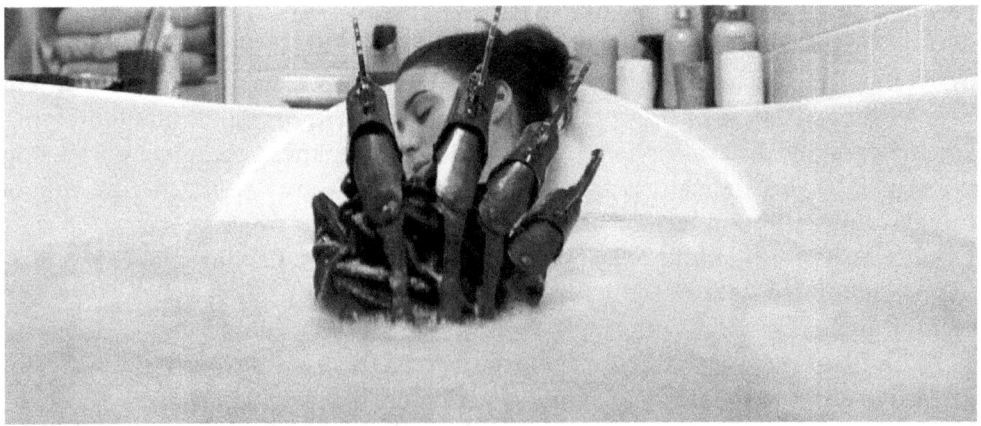

Freddy gets hands-on with Nancy.

Earle Haley. The versatile actor memorably appeared in *The Bad News Bears* (Michael Ritchie, 1976), *Breaking Away* (Peter Yates, 1979), *Maniac Cop III: Badge of Silence* (William Lustig, 1993) and *Watchmen* (Zack Snyder, 2009) before landing the coveted role as the iconic Krueger. Haley is suitably creepy here and does his best with the material at hand, but his interpretation of the role is wildly different from that of Englund's, as the actor plays it entirely sober, omitting any of the personality that made Krueger such a playful, teasing menace; Haley is given a low-bass gravel voice and rodent-like appearance, all of which contributes to make the darkly lit and joyless film an even more dour experience. Even in the weakest films of the formal series, one could always count on Freddy Krueger to bring some life to the screen.

"Jackie Earle Haley is not Robert Englund," former Fangoria editor Tony Timpone says, "He didn't bring any personality to it. It all comes back to Freddy and the great character that he is, if the movies didn't have such a great villain and such a great actor in Robert Englund to play that villain, I don't think the films would have been as popular. Unfortunately it is inevitable that there will be another *Nightmare on Elm Street* and I still think Robert Englund can play him, he is still in great shape and I'd love to see him do it again, but I'm sure there will be another film with another actor in the role of Freddy and it will never touch the greatness of the original film. They're not going to be able to capture the lightning in a bottle again and the remake was evidence of that, it was terrible. They could have expanded on the story a bit more and given that we've had so many advances in special effects they could have created really exciting dream sequences but the whole thing is flat and dreary and not very imaginative. The dream sequences were boring and with the technology that they had at their fingertips they really failed to exploit the possibilities that a *Nightmare on Elm Street* film can offer. The 1984 original had a much smaller budget and used practical effects and is far more effective than the remake."[7]

"With all due respect to the remake, there is no Freddy Krueger without Robert Englund," concurs *Freddy's Nightmares* director Mick Garris. "I don't think recasting Freddy worked particularly well in the remake because Robert has a personality that

The new-look Freddy Krueger (played by Jackie Earle Haley) in the remake of *A Nightmare on Elm Street.*

nobody else possesses and it shines through even under that makeup. Everything about Freddy Krueger as we know him is Robert Englund, whether it's the look, the line delivery, the physical mannerisms, they are so him. Robert truly owns that character, you can't just put somebody else in that costume and makeup."[8]

"Without Robert, it's not Freddy Krueger. Simple as that," says special effects man, Andre Ellingson. "When you put out a film with the words 'Elm Street' in the title and it doesn't have Robert Englund then you are just putting out product, you are not making movies. It is impossible to recapture what made *A Nightmare on Elm Street* so special. There has never been a richer, deeper, more colorful, more creative film series, both on an intellectual and aesthetic level, and no remake is going to be able to harbor all of those elements successfully."[9]

Evidently, regardless of who is behind the mask, the image of Freddy Krueger is still a financially potent one, as despite universally damning reports from critics and commentators, Bayer's *A Nightmare on Elm Street* accrued a significant $115 million in box office receipts. Which perhaps says a lot about the importance of the Elm Street brand and its universal themes which reach out to young audiences around the world.

"On a non-intellectual level Freddy is the logo of the whole experience," Robert Englund says, "Freddy is the great silhouetted logo, with the claw and his posture and his thrust pelvic walk and his snap-rim hat and the tattered sweater, and there's a certain sexual threat there. On an intellectual level he is certainly a contemporary bogeyman and represents all that is disgusting and evil that you have to confront in the world—'hey, it's time to move out, it's time to be a grownup, it's time to get laid, it's time to pay your own bills,' he is what's coming in life.... There's a great French poster [for *A Nightmare on Elm Street*] which depicts this one-story, classic early–1960s European version of the American tract suburban house. It's not the tract suburban house of today which a little bit boutiqued up, but it's the real plain, hard-edged one and we're looking at it very low angle and there's a lot of sky, and coming out of the sky is the claw.... That really sums it up. I think that Freddy is the evil that is coming to pollute suburbia ... you can't escape evil, you can't hide from it; it's everywhere."[10]

"It will always be hard to reboot a film as beloved as *A Nightmare on Elm Street*," Tom McLoughlin says, "because one problem is that by the time you get to a remake it has already become part of pop-culture and there will be less focus on the themes and ideas. But it will be financially successful because the franchise is so culturally important, people of a certain age grew up with and identified with these films. There will always be an audience there for it because it taps into dreams and nightmares, that feels universal and it always makes for very cinematic work. The great thing about the dream genre is you don't have to be literal with everything; you can be surreal instead of just real or hyperreal. I think the dream quality of Freddy Krueger, the guy who haunts your nightmares and who can take you in your dreams, is a pretty powerful and potent one and also a great metaphor for fear in general. Also, these films are relevant because they revolve around many issues that teenagers face, an age that can be the most dramatic time because there's an innocence where you're still kind of a kid and yet you have to start thinking a bit more like an adult and make decisions which can be far more dangerous, a time when you have to be careful about where you are putting your heart on the line. So I think that the films that involve those kind of issues are more relatable and universally understood. It gives these movies an opportunity to be grounded in humanity, rather than those which just go for the big set pieces but which have nothing emotionally or intellectually stimulating behind them."[11]

"There hasn't been a truly great horror character in all of these years since Freddy appeared," Tony Timpone states, "He is really the last of the great horror icons because nobody has been able to duplicate the success of the first film, and that is because it contained such great writing and had a deep psychological undercurrent that Wes Craven brought to it. The sequels had a lot of imagination and brilliantly brought all of these surreal scenarios to life in a very creative fashion; the filmmakers really put a lot into creating fantastical dream sequences and Freddy's kills, so they weren't slapdash in any way … well, the second one may have been a little slapdash, but for the most part they really wanted to give the fans what they craved and they delivered. At the height of the *Elm Street* phenomenon there were so many horror films trying to replicate it, even the major studios were trying but they couldn't get the formula right to capitalize on it. They were all desperate to create characters that had that same kind of staying power but they couldn't do it, and that is partly because they weren't played by Robert Englund and they weren't created by Wes Craven. Even Wes couldn't replicate it himself when he tried with *Shocker*, even he couldn't capture lightning in the bottle twice, and the actor from that film, Mitch Pileggi, is a really good actor but he didn't have that panache that Robert has, he was just another angry slasher and it just didn't work. Freddy had personality because Robert has personality."[12]

Indeed, the aesthetic failure of the remake is a sharp reminder of just how powerful and remarkable Wes Craven's 1984 film truly is. It is a story that addresses issues that lurk in every house and within every family, it speaks to the disenchanted kids of broken homes and to those struggling with the various issues—emotional, psychological, and sociological—that the average viewer can relate to on some level. It has heart and intelligence in abundance, and it was achieved with brilliantly inventive filmmaking that inspired and informed a most lucrative franchise, that which helped build a Hollywood studio and afford Robert Shaye and New Line Cinema the opportunity to become major players in the film industry. It created a modern horror icon in Robert Englund, a legend in Freddy Krueger, and launched Wes Craven into the pantheon of truly great American filmmakers. And in the end, those two powerful words "Elm Street" will linger long in the hearts and minds of fans to whom it is no mere movie location, but a microcosm wherein the fears, anxieties, hopes, and aspirations of all teenagers and parents remain. As Robert Englund put it, those words are emblematic of the "Nightmare of America," they allude to the great promise and great tragedy of not only a nation but to the great promise and great tragedy that resides in every home in every town, not just Springwood, because as Freddy Krueger put it, "every town has an Elm Street."

6

The Legacy of *A Nightmare on Elm Street*

In the four decades since Robert Shaye and his modest independent film distribution company gave Wes Craven the opportunity to realize his terrifying tale that was turned away from other studios, New Line Cinema went through an incredible ascent to become a power player in the film industry, competing with the long-established Old Hollywood studios. And due to the success of Craven's creation and subsequent impact it had on the company's finances, New Line would become colloquially known as "The House That Freddy Built." The film and its subsequent sequels have afforded New Line Cinema the opportunity to develop rich working relationships with maverick filmmakers such as John Waters, John Carpenter, Paul Thomas Anderson, and David Fincher, releasing highly acclaimed works and box office hits such as *Teenage Mutant Ninja Turtles* (1990), *The Mask* (1994), *Dumb and Dumber* (1994), *Seven* (1995), *Austin Powers: International Man of Mystery* (1997), *Boogie Nights* (1997), *The Wedding Singer* (1998), and *Rush Hour* (1998). And then with *The Lord of the Rings* trilogy, released in the first three years of the millennium, Shaye's once-fledgling company defied the odds once again in reaching commercial heights to rival any of the major studios in Hollywood. It was no longer the humble house that Freddy built, but a gleaming chateau resplendent in industrial might. Here, an esteemed assembly of filmmakers and horror experts reflect upon working with New Line Cinema and issue their ultimate thoughts on the importance and cultural impact of *A Nightmare on Elm Street*.

Tony Timpone (Editor, *Fangoria*): *Fangoria* wouldn't be the magazine it is or would never have become as popular as it is today if it wasn't for the *Nightmare on Elm Street* movies. Starting with *A Nightmare on Elm Street 2* in 1985, every time we put Freddy on the cover sales went through the roof, so we were positively ecstatic when every year a new *Nightmare on Elm Street* movie would roll around and we'd get Freddy on the cover, because those issues sold incredibly well and led to *Fangoria* really taking off in the late-80s. Only a few years prior, the magazine was on the verge of being canceled because sales weren't that good, but once Freddy came along he really elevated our popularity on the newsstands and *Fangoria* became a household name. And I also think that those movies owe a lot to *Fangoria* due to the way we covered and pushed them in the magazine and at the conventions; we really helped build the audience for those movies, so they kind of go hand-in-hand; *Fangoria* is what helped put Freddy on the map and Freddy increased our circulation.

New Line Cinema was great because they gave us everything that we wanted. They would do special photo shoots for us, they gave us exclusive access to the sets, they gave us access to any of the filmmakers, and they made our company be the ones to publish their official *Nightmare on Elm Street* movie magazines. So we had a great relationship with them. I used to go into their offices and go through all the photo books to pull the best images to illustrate our articles. They were amazing, and it was easy because we were a team player with them. If every studio was like New Line Cinema it would have been a constant joy going to work at *Fangoria*, but they weren't all like New Line Cinema. I've interviewed Bob Shaye and have gone to some of his parties down the years and he is a lovely man, always appreciative of everything we did for the movies and I've always enjoyed his company. New Line was the best.

Chuck Russell (Writer/Director, *A Nightmare on Elm Street 3: Dream Warriors*): The *Elm Street* series really helped New Line grow from a forward-thinking independent to this much bigger thing and then they finally became part of the major studio system. I have to give credit to Bob Shaye, Mike De Luca, Sara Risher, and Rachel Talalay for their teamwork when I was making *A Nightmare on Elm Street 3*. At that time at New Line I could go directly to Bob and make my case for taking some creative risks. I didn't always get approvals, but Bob supports his filmmakers and would hear me out. Bob wanted a new direction for the series, but would also challenge me about breaking *Elm Street* traditions, such as taking Freddy out of his traditional wardrobe and into a tuxedo, or body mods like "TV Freddy." But in the end he allowed me to do it. And then years later I made *The Mask* for them and it was initially supposed to be a horror film but I talked them into making it a comedy, which was a huge leap of faith. Casting Jim Carrey was also a leap at the time as he was not yet an established film star; *Ace Ventura* had not come out yet. But he was so brilliant in *In Living Color* and I found his work inspired my entire version of the film. So casting Jim was a big deal to me as was being allowed to cast Cameron Diaz, who had never acted before. She won the role, hands down through auditions, screen tests and the good, old-fashioned chemistry she had with Jim. That's the beauty of working with a really smart indie company, they relied on their filmmakers and you had full access to the boss. They were open minded, even if you wanted to flip a horror film into a comedy/dance/superhero movie. Pretty rare.

Steven Fierberg (Cinematographer, *A Nightmare on Elm Street 4*): I remember when New Line hired Renny Harlin for *A Nightmare on Elm Street 4*, they admitted that his first film *Prison* was not good but that there was something there, they saw talent and a vision in Renny and they thought, "if we give him the opportunity, he is going to soar," and he did, he became a major director after that and went on to do massive box office business for major studios early in his career. And that is to Bob Shaye's and Sara Risher's credit, because they ultimately gave him the job. That's the kind of chances they would take. Bob was a great executive, he would tell us what he thought of what we were doing and he would give us some ideas, but they were never strict directives, you didn't have to do what he said, they were just suggestions. Bob was a guy who brought out the best in you because you felt supported, it was a really positive experience. I really like Bob Shaye.

Bill Froehlich (Executive Producer, *Freddy's Nightmares*): Bob Shaye was very protective of the *Nightmare on Elm Street* brand. He did not have any input on the day-to-day aspects of *Freddy's Nightmares* when I was doing it, he had more impact on the first season, but I know he was careful about not letting the television series stray too far. He wanted the series and the character of Freddy Krueger to remain faithful to the films and he knew I would respect that. I would get a comment from him every once in a while saying that I was doing a really good job of keeping things within the feel of the *Nightmare on Elm Street* franchise.

Lisa Gottlieb (Director, *Freddy's Nightmares*): Freddy Krueger really helped New Line Cinema become the big studio that they did, because by the second and third films they had an international hit on their hands. When Sara Risher and Bob Shaye were running New Line I could pitch anything to them, and sometimes they would want to run stuff by me! I actually pitched a story for *A Nightmare on Elm Street 4* to them, and my pitch was that Freddy finds love and he has to romance somebody but be careful not to kill her by accident. They thought it was comedic but they decided they wouldn't accept me as an original writer, they didn't want me to write it or have my name on the credits, they just wanted to keep some of the ideas, so they promised that they were going to do a development deal with me and brought in some big writer to work on the film. I used to have lunch with Sara whenever I was in New York and I was very close friends with Bob's sister, Lin Shaye, so I would go to dinner parties at her house and Bob would be there. One year I went on vacation to St. Barts and I walked into a French restaurant with my family and there's Bob! But my in-laws instantly didn't like him, they said "that guy is snotty!" and I said "well, all the bosses in Hollywood are snotty! But Bob's been very good to me, so don't dislike him and don't give him dirty looks!" New Line would attract and nurture talent and were very open to people who weren't the usual suspects because they hung their initial success on *Pink Flamingos*, they started out as a scrappy little New York company and all of their early films were weird, outsider work. By the time Wes arrived with *A Nightmare on Elm Street* it was a little later and New Line already had an LA office. Sara and Bob were great people and New Line was a great company when they ran it, but then it became a different company run by very different people.

Craig Safan (Composer, *A Nightmare on Elm Street 4: The Dream Master*): New Line really took chances because they were an independent company and they were able to do that. They took risks on younger filmmakers and people who hadn't necessarily been hugely successful before but who had a great idea or were eager and talented. Ultimately, that is how they made their money, and with films like *A Nightmare on Elm Street* they were able to establish themselves in Hollywood.

Andre Ellingson (Special Effects Coordinator/Actor, *A Nightmare on Elm Street 4: The Dream Master*; *A Nightmare on Elm Street 5: The Dream Child*; *Freddy's Nightmares*): Bob Shaye is a good guy. When I started out in Hollywood I was a young ambitious kid who went up through the ranks pretty quick and I would come across

Bob often. There were a lot of parties back in the eighties and Bob was always there and even though he was the bigwig he always had time to talk to us and was always cordial. New Line was the kind of place where they took young talent and gave them work and Bob gave a lot of people great opportunities. I always felt like he was going to take me under his wing at any minute, that's how close it felt, but I ended up working on movies for different studios and when you do that you move on to a different circle of people, so I never saw Bob again after that. Had I been more aware at the time of the opportunities he gave people, I could have been more strategic in my interactions with him, but that's not the way it was, that's not how I rose through Hollywood, my work spoke for itself and I just climbed the ladder as the jobs presented themselves, rather than through working my connections.

Jacques Haitkin (Cinematographer, *A Nightmare on Elm Street*; *A Nightmare on Elm Street 2: Freddy's Revenge*): New Line was under tremendous pressure financially with the *Elm Street* films. I mean the budget on the first film was $1.8 million, and that's pretty low for the kind of film it was. We were running five units at some points but it was non-union, so the labor was a lot cheaper. But the ambitiousness and the organizational skill on a non-union show to run a five-unit factory was something else. This was back in the days when there was no Marvel or those kinds of film factories, with New Line we created our own factory with a bunch of industrious, creative, and happy people … and some crazy people! That's the way it was with New Line.

Dennis Maguire (Assistant Director, *A Nightmare on Elm Street 3: Dream Warriors*): The only *Elm Street* film I have ever seen is *A Nightmare on Elm Street 3* and that's because New Line sent me a VHS tape of it along with a bottle of champagne as a thank you present after the film came out and had a great opening weekend. We were a small little film, though conversely a big film for New Line at the same time, but they retained that low-budget, non-union mentality; they weren't used to working on a $4 million budget. And then of course they went on to become a mega-budget studio, but they really weren't and shouldn't have been and I think that's why they imploded, they just got too big. But I do think Bob Shaye is a very nice man. I worked on another film for New Line called *Torch Song Trilogy* and Bob was always very complimentary of me because they were very happy with that film. Bob's right hand, Sara Risher, was also present a couple of times and she was just as nice and supportive. Once you got everything on track they both really left you alone to get the work done.

Tony Timpone: The marketing people at New Line were great, beginning with a guy named Gary Hertz who worked on the first few movies and he was really good not only in getting the movie to the horror fans but reaching beyond those fans in trying to cultivate more of a mainstream audience, and this was helped when they started getting a lot of popular rock and rap artists on the soundtracks and bringing in stronger actors in supporting roles. Freddy was ready for the next step after a while and so they started making the films a little more mainstream, more comedic, more populist, and as the audience started extending they began to make the films more of a special effects extravaganza, the kind we saw with *A Nightmare on Elm Street 3:*

Dream Warriors, and from there they just kept escalating and getting more elaborate with the productions. They also began to lighten their tone, so the humor allowed them to find a wider audience, including people who wouldn't necessarily go and see a horror film. By the time they got to *Freddy's Dead* they had successfully broadened the base.

Robert Englund (Actor/Freddy Krueger): The Freddy fanbase is very wide and varied, it's not just hardcore horror enthusiasts and goth kids. I remember at one stage between *A Nightmare on Elm Street* parts 3 and 4 Bob Shaye told me that someone had done their PhD on the *Elm Street* films and at that time it was a pretty unbelievable thing to hear that, but now after all of these years and having talked to so many fans I know it to be absolutely true. I have met people who are now in their forties who got in trouble in elementary school for drawing pictures of Freddy Krueger with their crayons, and they tell me about the teacher asking the parents to come down to school to discuss their child's fascination with this horror character. And these may have been religious schools and the teachers not very hip, but the parents would go down and put it in context, they would tell the teacher that this is a great allegorical horror film and they ask the teacher if they would feel the same way if the child had drawn a classic character like Frankenstein. At least once in every convention I get that kind of story from a fan, where somebody had to defend their love of Freddy because it is important to them, and he is an important character to many people.

Tom McLoughlin (Director, *Freddy's Nightmares*): It's hard to say exactly what it is about Freddy, but to me he has become to a certain generation what Frankenstein and Dracula were to previous generations. The same thing happened with those Universal Monsters, their success meant that the studio kept making one movie after another and with that the monsters became less-frightening, but as the years went on they also became iconic. It is especially powerful when you see these movies when you are young, they speak to that sense of youthful alienation when you feel that nobody understands you, and the *Elm Street* series speaks to different feelings that teenagers go through and it crosses generations because there's always a powerful and timeless message in there. What Wes Craven did in the beginning was brilliant, and that was to establish a really horrific idea which is if you go to sleep then this guy is going to get you; we all need sleep, so how do you avoid that? You can't, and once you get into that dream realm anything can occur. That was a tremendous idea for a horror film. But once the budgets got bigger and they had to be less-inventive with how they achieved the imagery, the films became more elaborate and the set pieces became huge. When that starts happening it takes away from what was scary about the original film, which always feels more like a personal film rather than a big Hollywood production. But Freddy has been alive in pop culture for a long time and is still being discussed, whether it's by fans celebrating it or by studios looking to see if they can cash in on it somehow. It's always on different TV stations and reappearing on new home video formats, so Freddy just keeps on being discovered by new audiences.

Mick Garris (Director, *Freddy's Nightmares*): Wes was such a fertile mind and he influenced the genre in so many ways. He brought so much intelligence to everything that he did. I was so lucky to have him as a friend. We weren't close friends, but when he finished his film *My Soul to Take* he invited me to see it and when I got to the screening room at Universal Studios there was no one else in the room except him and Iya, his wife. I thought, "wow this is an incredible honor, I'm the first person he is showing this movie to and I get to watch it with just him." He would come to some of the regular *Masters of Horror* dinners and it was always great to see him, he was such a gentleman. When you have a certain amount of success within a certain genre you are almost consigned to that because it made you successful, in fact you get consigned not only to the genre but to the subgenre. So it was great to see Wes break out to do other things such as *Music of the Heart* and *Red Eye*, but the studios only really wanted him making horror films. But Wes made the most of his jail and turned it into his own wheelhouse and put his themes into play, though I do think he would have liked to have addressed those themes in work outside of that pool that he was consigned to. He was an extremely educated, intelligent guy who was very aware of his storytelling. For a lot of filmmakers it is about the scares, the flash, the grotesque imagery, and showing you things that have never been done before; and that can be great fun, but Wes was so much more than that. There wasn't a lot of gadgetry or gimmickry in his movies because he was devoted to the storytelling and his directing was misleadingly simple. Wes has left quite a legacy. He went on to become one of the most successful and rightfully lauded pioneers of contemporary horror cinema, a man who created two hugely successful film series, *A Nightmare on Elm Street* and *Scream*, when you are very lucky to have one! He reinvented the genre several times over and maintained his auteur vision whether working with the likes of Miramax or Universal. And while New Line Cinema became consumed by the Hollywood corporate machine and Wes Craven has passed on, the legacy of Freddy Krueger will endure.

Jack Sholder (Director, *A Nightmare on Elm Street 2: Freddy's Revenge*): Wes really researched his themes and you can see that in all of his discussion about sleep and dreams, but I don't think the filmmaking on the first one was especially good. Wes became a much better director later on. If you look at *New Nightmare*, that film is, in my opinion, a much better made film technically-speaking, he had really grown as a director by that point.

Roy H. Wagner (Cinematographer, *A Nightmare on Elm Street 3: Dream Warriors*): I love the film *Carnival of Souls* and I think Wes used that as a kind of benchmark for *A Nightmare on Elm Street*, the idea of this awful decadence of not really knowing what's real and what's not real, and the interesting thing is that the director of that film, Herk Harvey, knew as little about making films as Wes, but what they wanted to do was in their soul and they were able to communicate that through their films regardless. The tragedy about Wes is the fact that he never got to go as far as he could have gone, or should have gone, because he had the *Elm Street* baggage to carry around throughout his whole career. That happens to a lot of great filmmakers.

Tuesday Knight (Actress, *A Nightmare on Elm Street 4: The Dream Master*): I was so excited to work with Wes on *New Nightmare*. It was amazing, to finally work with the creator of the series and to see how he made movies was such a thrill; it put everything into place for me. He was such a gentle person, very soft-spoken, sweet, and funny! But also very intelligent, I kind of got the feeling that I was in the company of a college professor, he had that erudite kind of manner.

Andre Ellingson: Wes Craven was just a brilliant mind, he really was an intellectual guy and so he brought depth to his stories and to the horror genre. I had just come back from Thailand having worked on the Dolph Lundgren movie *Men of War* when Lou Carlucci called me and said he needed me to foreman on *Wes Craven's New Nightmare*; Lou was coordinating the special effects and I came in and took over as foreman but it was only for a few weeks toward the end of the production. I would have worked on an *Elm Street* film any time and I think part of the reason the series was so good is because of the people who worked on the films. There was such a great team of people putting those films together. Hollywood was a pretty compact unit back in the eighties, so to be working on a *Nightmare* movie, which had become the biggest horror show in town, you were pretty lucky, there was a lot of attention paid to those movies, a lot of people got to see your work. I was living on hot dogs and Ramen Noodles, working every hour of the day on a non-union job with no benefits, working to the point of exhaustion, but I didn't care. Some of us would just sleep on the sets, because who wants to spend two hours driving home after an eighteen hour day only to get up a couple of hours later and drive another two hours to do it all again. We would just pull up a bloody mattress that was used in a killing scene and sleep on that for a few hours in a corner of the stage. We had that fire and hunger in us to just keep working. The camaraderie of the crew helped, we were all in it together, a great group of people at a great time in the film business.

Lisa Gottlieb: I love the first *Nightmare on Elm Street* film in all its funky indie-ness, and of course you can't go wrong casting Johnny Depp in anything; I remember when it was released the whole world woke up and went, "who's that guy?" I think the third film, *Dream Warriors*, had a great script with such an interesting premise: these kids being admitted to a place to deal with their sleep issues but they can't go to sleep! It was just a fantastic concept. My friend Jack Sholder directed the second one and I love that movie. I watched my episode of *Freddy's Nightmares*, *Saturday Night Special*, again recently and there are some great moments in it. It's interesting, some stuff you work on has a long life while other stuff you did goes dormant and then comes back to you because people rediscover it. Young people love this kind of stuff and so every generation will see it and adopt it.

Tony Timpone: The original *A Nightmare on Elm Street* came at the tail end of the slasher boom and it was the next evolution of the slasher film, and subsequently the later films introduced a greater level of special effects and imagination and production values that weren't in the typical slasher film up to that point. But also important was the fact that it had this villain with personality and who had the same kind of qualities as the horror icons of the 1930s and 1940s: Boris Karloff, Bela Lugosi, Vincent Price, Christopher Lee, Peter Cushing, etc. You have a legitimate horror star in Robert Englund, he is a wild man with real colorful personality and was very game for the craziness of the character. He brought Freddy Krueger alive despite being buried under pounds of makeup and latex on his face; some actors go dead in makeup but Robert was able to bring his personality to this amazing character. He is also very physical, very funny, and he has this devious wink in his eye, so Freddy became larger than life. A lot of the success of Freddy becoming this pop culture icon is down to the sheer force of Robert's personality, he is a very charming person and he would be great with the press, he really knew how to sell himself and the character.

Chuck Russell: Robert Englund is a huge talent, and I find it interesting that he's so irreplaceable in the role. He's a wonderful guy and a great actor; a fearless actor. Robert will take incredible chances as he puts his whole heart into such an extreme character. In our discussions on set, we see Freddy's point of view as taking justified revenge. In his eyes he's The Good Guy dealing with these Elm Street brats. Robert brings this weird zest to being Freddy that makes the character seem to enjoy disrupting our reality. He is a true thespian who is willing to go through a more theatrical process to reach amazing solutions for a scene.

Dennis Maguire: Robert would sit in makeup getting the mask applied for hours, and then have to sit through another hour of taking it off, and not once did I ever hear him complain, nor has anyone ever heard him moan about the process. He is professional and he had already played the character twice before, so there is little directing that needs to be done with him because he knows exactly how the character should be played. That glove is like his six-shooter, and the way he wears that hat, it's like he is poised for a gunfight when he appears. He plays with that and just enjoys it.

Jack Sholder: I think one of the significant factors of the success of *A Nightmare on Elm Street* is that Freddy has a lot of personality and he takes a lot of glee in what he does, and that is because Wes cast a really great actor in the role of Freddy. If you look at the other horror monsters of the time, the actors are anonymous and interchangeable and the characters come and go without leaving much of an impression. Wes created this really interesting character and then he cast a really interesting actor in the role, not the guy that you would have ever imagined, I mean if you were looking at a bunch actors' profile photos you would never have picked this guy, but it was the combination of perfect character and the most ideal actor you could get. Robert was fearless, he would go wherever you would want him to go.

Bill Froehlich: Robert really does own that character on so many levels. I think that staying with that character for as long as he did meant he began to have an intuitive feel for how his character would behave, and that really makes the character unable to be played by anyone else, but another crucial thing that makes it impossible for anyone else to step into it is that he just loves doing it and that creative joy comes through on the screen. Even when I would watch the footage in dailies and in all the hours of editing, there were times when you would just laugh or break out into a smile because you could see that he was absolutely digging it and that energy is the key thing. Robert Englund as Freddy Krueger has entered the pantheon of the great horror icons such as Bela Lugosi as Dracula and Boris Karloff as Frankenstein; Freddy is as big and as important as any of those characters and it will remain that way.

Lisa Gottlieb: I think Robert is the reason that *A Nightmare on Elm Street* has lasted; even though the films got bigger and the production values were greater as they went along, Robert's power as a performer was the constant throughout it all. I do think Freddy and Elm Street will be around forever. They tried to do it again with Jackie Earle Haley, who is a very good actor and can be scary when he wants to be, but Robert brought humanity to the guy; yes, Freddy is evil, but every now and again a bit of humanity would slip out and that was all Robert. Look at his movements, especially the walk. Robert is not such a big guy but he is so full of himself, and that also worked great for him as the host of *Freddy's Nightmares* because he has got the quality of an impresario. He allows Freddy to have a great time even though other characters are suffering, but that's Freddy! They built the whole show around him, they told Robert that he would be working every week, he'd make millions of dollars, but for Robert it was really the idea of being a host that was very attractive, that he would be leading the audience through the story and maybe occasionally intruding upon the story in a very rude way; he loved that! It was so much fun being set up in front of that Green Screen with him, we laughed all day long. Another thing I used to tell Robert was "the story comes through you, you've designed these little tales" and he said, "Well that's a good way of looking at it as long as you don't cast me in an actual episode!" He said to me once, "I can't hate Freddy. The Freddy industry has made me a rich man, it allows me to fund theaters that I want to act in or support productions that I want my actor friends to be in, and whenever New Line wants to do another Elm Street I get to work and they make me very happy and secure … but I'll never get to play anything else." Essentially, he loved the work, he loved the money, he thought it was fun, and he loved Wes. I do love Robert.

Mick Garris: Robert is such a smart, funny, intelligent, dedicated guy. He knows the horror genre inside and out and tells some great Hollywood stories. In fact, Robert does like to talk, he's quite loquacious and always entertaining.

Nick Benson (Special Effects, *A Nightmare on Elm Street 4: The Dream Master*): Robert was such a pleasure to have around. He loves to tell stories and express himself, especially while he is having the makeup applied, and that is part of what makes him a lot of fun to be around him. I am impressed that he was able to remain as pleasant as he did after being in that make-up for sixteen hours a day. There was one time I was puppeteering some of the souls coming out of Freddy's chest and while we were filming it one of the armature wires popped through the fingers and poked Robert. I was nervous to begin with because here I am shooting Freddy's death scene, but then I ended up stabbing Robert and making him angry in the process. But he is such a nice guy and a phenomenal actor. Freddy is a difficult character and not everybody can pull it off, as we have seen, but Robert envelopes himself in that character and brings everything he can to it and he applies that to every character he plays. Before I knew him I was a fan of his on the TV show *V*, which I used to watch when I was in high school. I fell in love with his acting when he was on that and then to see him in *A Nightmare on Elm Street*, where he really brought all of that skill and personality, it really made me think "this guy has it!" So it was a thrill to be on set and seeing him become the character before my eyes.

Andre Ellingson: Robert Englund is a great storyteller and he loves to tell you about all of these great Hollywood experiences he has had. He is a super, super good dude, so gracious, he always treated me with respect, which I am especially grateful for considering how young I was back then. One time when I was in Santa Fe, New Mexico shooting a western with Robert Urich called *The Lazarus Man* I had to go to a Home Depot to look for a Hudson Sprayer, which is a self-contained pressure pot that you put water fertilizer liquid in to spray around and we use those on horror films all the time. But I needed one of these Hudson Sprayers for a blood gag in the western where a guy gets cut by a sword, and I'm standing there in the aisle looking at these pumps and I feel this presence next to me and I turn around and it's Robert Englund! Robert and I are the only two people in the whole aisle and we're both looking at Hudson Sprayers! I'm like, 'Robert!' and he says, 'Andre! What are you doing here?' We hadn't seen each other for years and there we are, both of us, in the same place at the same time on earth in a completely random Home Depot looking for Hudson Sprayers. He was getting one for his garden, and I say, 'you know why I'm getting one, right?' and he says, 'of course I do, you're getting ready to do a blood gag!' I met him again another twenty years later when he had a guest appearance on *Criminal Minds* and it was an opportunity to reminisce. He is a super good guy, you can't say a bad word against him.

William Malone (Director, *Freddy's Nightmares*): Robert Englund is great, he really created that character of Freddy Krueger and made it that nobody could possibly do a better job of it. Robert added a creepiness to it and yet he brings an element of fun, and that is a hard thing to pull off. It reminds me of the TV show *Kolchak: The Night Stalker* with Darren McGavin, and when you think about it, you could never replace Darren McGavin in that show because he just embodied Carl Kolchak and it is exactly the same with Robert and Freddy Krueger. He was fantastic on the show, a really good sport. I remember one time we were filming and it was my daughter's sixteenth birthday and I asked him if he could put a Happy Birthday message to her on camera and he was very gracious about it, so we made up something really fun, it's a birthday message from Freddy Krueger and I gave it to her. Of course she was the hit of her high school with that. I love Robert, so I felt very blessed to be working on *Freddy's Nightmares* with him.

Tuesday Knight: Robert is a very giving actor and so special, I mean he is Freddy! He is one of a kind. I couldn't even watch the remake, and Jackie Earle Haley is a great actor but it was not Freddy, nobody else is. Robert Englund as Freddy Krueger is iconic.

Declan Quinn (Cinematographer, *Freddy's Dead: The Final Nightmare*): I'm not sure at what point it became the thing to light Freddy out of the shadows, but I think that eventually became the thing to do because of Robert's personality made the character bigger, or perhaps because the audience wanted to see more of Freddy because of that. I was so up to my eyeballs in getting the movie made that I didn't have a big rapport with him except when I needed to, I had to keep things moving along and looking good, but any time I was around him I found him to be incredibly easy to work with. He came in hours before any of us and sat in the makeup chair for what I understood to be five hours, and we would try to get him in and out as early as possible because he needed the turnaround and the schedule was built to accommodate that. I would communicate with him when I needed him to do certain things and he was always very accommodating and understanding, he was a total pro. One of the things I really liked about Robert was that he knew how and when to bring the humor to the character, and he did it effortlessly; Rachel Talalay understood his sense of humor so well and knew how to parlay that into the film.

Jacques Haitkin: Working on these films certainly affected my career as I've gotten a lot of attention because of it, I'm not talking Roger Deakins level of attention but that's fine for me, I've never considered myself a "maestro," I always considered myself a journeyman, just a thankful, honest hard worker and that's as much of an artist as I can be. You know, when you're in the middle of making something, you don't realize it's going to be anything; to me, every film was the most important thing I worked on. Every film is *A Nightmare on Elm Street* to me because every project I go into I give 110 percent. But, I'm very thankful I got the opportunity to work on these films, it was a terrific collaborative effort.

Nicholas Pike (Composer, *Freddy's Nightmares*): I have become known primarily for my horror scores, but people find it a bit weird that I'm not a horror buff. I wasn't familiar with the *Elm Street* films but going into *Freddy's Nightmares* I did have the sense that this was something of a big deal. I was aware that the character of Freddy Krueger was the biggest thing in horror back then. So I knew it was an important job but not in an intimidating way because I hadn't seen any of the films and hadn't paid much attention to the franchise, but I enjoyed working on it because horror offers a composer the widest palette imaginable in terms of doing cool and unorthodox stuff.

Andre Ellingson: When I think back, what made working on these films so special was that people cared. I still get phone calls like this thirty-five years later and it is great because we have a story to tell, we're now part of horror history because Freddy Krueger is one of the most popular horror film figures ever. They were great times working on these films, I was in my twenties and I was right in the middle of it, but you didn't realize back then that you were working on something big or important, you were just working. When I think of all the props, some of which survived and others went in the dumpster. We probably threw away half-a-million dollars' worth of stuff, but I see props that I built selling online for tens of thousands of dollars, and some of those are things we got rid of but were rescued from the garbage by some enterprising person because now they are being sold as collector's items. We were working so hard building new things all the time and you never thought about the potential value of them. Who knew? It was a very special time and we were very fortunate to work on these productions.

Lisa Gottlieb: Through my film *Just One of the Guys* I'm always invited to '80s film conventions and Comic-Con kind of weekends. These events are always celebrating horror films but they also love '80s comedies, so it can be a little schizoid. But it means I have an audience who come for autographs and pose for pictures and what I have found is that they are initially there for *Just One of the Guys*, but then they see my poster that says who I am and what I've done and on that it says that I've directed *Freddy's Nightmares*. So when people realize this they would come back the next day to get their Freddy DVDs signed. People are watching a lot more stuff online now, so the access to the films and particularly to *Freddy's Nightmares* means it is a lot easier to watch than it was for many years. A lot of the shows that I have worked on or pitched for have vanished, but some things are forever, and that whole *Nightmare on Elm Street* enterprise really has longevity.

Craig Safan: You can see just how popular these films are with all the fan conventions. They don't be too interested in the composer but certainly some of the actors have made a career out of doing these signing events. The fan base for these films is just huge. Everybody knows what *A Nightmare on Elm Street* is. These films aren't just enjoying a second life, it is a least a second life, I think they are on their fourth of fifth life at this stage! I find myself always talking about it a lot, it is up there with *Cheers*, *The Last Starfighter*, and *Remo Williams* as the work that I get asked about most and which people write about a lot. *A Nightmare on Elm Street 4* is definitely a very well-remembered film and particularly so with my daughter's generation. Just this morning I was speaking to my daughter and I said, "oh, I have another interview for *Elm Street*!" and she asked me, "did you do the one with the waterbed? That was the best one!" and that is coming from a thirty year old, so that was really cool.

Roy H. Wagner: I get more attention about Freddy and this little horror movie than any of the big studio films that I have done. The *Elm Street* series became important because of the first film and the third one; they both deal with inner emotional themes which frighten us deeply. I think some of the themes in *A Nightmare on Elm Street 3* don't work quite as well now as they did when it was released, because we've gone through so much deeply introspective, intellectual and emotional things in cinema since we made it, but in the context of mid–1980s cinema, those ideas (teen mental health, generational conflict, etc.) weren't things that people were thinking about. But it worked at the time and it helped make the franchise what it became. The thing I admired so much about the original *Nightmare on Elm Street* is that it was an intellectual treatise and it poses the question: what if you couldn't escape your dreams? That to me is frightening. Wes was an intellectual. He hit upon something deeply emotional, something we are all afraid of, something that reaches into our deepest fears. The notion of being haunted in your dreams by an intangible force that can manipulate your worst fears and use them against you and you can't escape … well that is a terrifying idea.

Declan Quinn: The hook of not being able to fall asleep and that Freddy is going to get you while you are in a dream state is an overpowering idea. It is especially scary for a child but it applies to everybody because we know what it is like to be exhausted but still trying to stay awake. And so when you put that in the context of falling asleep meaning you lose control and become vulnerable to this thing that is terrifying or dangerous, that is a concept which, in a horror film, is a pretty damn good idea. It is the kind of premise that lends itself to multiple films because you can keep coming up with new scenarios. But Freddy is a memorable and horrific villain, the burnt man with a mechanical hand who lurks in the shadows and in your subconscious, it is a powerful image.

Nick Benson: The *Elm Street* franchise has become a legendary part of horror film history. When you say the words "Freddy Krueger" there aren't many people who don't know who you're talking about, even if they haven't seen the films they still know who the character is because he has become such an identifiable logo and such a huge icon of cinema. The series has lasted because it was a really original horror story which was developed really well from one film to the next. They each had great stories, especially the first four films. Did they do everything they could have done with it? Probably not. Maybe they got a little too wrapped up in its success rather than following through with better stories in the latter films. But it is such a creative premise that they could still pull something out and make a new *Elm Street* film. With Freddy you have a character that can be resurrected and utilized again and again because he is neither dead nor alive, he exists as long as there is fear, and there will always be an audience there for him.

Jack Sholder: To be perfectly honest, I understood why Wes Craven's first movie was a hit and I understood why the movie was original and interesting. The concept itself was a really great one because a lot of other horror films were just a maniac shows up at your door with an axe or a chainsaw and he kills you, or it's a summer camp and the kids are roaming the woods, in the dark of course, while there's a killer on the loose. But I approached *A Nightmare on Elm Street 2* not wanting to re-create anything that went before, I wanted it to be my film. And that's how we made it, the only rule we had to follow was "Freddy has to be scary," and we reprised some of the tropes like the little girls singing "One, Two, Freddy's coming for you…" and of course we wanted to use those in the same spirit as the first film but we didn't take the template of the original and try to replicate it, we went our own way with it. At that stage in my career I had done *Alone in the Dark*, which did okay but it didn't do great, and if *A Nightmare on Elm Street 2* didn't come along I don't know what would have happened, because the movie opened up and made more money than the first one and then my phone started ringing; then I found myself in Hollywood directing movies for the next twenty years. It worked out pretty well all because of *A Nightmare on Elm Street*.

Chuck Russell: There's two reasons why it has endured: one is that Wes hit upon something that is universal and very resonant to all of us, which is that at the ages of around 15, 16, 17 you come to realize that life is more dangerous than you're taught as a child. You become aware of mortality; you realize that the world is a dangerous place and your parents can't help you. Most kids are raised in fairyland, you grow up with Santa Claus and the Tooth Fairy, but then you see war on the news, or someone close to you dies, or you hear that someone has been shot at the local grocery store—then you realize you have been coddled and you are not going to get the truth from your parents. For me that is what lies at the heart of the *Elm Street* series: the fear of the world as it really is, which is that it's a large, confusing and scary place. And the other half of that idea is at that age you are not trusted, you have not earned respect, so people are not listening to the fact that you are having difficulties, in this case a nightmare that might be real. That is the brilliance of the original concept: that no one will believe you but your fellow teens. Your parents' natural desire to protect you and make you become a good citizen and not someone who is obsessed with nightmares is very dangerous for you in an *Elm Street* film.

Tuesday Knight: It is amazing to see the age range of people who come up to you at conventions wanting to talk to you about *A Nightmare on Elm Street*. It can be anything from twelve years old right up to people in their forties and fifties. Freddy and the *Elm Street* films always seem to speak to different generations. I get whole families coming up to me telling me that they watch the films together, so it is a wonderful thing to think that these movies have brought people together. I have my favorites too. Parts 5 and 6 I wasn't crazy about but I love *Wes Craven's New Nightmare*, that, the first one and the third one are incredible movies. I think the whole *Elm Street* thing has lasted because of Robert Englund and the way he presented the character of Freddy Krueger. And I think everybody is fascinated by anything to do with dreams; that's another important element, because it is a world we don't know much about and we are always wondering what dreams mean. The concept of having this character who lives in your dreams is brilliant, because how do you escape that? There is no escaping him. There's a surreal, mystical vibe to the films that is very appealing. And *A Nightmare on Elm Street* is now part of me, part of my soul; it is a huge part of my life. It is something I talk about almost every day. I am really grateful to be in it and that I get to be part of the world of *Elm Street*. It has made me realize that horror fans are the most devoted, amazing fans that you could have. These people really care about the films and the characters, it has really opened up the eyes of all of us who were in the films. We knew it would be something special but we never knew it would be something like this. For me it is always there, it is an intrinsic part of my life and has always lived with me. I've been in a lot of films but this is the one that keeps coming back to me and gets the most requests for interviews and brings me the most recognition. It's not the ones I was in with Robert De Niro or whoever, it's the one with Freddy, which I always find so funny, but I'm always very grateful to be in that family.

Robert Englund: I think part of the reason that the *Nightmare on Elm Street* franchise has proven to be so fascinating for so many people for over three decades is timing, and I'm not talking temporally but about technology. All the movies were hits in the theaters but even more so they took over the culture on video and later on DVD. The rise of Freddy coincided with the birth of the video generation and what I have learned over the past ten years from fans at conventions and film festivals is that *A Nightmare on Elm Street* not only entered the mainstream world of comic books, talk shows, merchandising, stand-up jokes, and has been referenced by all these cultural touchstones, but crucially, Freddy came home! Freddy came home with families all over the world because of the video phenomenon, and even before Blockbuster it was a hit in the mom and pop stores. Divorced parents trying to be cool by bringing it home for their kids, or older brothers going in to rent it out for their younger siblings, and this is when you kept the videotape for the weekend and you would watch it over and over again and you could hit the Pause button or rewind a scene and replay it, maybe scaring mom and dad while they sat and watched it while eating their TV dinners. It became a shared family experience, be it broken family or healthy family, from 1985 to 1995 because there was a film almost every year. When Part 3 came out in the theaters the family were renting Part 2 from the video store, that cycle continued, so it was always in their lives throughout those years and it got to the point where kids can have *Elm Street* marathons because there's enough of them available. And it just continued with *Freddy vs. Jason* and with the documentaries, DVD box sets, Blu-ray re-releases, and being shown on streaming services. People have these sophisticated home theater living rooms with the big flat screen TVs and they can watch these films and they look phenomenal, they are as beautiful as when they were released. What I've come to realize from the fans over the past ten years, and especially fans who were there in the early days when these films were new, is that their parents are old now or some of them have passed away, but these people discovered the series when they were young in the '80s and '90s and they associate the films with being at home, maybe eating some cold pizza and sitting around with all the lights off, the fireplace roaring, with the afghan quilt on the back of the couch, and the family is all there sitting around the video machine which is playing one of the *Nightmare* movies. Or perhaps the memory is associated with a loved one who has gone off to war, or who lives on the other side of the country, or who may have passed away; it is wonderful to hear that someone holds this memory so dearly of them being around their loved ones and sharing this moment of having fun being scared and laughing while watching one of my movies. The fans have a shared cultural memory of this spook show and this bogeyman which became a part of everybody's life. And there are eight films, each with their own huge audience. *A Nightmare on Elm Street* and Freddy Krueger have truly endured.

Chapter Notes

Chapter 1

1. Wes Craven "It Really Happened," DVD Supplement, *A Nightmare on Elm Street* Collection Bonus Disc. Warner Bros., 2011.
2. Robert Englund, *interview with author*, August 10, 2020.
3. Wes Craven "It Really Happened," DVD Supplement, *A Nightmare on Elm Street* Collection Bonus Disc. Warner Bros., 2011.
4. Robert Englund, *interview with author*, August 10, 2020.
5. *Ibid.*
6. Tom McLoughlin, *interview with author*, April 17, 2020.
7. Jacques Haitkin, *interview with author*, May 1, 2020.
8. Wes Craven, *Deformed and Destructive Beings: The Purpose of Horror* (Jefferson, NC: McFarland, 2011) p. 185.
9. Robert Englund, *interview with author*, August 10, 2020.
10. Tony Timpone, *interview with author*, August 27, 2020.
11. Wes Craven, Audio Commentary, DVD Supplement, *Shocker*. Momentum Pictures, 2011.
12. Mick Garris, *interview with author*, April 22, 2020.
13. Jacques Haitkin, *interview with author*, May 1, 2020.
14. *Ibid.*
15. *Ibid.*
16. *Ibid.*
17. Robert Englund, *interview with author*, August 10, 2020.
18. Bradford May, *interview with author*, June 24, 2020.
19. *Ibid.*
20. Wes Craven, "Never Sleep Again: The Elm Street Legacy," Documentary, 1408 Films, 2010.
21. Robert Shaye, "Heroes and Villains." DVD Supplement, *A Nightmare on Elm Street 2: Freddy's Revenge*, Warner Bros., 2011.
22. Jack Sholder, *interview with author*, Skype, May 11, 2020.
23. Wes Craven, "Heroes and Villains." DVD Supplement, *A Nightmare on Elm Street 2: Freddy's Revenge*, Warner Bros., 2011.
24. Jack Sholder, *interview with author*, Skype, May 11, 2020.
25. *Ibid.*
26. Robert Shaye, "Never Sleep Again: The Elm Street Legacy," Documentary, 1408 Films, 2010.
27. Jack Sholder, *interview with author*, Skype, May 11, 2020.
28. Jacques Haitkin, *interview with author*, Skype, May 11, 2020.
29. Jack Sholder, *interview with author*, Skype, May 11, 2020.
30. Jacques Haitkin, *interview with author*, Skype, May 11, 2020.
31. Jack Sholder, *interview with author*, Skype, May 11, 2020.
32. Jacques Haitkin, *interview with author*, Skype, May 11, 2020.
33. Jack Sholder, *interview with author*, Skype, May 11, 2020.
34. *Ibid.*
35. Jacques Haitkin, *interview with author*, Skype, May 11, 2020.
36. Mark Patton, "Never Sleep Again: The Elm Street Legacy," 1408 Films, 2010.
37. Jack Sholder, *interview with author*, Skype, May 11, 2020.
38. Robert Englund, *interview with author*, August 10, 2020.
39. Jack Sholder, *interview with author*, Skype, May 11, 2020.
40. Jacques Haitkin, *interview with author*, Skype, May 11, 2020.
41. Jack Sholder, *interview with author*, Skype, May 11, 2020.
42. Robert Shaye, "Never Sleep Again: The Elm Street Legacy," Documentary, 1408 Films, 2010.
43. Robert Englund, *interview with author*, August 10, 2020.
44. Jack Sholder, *interview with author*, Skype, May 11, 2020.
45. *Ibid.*
46. *Ibid.*

Chapter 2

1. Chuck Russell, *interview with author*, September 9, 2020.
2. Roy Wagner, interview with author, May 16, 2020.
3. *Ibid.*
4. *Ibid.*
5. *Ibid.*
6. Chuck Russell, *interview with author*, September 9, 2020.
7. Roy Wagner, *interview with author*, May 16, 2020.
8. Robert Englund, *interview with author*, August 10, 2020.
9. Dennis Maguire, *interview with author*, June 5, 2020.
10. *Ibid.*
11. Mick Strawn, *interview with author*, April 21, 2020.
12. *Ibid.*
13. Andre Ellingson, *interview with author*, June 23, 2020.
14. Roy Wagner, *interview with author*, May 16, 2020.
15. Dennis Maguire, *interview with author*, June 5, 2020.
16. Roy Wagner, *interview with author*, May 16, 2020.
17. Dennis Maguire, *interview with author*, June 5, 2020.
18. Roy Wagner, *interview with author*, May 16, 2020.
19. Chuck Russell, *interview with author*, September 9, 2020.
20. Roy Wagner, *interview with author*, May 16, 2020.
21. Chuck Russell, *interview with author*, September 9, 2020.
22. Robert Englund, *interview with author*, August 10, 2020.
23. Roy Wagner, *interview with author*, May 16, 2020.
24. Andre Ellingson, *interview with author*, June 23, 2020.
25. Dennis Maguire, *interview with author*, June 5, 2020.
26. Roy Wagner, *interview with author*, May 16, 2020.
27. Dennis Maguire, *interview with author*, June 5, 2020.
28. Roy Wagner, *interview with author*, May 16, 2020.
29. Dennis Maguire, *interview with author*, June 5, 2020.
30. Roy Wagner, *interview with author*, May 16, 2020.
31. Dennis Maguire, *interview with author*, June 5, 2020.
32. Roy Wagner, *interview with author*, May 16, 2020.
33. Dennis Maguire, *interview with author*, June 5, 2020.
34. Roy Wagner, *interview with author*, May 16, 2020.
35. Dennis Maguire, *interview with author*, June 5, 2020.
36. Roy Wagner, *interview with author*, May 16, 2020.
37. *Ibid.*
38. *Ibid.*
39. Chuck Russell, *interview with author*, September 9, 2020.
40. *Ibid.*
41. Roy Wagner, *interview with author*, May 16, 2020.
42. Mick Strawn, *interview with author*, April 21, 2020.
43. Chuck Russell, *interview with author*, September 9, 2020.
44. Dennis Maguire, *interview with author*, June 5, 2020.
45. Roy Wagner, *interview with author*, May 16, 2020.
46. Mick Strawn, *interview with author*, April 21, 2020.
47. Chuck Russell, *interview with author*, September 9, 2020.
48. Robert Englund, *interview with author*, August 10, 2020.
49. Chuck Russell, *interview with author*, September 9, 2020.
50. Renny Harlin, "Never Sleep Again: The Elm Street Legacy," Documentary, 1408 Films, 2010.
51. Robert Shaye, "Never Sleep Again: The Elm Street Legacy," Documentary, 1408 Films, 2010.
52. Mick Strawn, *interview with author*, April 21, 2020.
53. Nick Benson, *interview with author*, January 6, 2021.
54. Robert Englund, *interview with author*, August 10, 2020.
55. Steven Fierberg, *interview with author*, June 9, 2020.
56. Robert Englund, *interview with author*, August 10, 2020.
57. Nick Benson, *interview with author*, January 6, 2021.
58. Steven Fierberg, *interview with author*, June 9, 2020.
59. Nick Benson, *interview with author*, January 6, 2021.
60. Tuesday Knight, *interview with author*, July 27, 2020.
61. Steven Fierberg, *interview with author*, June 9, 2020.
62. Tuesday Knight, *interview with author*, July 27, 2020.
63. Mick Strawn with Blake Best, *Behind the Screams: The Dream Masters Revealed* (USA: Self Published, 2018), p. 179.

64. Mick Strawn, *interview with author*, April 21, 2020.
65. Craig Safan, *interview with author*, August 12, 2020.
66. *Ibid.*
67. Tuesday Knight, *interview with author*, July 27, 2020.
68. Nick Benson, *interview with author*, January 6, 2021.
69. Robert Englund, *interview with author*, August 10, 2020.
70. Mick Garris, *interview with author*, April 22, 2020.
71. Steven Fierberg, *interview with author*, June 9, 2020.
72. Tuesday Knight, *interview with author*, July 27, 2020.
73. Nick Benson, *interview with author*, January 6, 2021.
74. Craig Safan, *interview with author*, August 12, 2020.
75. Steven Fierberg, *interview with author*, June 9, 2020.
76. Robert Englund, *interview with author*, August 10, 2020.

Chapter 3

1. Robert Englund, *interview with author*, Phone, August 10, 2020.
2. Bill Froehlich, *interview with author*, Skype, December 18, 2020.
3. Robert Shaye, "Never Sleep Again: The Elm Street Legacy," Documentary, 1408 Films, 2010.
4. Bill Froehlich, *interview with author*, Skype, December 18, 2020.
5. Robert Englund, *interview with author*, Phone, August 10, 2020.
6. Tom McLoughlin, *interview with author*, Skype, April 17, 2020.
7. https://catalog.afi.com/Catalog/Movie Details/57548.
8. Mick Garris, *interview with author*, Skype, April 22, 2020.
9. William Malone, *interview with author*, Skype, October 5, 2020.
10. Bill Froehlich, *interview with author*, Skype, December 18, 2020.
11. Lisa Gottlieb, *interview with author*, Phone, August 1, 2020.
12. Mick Garris, *interview with author*, Skype, April 22, 2020.
13. Nicholas Pike, *interview with author*, Skype, April 15, 2020.
14. *Ibid.*
15. Bill Froehlich, *interview with author*, Skype, December 18, 2020.
16. *Ibid.*
17. Mick Strawn, *interview with author*, Skype, April 21, 2020.
18. Tom McLoughlin, *interview with author*, Skype, April 17, 2020.
19. Mick Strawn, *interview with author*, Skype, April 21, 2020.
20. Andre Ellingson, *interview with author*, Skype, June 23, 2020.
21. Bill Froehlich, *interview with author*, Skype, December 18, 2020.
22. Mick Garris, *interview with author*, Skype, April 22, 2020.
23. Tom McLoughlin, *interview with author*, Skype, April 17, 2020.
24. Lisa Gottlieb, *interview with author*, Phone, August 1, 2020.
25. *Ibid.*
26. Bobby Lesser, *interview with author*, Phone, July 25, 2020.
27. Lisa Gottlieb, *interview with author*, Phone, August 1, 2020.
28. Bobby Lesser, *interview with author*, Phone, July 25, 2020.
29. Andre Ellingson, *interview with author*, Skype, June 23, 2020.
30. Mick Strawn, *interview with author*, Skype, April 21, 2020.
31. Lisa Gottlieb, *interview with author*, Phone, August 1, 2020.
32. Bill Froehlich, *interview with author*, Skype, December 18, 2020.
33. William Malone, *interview with author*, Skype, October 5, 2020.
34. Andre Ellingson, *interview with author*, Skype, June 23, 2020.
35. Mick Strawn, *interview with author*, Skype, April 21, 2020.
36. Mick Garris, *interview with author*, Skype, April 22, 2020.
37. William Malone, *interview with author*, Skype, October 5, 2020.
38. Tom McLoughlin, *interview with author*, Skype, April 17, 2020.
39. Mick Strawn, *interview with author*, Skype, April 21, 2020.
40. *Ibid.*
41. Mick Garris, *interview with author*, Skype, April 22, 2020.
42. Tom McLoughlin, *interview with author*, Skype, April 17, 2020.
43. Mick Garris, *interview with author*, Skype, April 22, 2020.
44. B.J. Del Conte, "TV Station Cancels 'Freddy's Nightmares,'" UPI Archives, June 15, 1989, https://www.upi.com/Archives/1989/06/15/TV-station-cancels-Freddys-Nightmares/5745613886400/.
45. Mick Strawn, *interview with author*, Skype, April 21, 2020.
46. Robert Englund, *interview with author*, Phone, August 10, 2020.
47. Mick Garris, *interview with author*, Skype, April 22, 2020.

48. William Malone, *interview with author*, Skype, October 5, 2020.
49. Robert Englund, *interview with author*, Phone, August 10, 2020.
50. Tony Timpone, *interview with author*, Phone, August 27, 2020.
51. Tom McLoughlin, *interview with author*, Skype, April 17, 2020.
52. *Ibid.*
53. Mick Garris, *interview with author*, Skype, April 22, 2020.
54. Lisa Gottlieb, *interview with author*, Phone, August 1, 2020.
55. Andre Ellingson, *interview with author*, Skype, June 23, 2020.
56. Lisa Gottlieb, *interview with author*, Phone, August 1, 2020.
57. Nicholas Pike, *interview with author*, Skype, April 15, 2020.
58. William Malone, *interview with author*, Skype, October 5, 2020.
59. Tom McLoughlin, *interview with author*, Skype, April 17, 2020.
60. Bill Froehlich, *interview with author*, Skype, December 18, 2020.

Chapter 4

1. Robert Englund, https://www.youtube.com/watch?v=xlWNX6-gJMU (*Freddy's Dead: The Making of the Final Nightmare*)—Accessed 1/11/20 (Uploaded by Nightmare Tributes, 1 July, 2016).
2. Rachel Talalay, "Womb Raiders." DVD Supplement, *A Nightmare on Elm Street 5: The Dream Child*, Warner Bros., 2011.
3. Andre Ellingson, *interview with author*, Skype, June 23, 2020.
4. Mick Strawn, *interview with author*, Skype, April 21, 2020
5. Andre Ellingson, *interview with author*, Skype, June 23, 2020.
6. Stephen Hopkins, quoted in article by Marc Shapiro, *Fangoria*, Issue #99, 1990.
7. Stephen Hopkins, "A Slight Miscalculation." DVD Supplement, *A Nightmare on Elm Street 5: The Dream Child*, Warner Bros., 2011.
8. Robert Englund, *interview with author*, Telephone, August 10, 2020.
9. *Ibid.*
10. *Ibid.*
11. Rachel Talalay, https://www.youtube.com/watch?v=xlWNX6-gJMU (*Freddy's Dead: The Making of the Final Nightmare*)—Accessed 1/11/20 (Uploaded by Nightmare Tributes, 1 July, 2016).
12. Rachel Talalay, "Rachel's Dream." DVD Supplement, *Freddy's Dead: The Final Nightmare* DVD. Warner Bros., 2011.
13. Quinn, Declan, *interview with author*, Skype, August 4, 2020.
14. *Ibid.*
15. *Ibid.*
16. *Ibid.*
17. Rachel Talalay. "3D Demise." DVD Supplement, *Freddy's Dead: The Final Nightmare* DVD. Warner Bros., 2011.
18. Declan Quinn, interview with author, August 4, 2020.
19. Shon Greenblatt, "Never Sleep Again: The Elm Street Legacy," Documentary, 1408 Films, 2010.
20. Rachel Talalay, https://www.youtube.com/watch?v=xlWNX6-gJMU (*Freddy's Dead: The Making of the Final* Nightmare)—Accessed 1/11/20 (Uploaded by Nightmare Tributes, 1 July, 2016).
21. Rachel Talalay. "Rachel's Dream." DVD Supplement, *Freddy's Dead: The Final Nightmare* DVD. Warner Bros., 2011.
22. Bob Poole, *Los Angeles Times*, September 13, 1991—https://web.archive.org/web/20150915011752/http://articles.latimes.com/1991-09-13/local/me-2351_1_people-freddy-krueger.
23. Robert Shaye, "3D Demise." DVD Supplement, *Freddy's Dead: The Final Nightmare* DVD. Warner Bros., 2011.
24. Declan Quinn, *interview with author*, August 4, 2020.
25. https://www.latimes.com/archives/la-xpm-1988-09-15-mn-2834-story.html—Accessed 2/7/20.
26. https://www.movie-censorship.com/report.php?ID=665—Accessed 22/11/2020.
27. Wes Craven. "Filmmaker." DVD Supplement, *Wes Craven's New Nightmare* DVD. Warner Bros., 2011.
28. Jon Lewis, *Hollywood V. Hard Core: How the Struggle Over Censorship Created the Modern Film Industry* (New York: NYU Press, 2002) p.179.
29. Wes Craven. "Filmmaker." DVD Supplement, *Wes Craven's New Nightmare* DVD. Warner Bros., 2011.
30. Robert Englund, *interview with author*, Telephone, August 10, 2020.
31. *Ibid.*
32. Wes Craven. "Filmmaker." DVD Supplement, Wes *Craven's New Nightmare* DVD. Warner Bros., 2011.
33. Robert Englund, *interview with author*, Telephone, August 10, 2020.
34. Tony Timpone, *interview with author*, Phone, August 27, 2020.

Chapter 5

1. Robert Englund, *interview with author*, Telephone, August 10, 2020.
2. Tom McLoughlin, *interview with author*, Skype, April 17, 2020.

3. Ronny Yu, https://movieweb.com/director-ronny-yu-talks-freddy-vs-jason/.

4. Tom McLoughlin, *interview with author*, Skype, April 17, 2020.

5. https://www.youtube.com/watch?v=-AP2_DNFhOA (Freddy vs. Jason Weigh-in at Bally's in Las Vegas (July 15, 2003)—Accessed 3/10/20 (Uploaded by Bloody Disgusting, 21 March, 2017).

6. Tony Timpone, *interview with author*, Phone, August 27, 2020.

7. *Ibid.*

8. Mick Garris, *interview with author*, Skype, April 22, 2020.

9. Andre Ellingson, *interview with author*, Skype, June 23, 2020.

10. Englund, Robert. "Freddy on 8th Street." DVD Supplement, *A Nightmare on Elm Street 2: Freddy's Revenge*, Warner Bros., 2011.

11. Tom McLoughlin, *interview with author*, Skype, April 17, 2020.

12. Tony Timpone, *interview with author*, Phone, August 27, 2020.

Bibliography

Craven, Wes. "Audio Commentary." DVD Supplement, Shocker. Momentum Pictures, 2011.

Craven, Wes. "Filmmaker." DVD Supplement, *Wes Craven's New Nightmare* DVD. Warner Bros., 2011.

Craven, Wes, "Heroes and Villains." DVD Supplement, *A Nightmare on Elm Street 2: Freddy's Revenge*, Warner Bros., 2011.

Craven, Wes. "It Really Happened." DVD Supplement, *A Nightmare on Elm Street Collection* Bonus Disc. Warner Bros., 2011.

Craven, Wes. "Never Sleep Again: The Elm Street Legacy." Documentary, 1408 Films, 2010.

Craven, Wes. "Two Worlds." DVD Supplement, *Wes Craven's New Nightmare* DVD. Warner Bros., 2011.

Del Conte, B.J. "TV Station Cancels 'Freddy's Nightmares'" UPI Archives, June 15, 1989, https://www.upi.com/Archives/1989/06/15/TV-station-cancels-Freddys-Nightmares/5745613886400/.

Englund, Robert. "Freddy on 8th Street." DVD Supplement, *A Nightmare on Elm Street 2: Freddy's Revenge*, Warner Bros., 2011.

Englund, Robert. "Freddy's Dead: The Making of the Final Nightmare." Electronic Press Kit, 1991.

Englund, Robert. "Never Sleep Again: The Elm Street Legacy." Documentary, 1408 Films, 2010.

Englund, Robert. "Psycho Sexual Circus." DVD Supplement, *A Nightmare on Elm Street 2: Freddy's Revenge*, Warner Bros., 2011.

Greenblatt, Shon. "Never Sleep Again: The Elm Street Legacy." Documentary, 1408 Films, 2010.

Harlin, Renny. "Never Sleep Again: The Elm Street Legacy." Documentary, 1408 Films, 2010.

Hopkins, Stephen. "A Slight Miscalculation." DVD Supplement, *A Nightmare on Elm Street 5: The Dream Child*, Warner Bros., 2011.

Hutson, Thommy, *Never Sleep Again: The Elm Street Legacy—The Making of Wes Craven's a Nightmare on Elm Street,* New York: Permuted Press, 2016.

Jackson, Robert L. "Reagan Likens Carter Years to Horror Film: Democratic Policies Resembled 'Nightmare on Elm Street,' He Says." *Los Angeles Times*, September 15, 1988—https://www.latimes.com/archives/la-xpm-1988-09-15-mn-2834-story.html.

Lewis, Jon. *Hollywood V. Hard Core: How the Struggle Over Censorship Created the Modern Film Industry.* New York: NYU Press, 2002.

Ochoa, George. *Deformed and Destructive Beings: The Purpose of Horror.* Jefferson, NC: McFarland, 2011.

Patton, Mark. "Never Sleep Again: The Elm Street Legacy." Documentary, 1408 Films, 2010.

Poole, Bob. "Sharp Edge: Mayor Proclaims 'Freddy Krueger Day' but Not Everyone Is Celebrating." *Los Angeles Times*, September 13, 1991—https://web.archive.org/web/20150915011752/http://articles.latimes.com/1991-09-13/local/me-2351_1_people-freddy-krueger.

Shaye, Robert. "86'D." DVD Supplement, *Freddy's Dead: The Final Nightmare* DVD. Warner Bros., 2011.

Shaye, Robert. "Heroes and Villains." DVD Supplement, *A Nightmare on Elm Street 2: Freddy's Revenge*, Warner Bros., 2011.

Shaye, Robert. "Never Sleep Again: The Elm Street Legacy." Documentary, 1408 Films, 2010.

Strawn, Mick, with Blake Best, *Behind the Screams: The Dream Masters Revealed,* USA: Self Published, 2018.

Talalay, Rachel. "Rachel's Dream." DVD Supplement, *Freddy's Dead: The Final Nightmare,* Warner Bros., 2011.

Talalay, Rachel. "3D Demise." DVD Supplement, *Freddy's Dead: The Final Nightmare,* Warner Bros., 2011.

Talalay, Rachel, "Womb Raiders." DVD Supplement, *A Nightmare on Elm Street 5: The Dream Child,* Warner Bros., 2011.

YouTube Videos

"Freddy Vs. Jason Weigh-in at Bally's in Las Vegas (July 15, 2003)." uploaded by Bloody Disgusting,

21 March, 2017. https://www.youtube.com/watch?v=-AP2_DNFhOA.

"Freddy's Dead: The Making of the Final Nightmare." uploaded by Nightmare Tributes, July 1, 2016. https://www.youtube.com/watch?v=xlWNX6-gJMU.

Websites

https://catalog.afi.com/Catalog/MovieDetails/57548.

http://filmireland.net/2020/05/27/making-nightmares-with-mick-strawn/.

https://www.movie-censorship.com/report.php?ID=665.

https://movieweb.com/director-ronny-yu-talks-freddy-vs-jason/.

https://www.screamqueendocumentary.com/.

Interviews with Author

Benson, Nick, Zoom, January 06, 2021.
Ellingson, Andre, Skype, June 23, 2020.
Englund, Robert, Telephone, August 10, 2020.
Fierberg, Steven, Skype, June 9, 2020.
Froelich, Bill, Skype, December 18, 2020.
Garris, Mick, Skype, April 22, 2020.
Gottlieb, Lisa, Telephone, August 1, 2020.
Haitkin, Jacques, Skype, May 11, 2020.
Knight, Tuesday, Skype, July 27, 2020.
Lesser, Robert, Telephone, July 25, 2020.
Maguire, Dennis, Skype, June 5, 2020.
Malone, William, FaceTime, October 5, 2020.
May, Bradford, Telephone, June 24, 2020.
McLoughlin, Tom, Skype, April 17, 2020.
Pike, Nicholas, Skype, April 15, 2020.
Quinn, Declan, Skype, August 4, 2020.
Russell, Chuck, Telephone, September 9, 2020.
Safan, Craig, Skype, August 12, 2020.
Sholder, Jack, Skype, May 11, 2020.
Strawn, Mick, Skype, April 21, 2020.
Timpone, Tony, Telephone, August 27, 2020.
Wagner, Roy H., Zoom, May 16, 2020.

Index

Alfred Hitchcock Presents 123, 127
Alone in the Dark 27, 33

BBFC 177; see also censorship
Black Tickets (Freddy's Nightmares episode) 129
The Blob 45, 76, 110
Blue Velvet 21

Cabin Fever (Freddy's Nightmare episode) 118
Carnival of Souls 199
censorship 144, 160, 177–179
Chaskin, David 27–28, 36
class 12–13, 16–17, 165
Critters 2 119, 123, 129

Darabont, Frank 46, 93
Deadline (Freddy's Nightmares episode) 129
Deadly Friend 16–17, 24
Do Dreams Bleed (Freddy's Nightmares episode) 149
Do You Know Where Your Kids Are (Freddy's Nightmares episode) 139
Dokken 92, 115
Dust to Dust (Freddy's Nightmares episode) 138

Easy Come, Easy Go (Freddy's Nightmares episode) 119

The Fat Boys 106–108, 115
Freddy Krueger Day 172–173
Freddy's Dead: The Final Nightmare soundtrack 171
Freddy's Nightmares soundtrack 123–125, 149–150
Freud, Sigmund 36–37
Friday the 13th: The Series 116, 146–147

The Goo Goo Dolls 171–172

Hargitay, Mariska 122
Heartbreak Hotel (Freddy's Nightmares episode) 119

Her Pilgrim Soul (The Twilight Zone episode) 23–24
The Hidden 42, 106, 158
The Hills Have Eyes 3, 10, 12
Hooper, Tobe 115–116, 119, 128, 143, 145 5
Hornrich, Junior 125
Huff, Dann 123–124

I Want Your (Hands on Me) 106–107
I'm Awake Now 171
It's a Miserable Life (Freddy's Nightmares episode) 119, 136, 143

Jung, Carl 36
The Junk Monkeys 171

Killer Instinct (Freddy's Nightmares episode) 121, 143

Lafia, John 136
Lange, Michael 129
The Last House on the Left 3, 10, 12
The Lion and the Cobra 107
A Little Peace and Quiet (The Twilight Zone episode) 23
Lucky Stiff (Freddy's Nightmares episode) 119, 151
Lynch, David 21–22
Lynch, George 92

Mother's Day (Freddy's Nightmares episode) 129, 136
MPAA 160, 177; see also censorship
Music of the Heart 199
My Demon Lover 106, 110
My Soul to Take 199

Never Sleep Again: The Elm Street Legacy 36
A Nightmare on Elm Street 3: Dream Warriors soundtrack 92
A Nightmare on Elm Street 4:

The Dream Master soundtrack 106–110
No More Mr. Nice Guy (Freddy's Nightmares episode) 115

O'Connor, Sinead 106–107

The People Under the Stairs 3, 12, 16, 25
Pitt, Brad 35, 129
Pop, Iggy 171

Quiet Cool 51

Rebel Without a Car (Freddy's Nightmares episode) 136–137
Red Eye 199
Reefer Madness 26
Return to Horror High 46, 150
Risher, Sara 29, 38, 195–196

Saturday Night Special (Freddy's Nightmares episode) 121, 133–136, 149
Scream, Queen! My Nightmare on Elm Street 36
Scream 3, 16, 24–25, 186–187
Serling, Rod 22, 129–130
The Serpent and the Rainbow 12, 25
Shatterday (The Twilight Zone episode) 23
Shocker 3, 17–18, 25
splatterpunk 155–156

Tico, Randy 125
Tippett, Phil 56
The Twilight Zone 22–24, 118, 127, 130–131

Vampire in Brooklyn 25
Vietnam 12

Wagner, Bruce 46, 93

Yagher, Kevin 31, 38, 72–73

www.ingramcontent.com/pod-product-compliance
Lightning Source LLC
Chambersburg PA
CBHW060342010526
44117CB00017B/2936